A retired cross-cultural worker was onc
cross-cultural work?" He wisely replied, "Nothing". This is particularly the
case when you leave behind everything that's familiar for a country where
almost nothing is familiar. With remarkable recall of their first months in
Samoa Ian Reilly writes honestly (almost painfully so), insightfully, hum-
bly, vividly and yet lovingly of their attempts to understand and adapt to
the Samoan way of life. Artfully written, Encounter will stimulate your
thinking, at times move your heart, and hopefully deepen your faith. This
story will be a rich resource for anyone anticipating the challenges and joys
of serving cross culturally.

Mike Raiter, *Director, Centre for Biblical Preaching, Author*

ENCOUNTER

A JOURNEY INTO CHAOS,
CULTURE AND COMPASSION

IAN REILLY

Ark House Press
arkhousepress.com

Unless otherwise stated, scripture quotations are from The ESV® Bible (The Holy Bible, English Standard Version®), © 2001 by Crossway, a publishing ministry of Good News Publishers. Used by permission. All rights reserved.

Some names and identifying details have been changed to protect the privacy of individuals.

Cataloguing in Publication Data:
Title: Encounter
ISBN: 978-1-7640542-9-4 (pbk)
Subjects: REL045000   RELIGION / Christian Ministry / Missions; REL012170
RELIGION / Christian Living / Personal Memoirs; BIO018000   BIOGRAPHY &
AUTOBIOGRAPHY / Religious.

Cover illustrated by Ian Reilly
Design by initiateagency.com

For our daughters
Rosemary and Elizabeth
In the hope they make their way through life making
fewer mistakes than I did.

NOTES

Except for the word 'palagi' (pronounced like Pah-Lung-y) Samoan words are italicised.

Samoan is pronounced phonetically with;

G pronounced like NG (as in 'sing') in English

A – ah

E – e as in air

I – as in ship

O as in Bore

U as in Fruit

So, *Talofa e* sounds like Tah-Low-Fye

The glottal stop (') is a consonant that does not appear in standard English. It is pronounced like 't' in cockney for 'bottle.'

AUTHOR'S NOTE

In this book, I do not claim to write authoritatively about Samoan culture. Rather, this book is the story of my collision with Samoan culture, when my wife Heather and I were part of an international aid programme to developing nations.

However, it's necessary to provide sufficient Samoan cultural background for readers to understand what we collided with. I apologise to any Samoan readers who think my explanations of Samoan culture are too simple or misleading. While I don't intend to mislead, telling an honest story demands sharing what we were told, including what was misleading or false, because being misinformed and mislead is an essential part of the experience.

Instead of merely informing you, I hope to give you a vicarious experience. Reading this book, you can live through a true to life cultural collision, including all the misunderstandings, mistakes, face-saving misrepresentations, and outright falsehoods that are common to such cultural encounters. I share what I was told about Samoan culture by Samoan people, and by other non-Samoans who were fellow travellers on our journey. Admittedly, help from fellow travellers was sometimes like the blind leading the blind, but two blind people can successfully combine their efforts to avoid falling in a hole. Inevitably, there are more questions than answers, and while I share my thoughts, I deliberately leave you to reach your own conclusions.

The problem faced by anyone who wants to grasp an understanding of another culture, is that they typically find their available time and experience too limiting. It is easier to think we understand something when we're short-term visitors, like tourists. Our cultural faux pas are excused, ignored or overlooked, and we don't have the simple messages we hear challenged or contradicted, or have the host culture place any demands or expectations upon us.

But when we stay longer term, when we live, work, and participate in the life of a community, cultural engagement is a difficult road to travel. It is hard, because when we uncover more learning layers, our host culture expects more of us. But also, because we only acquire the wisdom we need by integrating learning into lived experience, and the trial and error of that learning process can be painful. It's painful because we often make mistakes in response to hearing conflicting messages from the people who call that culture their home - people we think should know how to put us on a right path. Conflicting messages arise because all cultures are changing, and because diverse subcultures exist in even the most monolithic culture. Also, in practice people often behave in ways that conflict with their culture's norms. For example, people sometimes behave rudely, even in cultures that value politeness above all else.

However, the struggle to sort out fact from fiction, to understand the difference between the way things once were, the way they are, or the way we want them to be, can also make the experience an exciting adventure. Adventure or not, we are compelled to sift and sort, and make decisions about people, places and things, from the moment we step off the plane. Who is trustworthy? Are cockroaches harmful or just unsightly? Should I ride in the pickup of this person I just met? Can I trust this policeman?

While sound judgements are essential for survival and a productive life, we must also make room for provisional views, and sometimes suspend judgement to another time.

As you read Encounter, I challenge you to watch, wait and wonder. For today's culture too easily judges the actions of people in the past, by the values of our present time and place, secure in the knowledge our contemporary wisdom is superior to past generations.

FOREWORD

I first met Ian and Heather Reilly in 1990 when I was a young teacher at Leulumoega Fou College. Having recently completed a postgraduate degree in Social Anthropology at Otago University in New Zealand, I returned to Samoa in the wake of Cyclone Ofa. I found my country recovering from the devastating impact of a national disaster, and teachers struggling to run a high school without power and water. Newly arrived from Australia, Ian and Heather were not only grappling with the chaos of disaster aftermath but were also struggling with a new culture and climate.

We worked together throughout 1990 – 91, living in the same school community, and worshipping at Malua, where my father, the Reverend Oka Fauolo, was Principal of the Malua Theological College. In 2006, I was appointed to the position of Principal of Leulumoega Fou College and served in that capacity until I resigned in 2021.

For many decades, international volunteers like Ian and Heather have made an important contribution to the education of Samoan children. Samoa has welcomed and embraced these overseas volunteers, and many volunteers work hard to understand and adopt Samoan ways, learn the language, and immerse themselves in Samoan life and culture. Regardless of how deeply they engage, they all discover there are responsibilities and expectations that can seem daunting.

Encounter gives us the lived experience of a volunteer's personal struggles to grapple with these issues, trying to understand and fit in, and provides us with a rich source of unforgettable experiences. We journey into another world - to a different time and place - filled with intense life, love, laughter, and tragic loss. Life lessons from these experiences transcend culture, place, and time, and demonstrate how much we can learn from engaging with a different culture.

I admired Ian and Heather's commitment and energy to teaching, as well as their tolerance and acceptance of difficulties, due to the impacts of the cyclone. They were true Christians, not only dedicated to their calling, but they were also able to immerse into the fa'asamoa (way of life) – religion, language, and culture. Encounter shows how being immersed into a different culture can teach us a great deal in a very short time. For we not only learn about a different culture and people, but we also learn a lot about ourselves.

Encounter gives us a grass roots, on the ground experience, seeing Samoa through the eyes of people seeing it for the first time. When we look through the eyes of another person, we too notice things we never saw before, and what we thought was ordinary and taken for granted, can suddenly become valuable and precious.

This is a heart-warming testament of 'palagi engagement' with Samoa and its culture. Samoa was very different in the 1990s. Ian's journey may inspire others to recall the experience and circumstances of the time. For Encounter opens a window into the past, forming an important historical snapshot of a critical moment in Samoa's history, sandwiched between two very destructive natural disasters.

Fauolo Apevai Karisi Mataafa
Fusi, Safotulafai
Savai'i, Samoa

GLOSSARY OF SAMOAN WORDS

'ava	Ceremonial narcotic drink made from the root of the kava plant.
afa	Sinnet, coconut fibre twine
afakasi	Mixed race person
aiga	Extended family
alofa	Love
aso	Day
aso to'ona'i	Saturday
aua le pisa	Be quiet
Ausetalia	Australia
fa'afafine	Man or boy who behaves like a woman
fa'afetai	Thank you
fa'amolemole	Please
fa'asamoa	Samoan language, Samoan culture
faia'oga	Teacher
faife'au	Pastor
fala	Floor mat made from woven pandanus
fale	House, building

fiafia	Happy, or celebration, feast
i'a	Fish
ie faitaga	Men's formal wear - tailored wrap around skirt
ie, or *ie solosolo*	Casual wrap around skirt made from 1m x 2m cotton cloth
ili	Samoan fan
ioe	Yes
ke le iloa	(I) don't know
keke	Cake
kilikiti	Cricket
lakapi	Rugby
le'i sau	Not come
leaga	Bad
leai	No
lelei	Good
ma'i	Sick, ill
malaga	Journey
malo	Hi, casual greeting
manaia	Nice, pleasant
manuia	Blessings
masi	Biscuit, cookie
matai	Titled head of an extended family
mea	Thing
mea alofa	Gift
mea'ai	Food
miti	Dream
niu	Green drinking coconut
Niusila	New Zealand
nu'u	Village

palusami	A Samoan delicacy. Umu baked coconut cream in taro leaves
paopao	Samoan style dugout canoe
pe'a	Flying fox
pisikoa	Peace Corps Volunteer
pisupo	Tinned corned beef
poko, poto	Clever
popole fua	Don't worry
puletasi	Women's formal wear – tailored top and matching ankle length skirt
saina	China, or Chinese
se'e vae	Shoes, flip-flops, thongs (Aust.)
sene	Cent, cents in Samoan currency
soia	Stop
soifua	Good health
supageti	Spaghetti
ta'ele, ka'ele	Bath, shower, or swim
tafao	Wander around
tala	Samoan currency, dollar
talofa	Hello, formal greeting on first meeting
talofa e	What a pity
tatou o, kakou o	Let's go
tele, kele	Very, much, a lot
toeitiiti	Soon, almost
tofa	Goodbye
tulou	Excuse me
Tusi Pa'ia	The Bible
umu	Traditional above ground oven using hot stones to bake

vai aisa	Ice water
vaiaso	Week
vaofefe	A thorny, noxious weed that folds its petals when touched
vevela	Hot
volipolo	Volleyball

CONTENTS

TAPESTRY

All of life beckons, and calls us to run,
To the step of a dance, and the beat of a drum,
We spin bright yarn, and weave dark thread,
Through the fabric of life, and all that we dread.
Through stormy chaos, and crumbling plans,
We suffer, and seek to understand,
While nurturing new, we cherish the old,
And clutch our tattering hopes we hold,
Down the road less-taken, on paths not seen,
Round the twist of our thoughts, and shape of our dreams.
There mem'ries linger, and turn in our minds,
Mem'ries that hold us, and round us entwine,
*   So all of our yesterdays, are with us tomorrow,*
*   All of our joy, and all of our sorrow.*

Ian Reilly, 2024

"Open your eyes,
shut your mouth,
keep your hands to yourself,
and listen."

Parting advice to volunteers from Bill Armstrong,
Director, Overseas Service Bureau,
13th of January 1990.

1

SHOCK

*"For the gate is narrow and the way is hard that
leads to life, and those who find it are few."*
Matthew 7:14

Maybe it's our nervous naïvete that triggers the gatekeeper because everything spirals out of control before we even get on the first plane.

"That bag looks oversize," she says, as we board our flight from Melbourne to Sydney.

It isn't.

"Well, it's too heavy then," she adds, undeterred and irritated.

As she transfers the bag to the hold, she tells us it's checked through straight to Samoa.

"You won't need to collect it in Sydney," she assures us with a satisfied smile. Like she knows what's best for people like us.

Sounds reasonable, I guess. In Sydney, we're boarding a Polynesian Airlines flight that will take us to Samoa. Our first ever overseas flight. But as we settle into our seats, I remember our passports are in that bag.

Passports we need to get through Immigration to leave Australia.

In Sydney.

Worried we might be stuck in Australia while our friends wing their way overseas, we frantically run around Sydney's domestic and international airport terminals, desperately trying to retrieve the checked bag. With half an hour to spare, we're finally reunited with our passports, in time to hear the flight has been delayed a few hours. Then, when we finally board the plane, they confiscate another cabin bag at the gate, transferring it to checked luggage. But when we see others board hassle free, carrying too many or oversized bags, we wonder why they picked on us. Do we look suspicious, or dodgy?

At least they didn't take the Hepatitis B vaccine cold pack. We carry serum because there wasn't time to have the final injection in Australia. We plan to have a Samoan nurse administer the vaccine in a month's time.

"The airline will put the pack in the galley fridge," they assured us.

But the airline seems antsy about putting serum alongside passengers' food and claims there's no room in the fridge.

We wonder what else we've been told that will turn out to be untrue.

In our late twenties, my wife Heather and I are keen to live in another country, learn a language, and experience another culture in depth. Short term tourism or backpacking seems to offer a shallow, and perhaps selfish, experience, and being committed Christians we want to serve God in whatever we do. We know it's a harder road, and we might risk life and limb, but we think living out our faith and making a positive impact on other people's lives will enrich our own.

We joined the Australian Volunteers Abroad (AVA) programme run by the Overseas Service Bureau (OSB); a non-Government international aid organisation that matches up volunteers with roles in developing countries. In October 1989 the OSB called to offer us a two-year teaching post at a rural high school in Samoa (then known as Western Samoa) - giving us three days to accept.

Knowing almost nothing about Samoa, we scoured books in our local library for information (there being no internet in 1989). While we saw pictures of peaceful villages, coral reefed lagoons and happy, dancing Samoans in traditional dress, we knew that wasn't the whole story, and that Samoa was one of the least developed countries in the Pacific. As volunteers we'd live in local conditions and be paid a local salary - less than a tenth of what we earned in Australia. But we'd never been overseas before, and it seemed less risky than stepping on a land-mine in Mozambique or being shot by the Khmer Rouge in Cambodia. We accepted the offer, becoming teachers at Leulumoega Fou College, and employees of the Congregational Church of Western Samoa.

The OSB brought all volunteers (going to countries in Africa, Asia, and the Pacific) to Melbourne for a week of training before departure. We were advised on how to adapt to different cultures, given tips on how to evade serious illness and untimely death, and were admonished to be well behaved and avoid being sent home in disgrace. The next day, Jane, our Field Officer, saw us onto the plane and waved goodbye.

We are now on our own, along with four other volunteers also going to Samoa. However, apart from Erin, a teacher of children with disabilities, everyone else has lived and travelled overseas before. Carrying overweight and oversize hand luggage, they pass through airport gates hassle free - veterans in the cunning arts of deception, distraction, and evasion.

"I got most of my stuff in my coat," says Bruce, a motorcycle mechanic from Cairns. Grinning, he opens his coat like a flasher, showing pockets full of books and tools.

"An' ya gotta look confident," says Emma, a high school teacher from Perth. "If ya don't, they pounce on ya."

The others nod sagely with the assured wisdom of the cognoscenti.

"Don't worry," says Hannah, who always seems cheerful and encouraging. "You made it this far, and you'll know better next time."

We appreciate their support, but after our bag and passport debacle, we feel like we can't do anything right - like we're magnets for trouble, or just incompetent.

After an unscheduled stopover in Fiji to get more fuel (what plane flies across the Pacific without enough fuel?), we arrive in Samoa.

The hot, humid air slaps us hard in the face, as we cautiously exit the plane and step onto the tarmac. Inhaling the thick humidity into my cool, dry lungs, I feel a tightness that says an asthma attack is coming. But my Ventolin puffer is inside the cabin bag confiscated in Sydney.

"It's beautiful," says Heather, as she stops to look around her.

Behind us, the tropical lagoon glistens in the morning sunlight. Beyond the lagoon, a thin strip of deep blue sea stretches to the horizon. Coconut palms lean over bright green grass near the runway, and in the distance, green-blue mountaintops fade into a cloudy mist.

Unforgettable.

So this is Western Samoa.

Not a bad place for our first time overseas.

The sun beats down and we sweat. It's not even seven in the morning. In minutes, our clothes stick to our skin. If this is the cool part of the day, what's it going to be like by late afternoon?

I don't think I want to know.

Are we going to strike more trouble as we go through Samoan Customs and Immigration? It's only a few days since we heard about the volunteer rejected by Vietnamese Immigration, and nearly sent back to Australia.

We carry bags of duty-free goods - including an expensive camera. Will an unscrupulous official ask for a gift to 'help'?

And what about our vaccine serum? The ice has all melted now, so who knows if it's even still useable? Heather's an English teacher and I'm an engineer - what do we know about preserving serum?

Apparently, another volunteer named Mick will meet us at the airport.

"But he might not come," said Jane, "so make your way to the Seaside Inn any way you can."

Only a few days earlier, we heard a story about a volunteer who arrived in Jakarta to find no one there to meet him, no job, no accommodation, or anyone who'd even heard of him. They told us the story to lower our expectations. They succeeded.

A cart stacked with luggage appears nearby. Taking this to be the 'luggage carousel', we locate our suitcases and pull them off the cart. With relief, I find the confiscated cabin bag and locate the puffer.

Standing with our friends, we join a long line of passengers snaking its way out of the terminal building.

Looking back, I see our boxes of unaccompanied baggage being unloaded and taken to another part of the terminal building, which appears completely open, like a large pavilion. How do they maintain airport security here?

The boxes contain household belongings to get us started in Samoa - a frying pan, a fan, teaching reference books - things too big or heavy to be carried in our checked luggage. If we're worried about our duty-free coming under scrutiny, the unaccompanied baggage poses a fresh problem. We've heard so many horror stories about luggage being stolen, or customs officials extorting bribes out of passengers from rich countries. We want to retrieve our luggage before it's pilfered by a baggage handler or walks out on the arm of an airport official. I know we can't collect our unaccompanied baggage today (won't fit in a car boot), but every day it sits here is another day of temptation.

The queue inches forward again.

This queue is already the end of a long journey, even if it's the start of another. We spent the last six months having medical checks and vaccinations, leaving our jobs, and packing up our house.

As the puffer does its work, the asthma feeling fades, and my lungs adjust to the new climate. We're standing in the roof shade now, but we still feel the heat increasing.

The queue moves forward steadily until all six of us approach the Immigration desk together. Hannah hands over our passports and letters from our Samoan employers.

We wait nervously while the official carefully checks our faces against our passports. He slowly reads the accompanying letters before handing the stamped passports back without fuss.

We move forward to the next tricky step - Customs. But the Customs official nods at our duty-free bags, and after confirming we have nothing else to declare, waves us through with a smile.

Feeling relieved, we stand with our luggage on the pavement outside the terminal building.

That wasn't hard. Maybe we're not so daft after all?

A bewildering array of people bustle around us, including men in brightly coloured skirts and bare feet. Standing in the sun, the light is intense and the air thick.

A short, curly-haired man with a wispy beard, walks up and says: "G'day, I'm Mick," and reaches out a hand.

Maybe everything is finally going according to plan? What were we worried about?

"We got two cars here, so we can take youse all to Apia," says Mick. He picks up a case and begins loading luggage into a car boot.

A skirted Samoan man puts our luggage in another car, handling heavy cases like light packs. Is he with Mick? I guess so, but Mick doesn't introduce him.

When we slip into the rear seat, I can't find any seatbelt. Should I take the risk? I guess so. Surely, we won't be in an accident on our first day.

"Good flight?" asks Mick, as we move away from the curb.

"Not bad," says Hannah, sitting in the front passenger seat.

"Except we left late," adds Heather. "And had an unscheduled stopover in Nadi."

"Sounds pretty normal," says Mick.

"Is this your car?" asks Hannah.

"Nah - borrowed this one and rented the other. We've got 'em for the day, so it doesn't matter what 'appens - we c'n get around."

"Jane said we're going to The Seaside Inn," says Hannah.

"Yeah, we booked it, but I dunno whether youse can all stay there yet. They might be havin' a lend of us."

"Even with a booking?"

"Yeah, nah, they'll prob'ly have rooms for most of ya."

"Most of us?"

"Yeah, don' worry, we'll find somethin' else if y'se can't all fit in."

Mick's casual attitude to our accommodation is unsettling. If the OSB booked the hotel weeks ago, why aren't there rooms?

Turning onto the road, we pick up speed and a cool breeze blows through the windows. Although only travelling sixty kilometres per hour, Mick works hard to dodge large potholes and avoid people and animals on the road.

In Western Samoa, people drive on the right, like in Europe and the US - a remnant of their German colonial past. It feels odd travelling on the wrong side of the road, but Mick's slow pace eases our discomfort.

Putting aside our accommodation concerns, we feast our eyes on the surrounding sights. In the soft sunlight and deep shadows of early morning, we encounter a new and enchanting world waking to a new day.

We see houses made of brightly coloured posts and a roof, but without walls - Samoan *fales*.

Three teenage boys walk on the edge of the road. They wear faded, dirty tee-shirts, with colourful cloth wrapped around their waists. One boy swings a machete in his hand. They glance at the passing car, but don't move off the road.

Blue woodsmoke drifts across the road smelling strangely pungent and earthy. There are unfamiliar cooking smells too, suggesting strange foods.

Dark-haired, shirtless children, run across green grass between *fales*, carrying metal dishes and plates.

A large, ornate church towers over simple village *fales*, its white walls shining in the morning sunlight. Women and children walk towards the church wearing white dresses and lacy white hats - like old photos of my great-grandparents. We hear a 'clang, clang' noise as a boy bangs a rusty gas cylinder hanging from a tree.

"What are youse gonna be doin' here?" asks Mick.

Says Hannah, "Computer programming in the public service."

"We're teaching at Leulumoega Fou," adds Heather, struggling to pronounce the name.

"I know the place," says Mick. "We'll pass it soon."

Several dark-coloured pigs scamper across the road and seemed unconcerned by the approaching vehicle.

A teenage girl sweeps the steps of her family *fale*, bent over and using what appears to be a large hand broom.

We see a few traditionally thatched *fales*, with rounded, domed roofs. Most appear rectangular; built on concrete bases, with low peaked, corrugated iron roofs. The bright colours of posts and roofs - orange, yellow, aqua blue, and green - mix with intense colours of flowers and foliage.

A lonely horse stands tethered under a tree.

Dogs run across the road in front of the car, and a few vehicles pass in the opposite direction.

We're suddenly startled by the noise of a brightly coloured bus passing in the opposite direction. Music blares from loudspeakers and quickly fades into the distance.

The road wanders in gentle curves, lined here and there with white flowering frangipani, pink cascading fuchsias, and bright red hibiscus bursting between dark green leaves. We can't tell where each village ends and another begins, but we're captivated by one scene after another filled with curious buildings and tropical plants. Scattered between the bright colours and green leaves, the earthy tones of traditional thatch and unpainted wooden structures frame the bright blue sea.

We pass a group of two-storey school buildings painted bright blue beside a rugby field.

Everywhere, majestic coconut palms tower over everything, reaching for the white clouds, and the soft, blue sky.

The colours and smells seem intense.

"Y'school's over there," says Mick, gesturing to our right.

In the distance, we see a wide expanse of green grass and some buildings behind a long white fence. As we ponder where we'll live for the next two years, the vision vanishes when the car enters another village.

It's awe-inspiring to think we're on a tiny dot in the middle of the world's largest ocean. But the tiny dot is a wondrous place of extravagant, natural beauty. Its splendour overcomes our weary fatigue caused by all the travel stress and sleepless night.

When Mick points out a large industrial building on our right, he breaks the spell of enchantment. "Vailima beer factory," he says. "Biggest industry here is making the local beer."

"Any good?" asks Hannah.

"Not bad. It's made under licence from CUB, so it's sorta Australian beer."

We make a left turn and travel down a road looking more like an Australian street. Discarded plastic bottles float in large open drains lining each side of the road, and unsightly litter collects on fences. Unkept buildings in lots in various states of wear and decay mingle with *fales*, a ramshackle collection of shops, workshops, and storage areas enclosed by decrepit looking fences and gates.

"My joint's on the left," says Mick as we pass more dilapidated buildings, *fales*, and large open drains filled with stagnant water.

I hope Mick's place is in better shape than these buildings.

We turn right at the town centre, passing the clock-tower we've seen in tourist brochures. The main street of the capital is rough; Mick sometimes veers to the wrong side of the road to dodge potholes.

Opposite the shady trees and grassy expanse on our left are more tattered buildings covered with discoloured and peeling paint. With rusty roofs, and broken siding hanging off shabby walls, some buildings look like they're falling down.

Standing out against this visual decay, are the imposing Catholic church, the Australian and New Zealand High Commissions, and the Congregational Church building. Heather looks visibly shocked. If this is the best street in the capital, what's the rest of it like? It seems the books in our local library were hopelessly out of date, and portrayed a pristine ideal, not the hard reality of a developing country. My family came from rough and ready outback Australia, but this feels different - like no one cares.

As the road curves around the harbour's edge, we pass a large multi-story building that looks spectacularly modern, clean, and smart.

"Aggie Grey's Hotel," says Mick. "Best place in town. Just rebuilt and renovated."

"Not the Seaside Inn then?" suggests Hannah wryly.

"'Fraid not."

"If there's no room at the Seaside Inn, maybe we can stay there?"

"You wish," says Mick sardonically.

A little further on, we stop near a cargo ship looming over some rusty shipping containers and a few large shady trees. In front of us is a ramshackle place of peeling white paint, red trim, and a rusty iron roof. A peeling sign attached to two posts in the front garden declares it to be 'The Seaside Inn'.

"Here y'are," says Mick. "Youse can get out now."

As we spill out of our car, the second car pulls up alongside, bringing Erin, Matt, and Emma.

The small front garden looks inviting. White cafe-style tables and chairs sit amongst a scattering of small flowering shrubs and bushes. But wafting over the unkept building are diesel fumes and industrial odours from the wharf, and the fulsome smell of a septic tank.

"Wait here while I sort things out," says Mick, threading his way through the garden to the entrance. Meanwhile we stand in the street.

"What are we waiting for?" asks Bruce.

"Mick is checking whether we can stay," says Hannah.

"I thought we had a booking?" says Erin, looking puzzled.

"We do - but that doesn't mean we can stay."

"Oh," says Erin, her face falling. "What sort of place is this if they don't take bookings?"

"Knowing the OSB, I'd say it's a cheap one," says Bruce, grinning.

"It says, 'Private Hotel' on the sign," says Emma dubiously.

Lower your expectations, I think to myself. *That's what they said. Is this what they meant?*

"Maybe we can have breakfast here?" suggests Erin hopefully.

Arriving on a delayed overnight flight, we had no dinner the previous evening, and nothing to eat on the plane. Not only are we sleepless in Samoa, but we're also starving.

Mick is soon back. "It's like I thought," he says. "They 'ave rooms for five of ya, but don't have any free yet. We'll have to come back after lunch - and one of yous'll hafta stay somewhere else."

"Where else is there?" asks Erin, keen for something better.

"There's another place down the road - sorta bed-and-breakfast - where other volunteers stay. Anyway, too early to check now. We'll 'afta come back later."

Our weary faces look at him dubiously.

"Don' worry," he says to reassure us. "Should be able to find somethin' else for one of y's. They've got a double room 'ere," he adds, looking at Heather and me. "So you two should probably stay 'ere. We can sort the rest of y's out when we come back."

While we ponder whether we're lucky or unlucky, at least something is certain.

"What are we going to do till then?" asks Erin, her voice betraying frustration.

"You can all come to my place if y'like," says Mick. "Might be able to knock up some brekky if you're not fussy."

Relief floods our faces - something to eat at last. So far, it's about the only thing Mick has said with any certainty.

"You can leave your luggage 'ere - they said they'd hold it till you come back. They said they'd lock it in a room - it should be okay."

I feel alarm at the thought of being separated from our luggage again. But Mick has been here a year already - he should know, right? There's a pause while we all look at each other doubtfully. Then Mick opens the car boot and says, "So if you're all 'appy - youse can bring ya cases in."

Carrying our suitcases from the cars, we enter a lounge area the size of a large home living room, with a few armchairs and coffee tables scattered about. Old, framed prints decorate the timber walls, and some elegant antique lamps hang from the ceiling. It looks more like a quaint 1930s movie set than the 1990s 'private hotel' it claims to be. All it needs is Hemingway in a chair with whisky in one hand, a Cuban cigar in the other, and a spittoon in the corner.

A tall Samoan woman stands behind a reception desk. She's beautifully dressed in a brightly patterned top and long skirt. A bright red hibiscus flower pinned into her dark hair sets off a beaming smile as she calls out, "*Talofa*" (hello).

That's encouraging.

She opens an ancient door behind the reception desk, revealing a tiny, dusty room with decayed and splintered boards, leaving gaping holes in the floor.

Not encouraging.

Is this a good idea? Probably not, but we're too tired and hungry to voice any concerns. What can we do?

Putting our luggage down, I grasp a straw of reassurance when the lady turns a very large key in the lock.

But the time between decision and regret turns out to be short.

A few minutes later, Mick drives down a short, dusty road, and stops in front of a haunted house - a lonely, double-storey building, in bad repair, and partially covered by overgrown creepers.

"I got upstairs," says Mick, gesturing towards a rickety wooden staircase.

As he bounds up the weather-beaten stairs and opens his front door, we follow slowly and tentatively. While the worn steps feel solid, a few bent nails hold the wobbly railing together, and I see evidence of a succession of make-do repairs.

Entering Mick's flat, the bright yellow Laminex benchtop in the small kitchen stands out against a mishmash of patched grey Masonite walls, and a cracked and curled linoleum covered floor. It looks like a hovel to me. In Australia, it would be unfit for human habitation, condemned by the authorities, and demolished. We don't know it yet, but Mick's lucky; in Apia it's highly valued volunteer accommodation.

"Make yourselves at home," he says, gesturing towards a few odd pieces of furniture - a small couch and some wooden chairs. "Sorry we don't have 'nuff chairs. Loo's there if anyone wants it," he adds, pointing to a door on the left. Two other doors suggest bedrooms.

We wearily sit on Mick's chairs, or on the floor with our backs to the wall, where we hope it's cooler.

After checking with Mick, I put the two precious serum vials in his fridge and wonder if they'll still work after being so long at room temperature.

Meanwhile, Mick pulls a container from his fridge, and then stands up and waves it like a long-lost treasure.

"We're back in margarine," he says triumphantly.

"You ran out?" asks Emma.

"Yeah - butter and margarine, 'cos we ate it all before the margarine ship came back."

"Does that happen much?"

"The country's always runnin' out of somethin'. We'll be in real trouble if we run outa somethin' serious - like loo paper."

Mick gets to work slicing bread to make toast and turns on his electric kettle.

"Hey Mick, is the water here okay to drink?" asks Hannah.

"Yeah," says Mick. "Doesn't seem too bad - pick up the occasional bug, but that 'appens everywhere."

Only a few days earlier, during our training, a doctor had repeatedly admonished us to always drink clean water.

"To avoid cholera or gastroenteritis, boil your water for twenty minutes. It's the best way to kill pathogens. You can treat it with iodine or other purifiers too, but they're not as good," he said.

"Do you boil it for twenty minutes?" asks Hannah.

"Twenty minutes?" says Mick, aghast. "Bloody hell, not that long! Can't anyway - the kettle turns itself off once the water boils."

"That's what they told us we should do to kill all the bacteria," says Erin.

"Yeah, well, maybe if you're tryin' t' drink water out of some river full of giardia somewhere then … yeah, maybe … but this's about all we do 'ere."

"No fresh milk," he adds, "only powdered."

Did Mick use boiled water to make the powdered milk? I don't have the energy to ask. Mick says he doesn't "get sick much." Maybe we should take the risk?

Eating Mick's toast topped with jam, and washing it down with tea and coffee, we start to relax. But the hot drinks make us sweat more, and our skin turns red and blotchy.

We flap our shirts off our sweaty skin.

It doesn't do any good.

It's already stiflingly hot, but it's only nine in the morning.

And it's only going to get worse.

People told us polyester is bad in high humidity. Wear cotton they said!

But we're wearing polyester clothing because it was great in the cold, dry air of the plane.

But seriously, does cotton make that much difference?

Well, I hope so. Otherwise, we're doomed! Unfortunately, our cotton clothes are in our luggage, safely locked away at the Seaside Inn.

"Who lives downstairs Mick?" asks Emma, wiping the back of her head with a towel.

"The landlady," says Mick, as he sits on the floor with us. "Elena's *afakasi* of some sort - father was a yank who ended up 'ere somehow."

"What do you mean, *afakasi*?" asks Erin.

"Half-caste - mother was a Samoan girl."

"Oh," says Erin, frowning with distaste, "I don't like that word."

"Well, you betta get used to it 'cos they use it a lot 'ere. Anyone who looks a bit Chinese is *afakasi*. 'S not an insult, necessarily, sorta like a description."

"Well, I don't like it."

As we ply Mick with more questions, we discover he's on his second tour of duty after two years in Papua New Guinea (PNG). He explains that while there "might be a bit of breakin' and enterin' in Apia sometimes," PNG is bigger and has a lot more crime.

"Mind you, if y' leave stuff lyin' around 'ere it's gonna walk. But takin' your stuff without asking and never bringin' it back is called borrowin' or sharin' here. And if you lend somethin' to 'em, you'll never see it again."

"Sounds like stealing," says Erin.

"Yeah, but they see it different like. Everything belongs to the *aiga* - the family, or the village - at least traditionally."

"Sounds like communism," comments Hannah.

"Bit like that - sorta cultural communism."

Mick says he's organised some training for us at the UNDP (United Nations Development Program) building. "Ya gotta be there at eight o'clock tomorrow, so that'll test youse all out."

It's getting hotter. Everyone's sweating. No matter where we sit or stand, the air in Mick's flat is breathless and stifling. As though constructed with deliberate malevolence, the building design ensures no life-giving breeze can enter, or God forbid, pass through the place. Seeing a breeze blow the leaves on the nearby trees, Heather and I step outside onto the front door landing. We desperately hope for the refreshing feeling of cool wind on our sweaty faces. But the balcony is in the full glare of the tropical sun. Feeling a few whispers of air, we soon sweat even more, and despondently return inside.

"Jane said we're doing some language training?" says Erin.

"Yep - starts Wednesday," says Lance. "Got some Peace Corps language teachers comin' - if they turn up."

"What do you mean?"

"Well … jus' because they say they're comin' doesn't mean a lot here. Pretty sure Fagalele'll be there, but Jake can be dodgy. The OSB's payin' 'em, so that should help."

"I'm looking forward to that," says Erin.

We've been told we need to teach using English. But being at the country's only school for people with disabilities, Erin needs to speak some basic Samoan.

While there's training in the morning, we'll have the rest of the day free.

"There's a *fiafia* Sat'dy night," adds Mick. "That's a feast or party. They're goin' t' cook an *umu* so you can eat traditional food cooked on hot stones."

While Mick assures us "a lotta people might come," he can't say who. For someone who's organising the event, he doesn't seem to know very much.

When Erin expresses her belief, she'll soon move to a house provided by Loto Taumafai (her school), Mick is sceptical.

"You don't think they will?"

"Well, I'm jus' sayin that most times things don't work the way we expect 'ere. You might 'afta stay at the Seaside Inn for a while - or find somethin' else somewhere."

As the heat and humidity continue to rise, and Mick casts a dark cloud of uncertainty over everything, I feel faint and discouraged. The wet and matted hair around Heather's red face says she's also flagging. Seeing us all wilt, Mick says we can rest on his bed under a fan. But the small, rusty fan fixed to the wall in Mick's spartan bedroom turns out to be too inefficient, and too far away, to make any difference. As we wipe sweat from our sleep-deprived eyes, we stew in a nauseous fog of fatigue and lethargy. We've only been in the country a few hours. The heat is unbearable, and we're just sitting around.

How can anyone work in this oppressive climate?

Sleep is impossible. But sweating in a shabby room, in a decrepit, falling down house in Western Samoa, I think about the decisions that led us to this point.

Hearing God's call on our hearts, we left the certainty of the dance to the steps and music of our culture, secure employment with a bright future, the comfort of our mortgaged home, in one of the world's safest countries, and most liveable cities. While some friends think we're mad, and we expect hardship, the words of Jesus ring true for us - this time we choose the hard, narrow way we believe leads to life.

We expect the hard road means self-denial, discipline, sacrifice, and maybe risk to life and limb. But what about the life Jesus promises? Eternal life for sure, but what about life here and now? What does that life look like? Because our every step, taken in faith, hope and prayer, seems risky, and something always seems to go wrong, beginning with our passport fiasco in Sydney. Now Mick's comments add darkness to the already thick fog of our uncertain future. I'm not sure we can make it through our first day, let alone two years.

Have we made a grave mistake?

2
THE SEASIDE INN

*"Therefore do not worry about tomorrow, for tomorrow will
worry about itself. Each day has enough troubles of its own."*
Matthew 6:34

"What do you do at the YMCA?" Bruce asks Mick while he
gets lunch.

"Teach carpentry, and some admin. We wanna offer
more trades, so you're here to teach motorcycle maintenance. Tapua runs
the place - or e's supposed to - but I end up organisin' a lot, or it won't
'appen. Tapua's good at oilin' wheels though. Ya need someone like that to
get around the politics of the place."

"Are kids keen to learn trades?" asks Hannah.

"No. Problem is people here see trades as crap work. They want their
kids to go to high school and get jobs in town, or New Zealand - which
they got Buckley's of, really."

"Is there much carpentry work here?"

"There's plenty of shitty carpentry goin' on, that's for sure. But I reckon
trade skills are better than learnin' some of the crap they do at school."

Being the teachers of 'crap' we're taken aback by Mick's cynical disdain for our work but say nothing.

Mick's Samoan mate returns after lunch. Feeling relieved, but not hopeful, we escape Mick's residential sauna and pile back into the cars.

At Betty Moors Accommodation (a guest house) Mick finds a room for Erin, who's pleased to find the place looks out on coconut palms and ocean waves.

Returning to the Seaside Inn, we retrieve our luggage intact. Another Samoan woman, chewing gum, takes us to a large open area with many open doors leading to rooms at the back of the hotel.

"Bathroom - there," she says, vaguely waving towards an open door opposite.

"Your room," she adds, vigorously masticating gum while pushing open a rustic wooden door.

It's small and sparsely furnished, with a simple double bed and a wooden chair in the corner. The bed has a top sheet and pillows, but no blanket. Cracked and curled yellow linoleum covers the floor. The painted walls have the pattern of dark fungus we're seeing everywhere. Above the bed is an open louvre window, but no movement of air. It feels like an oven, but there's a fan on the wall.

I immediately flick a switch and the fan bursts into life.

A cool breeze. What a relief.

Finally changing into some life-saving cotton clothing feels wonderful. But when I close the door, it doesn't shut properly, and there's no lock. How do we keep our things secure? I jam the door in place, lie down on the bed, and close my eyes.

After thirty minutes of turning and sweating, we conclude the room is actually a fan-forced oven. In the full glare of the afternoon sun, the hot iron roof radiates from above, while the fan stirs the hot air to roast us evenly on all sides.

Finally abandoning any hope of sleeping, we try sitting under shady trees in the front garden. After all, 'The Seaside Inn' must surely be close to the seaside, where there might just be a sea breeze.

Since we can't lock our room, we put everything in our suitcases and lock those instead. The suitcases are heavy (without wheels), so we can't imagine a bandit bolting off with our belongings.

Outside, we find Bruce, Hannah, and Emma already sitting at one of the cafe tables in the shade. There is indeed a sea breeze, and our discomfort fades as we sit in cotton clothes in the shade. For once, we have made the right call.

Heather begins writing a letter to her parents describing our departure fiasco and arrival.

But while it is indeed by the seaside, the Seaside Inn does not afford the picture-postcard views the name might suggest - like a beautiful sandy beach, fringed with coconut palms, where holiday makers lounge on deck chairs sipping pina coladas. Instead, across the street a cargo ship obscures the sea view, and looms over rusty shipping containers and shabby buildings.

But to our left, we have a grand view of Apia across the harbour. Dwarfing the town below, dark mountains rise over a thousand metres into the clouds. The sinking evening sunlight reflects beautifully off prominent buildings and the white Catholic church.

Above the buildings, I think I see Mount Vaea, the last resting place of the man Samoans call Tusitala (teller of tales), known to the rest of the world as the author Robert Louis Stevenson. His famous novels, *Treasure Island* and *Kidnapped*, had enthralled me as a child. I look forward to visiting the author's grave one day soon.

"Reminds me of Malaysia," says Hannah. Her father, being a diplomat, she grew up in some interesting places.

"When I was a kid, I thought Malaysia was a magical place - full of exotic colours and plants, and amazing people. When I went back a few years ago, I was surprised how dirty, run down and chaotic it all seemed. You remember things differently as a kid."

"Yeah, I've backpacked through parts of Asia," says Bruce. "This place looks pretty quiet."

"It's Sunday," says Hannah. "I guess places are closed."

"Like France," says Emma. "God, 'alf the time the place is dead as a doornail 'cos everythin's closed."

Emma comes across a little blunt, but like Hannah and Bruce, she has a down-to-earth friendliness, and seems unfazed by a little hardship.

Relaxing with friends, our spirits rise, but now we're thirsty. What we need is a cold drink.

Today, even budget places provide complementary bottles of water in a room, perhaps with a welcome note. In 1990, the concept of bottled water is unknown in Samoa, and it's a wild fantasy to expect such courtesies at the Seaside Inn.

The hotel staff have all disappeared - apparently leaving the guests to fend for themselves.

Perhaps there's a jug of cold water in the kitchen fridge?

No such luck.

There's some cold water left in an electric kettle on the bench, but we don't know its history.

"Should we drink it?" I ask. "Or boil it first?"

"It'll be hot then," says the ever-practical Emma. "Don' worry about it."

In the comfort of our training course in Melbourne a few days ago, we were determined to diligently follow the doctor's orders about only drinking safe water. But in the hot and sweaty fog of real-world fatigue, our inhibitions melt like butter.

Pouring the water into chipped cups, we justify our actions by using Mick's stamp of approval (the water "doesn't seem too bad") and convince ourselves it's a once-off decision.

Henceforth, we will only drink water we know is clean; we don't want to become violently ill when we've only just arrived.

Sipping our suspect water, we hear church bells ringing in the distance. Perhaps the start of an afternoon church service? The bells remind us of ordinary life, and in the company of friends, we quietly absorb our new surroundings, and reflect on our journey so far.

By gossiping about Mick.

For someone who's lived in Samoa for a year now, he doesn't know very much. Mick books accommodation, but there's no room at the inn. He seems blasé about drinking potentially contaminated water. Mick organises language trainers and then doubts they'll turn up. He thinks teaching high school is 'crap', and couches everything with 'hopefully', 'maybe', or 'dunno'.

At the point when we're most vulnerable, Mick has shredded our last crumbs of confidence. While we accept that in Samoan culture things might not work the way we expect, Mick is an Australian! He should know better. An Australian organisation, the OSB, organised and paid for our accommodation. Surely, we can't blame these failures on Samoan culture.

"Lower your expectations," they said. But how low are we supposed to go? Isn't there a limit?

What we don't know is that it's only the beginning, and it isn't long before the penny drops; Mick is an optimist.

That evening we attend a barbeque but are too sleep deprived to remember anything about it and return to the Seaside Inn utterly exhausted.

The single bathroom turns out to be shared by all the hotel guests and breaks new ground in minimalist design. There's a small hand basin and a large shower at one end. We hang towels on nails hammered into the wall beside a splintered mirror shard - somehow affixed to the wall. If we lean in close and close one eye, we can just see ourselves reflected in the glass splinter. We feel annoyed, not realising that even a glass mirror shard is a bonus in Samoa.

How do we clean our teeth with 'safe' water?

We use the tap water again. Rationalising our decision with Mick's hearty endorsement ('not too bad'). After all, we're not drinking the stuff!

We become alarmed by a loud knocking sound coming from the front. Tentatively opening the front door, I find three men standing there. They immediately walk in like they're hotel guests.

"We go for walk," says one, with a German accent, "but we are locked out."

They must be telling the truth - I can't imagine tourists freeloading at the Seaside Inn. Aggie Greys, maybe, but not here.

They thank me for opening the door and lock it behind them. I suggest leaving it unlocked - maybe there are other guests?

"Nein," says another, shaking his head. "They tell us to lock at night - people steal things."

Hearing about thieves visiting in the night is another blow to our sense of security. While the hotel front is secure behind a locked door, our end of the building is completely open and unlockable.

And we can't lock our room door.

Will we be robbed while we sleep?

But back in our room, Heather's worried about something worse.

"What should we do about mozzies?"

A few days earlier, a doctor described the terrible suffering caused by dengue fever, and other deadly mosquito-borne diseases.

Thankfully, Samoa is malaria free; but dengue fever is endemic.

"Don't worry," said the doctor, "it's really only children and adults with complicating factors who die."

But then we heard about the unfortunate demise of a field officer, who contracted dengue in an undisclosed country and died.

Last year.

Erin ferrets around and discovers the 'undisclosed country' is Samoa. Apparently trying to reassure us, the doctor then explained she only died because she also had a nasty coral cut infection.

But they also warned us it's easy to get coral cuts. Since coral has some very nasty bacteria, a small nick on the skin can easily turn into a tropical ulcer.

Complications aside, the fact is, the poor woman was only in Samoa a few days and she died!

Then Jane, our current field officer, told us how she got dengue fever on her first, brief visit to Samoa, only a few months earlier. Taking precautions and staying in the pampered luxury of the brand-new Aggie Greys Hotel wasn't enough to protect her. She got on the first plane back to Australia and spent two weeks in hospital - being a curiosity to medical staff unfamiliar with the tropical disease.

"Be vigilant," they said. "Apply plenty of mosquito repellent. Always sleep under a mosquito net. Check insect screens for small holes. Every mosquito is a vicious predator - one bite might prove fatal. But don't worry, the risk of death is small."

How small is that?

"Oh, and don't touch the mosquito net while you sleep. Mosquitos can bite through the netting."

How are we supposed to do that when we toss and turn in the heat? We realise we should have packed our mosquito nets in our checked luggage. We shipped them in our unaccompanied baggage because they were bulky, and we understood we'd be staying in a 'hotel' in Apia.

And so we are.

A 'private hotel' no less - the Seaside Inn.

Since there are no mosquito nets, I inspect the insect screens over the windows. Fortunately, they're so coated with dirt, spider webs, and fungal growth, there's no way anything's getting through those screens - neither mozzies, nor cool night air.

"What about the door?" asks Heather. "Maybe there are mosquitos in the room already?"

Mercifully, the room appears mosquito free.

For the moment.

"Maybe we just close the door and apply lots of RID (insect repellent)?"

"I suppose so," says Heather wearily.

Hopefully, that'll be enough to thwart all but the most determined mosquito hunting for our blood.

Following all our training advice now seems too hard - now that we're in Samoa. And since we can't follow our trainer's well-meaning advice, we instead rationalise what we do. It may not work, but it makes us feel better.

As we lie down to rest under the oscillating fan, sleep feels so tantalisingly close.

But not close enough.

In the dark, a loud clanging pierces our ears. A ship dragging its anchor chain? Dogs bark close by, and we hear people talking and laughing in the street. But our exhaustion eventually overcomes our anxiety, and our minds settle in peace and stability.

BANG, BANG, BANG - the floor, walls and bed all shake. With peace and stability shattered like the mirror shard, Heather grabs my arm in fright. "What's that?"

It sounds so close. Are we being attacked? Are thieves breaking in?

Raised voices and yelling in a language we don't understand.

Is it outside our door?

I tentatively push the door ajar and look outside.

No, I think the voices are coming from the kitchen.

BANG, BANG, BANG - the building shakes again.

I cautiously creep down the passage towards the kitchen and peek round the corner.

The three Germans stand around the kitchen bench looking excited. One swings a large knife down, and with a "thud", buries it in the soft husk of a coconut. He then lifts the knife and coconut together, swinging them down hard on the bench with a terrific BANG, shaking the bench, floor, and walls. The other two call out encouragement.

"Hey! What are you doing?"

"We open this coconut," says the man holding the knife, visibly excited. "Can you open coconuts?"

"Dis is not right - I'm sure," says another man doubtfully.

"Ja - ist too hard," says the other, shaking his head.

"No, I don't know," I say, feeling relieved that no gangs are storming the building. "We're trying to sleep. My wife was frightened by the noise you're making."

"Oh, we are very sorry," says the first man, looking contrite and releasing the knife.

"What was it?" asks Heather, as I lie down again.

"Three Germans trying to open a coconut."

"Open a coconut?" She sounds astonished in the darkness.

"They were banging it on the kitchen bench. They said they're sorry and they'll open it tomorrow."

Shaking her head in dismay, she lies down again, relieved to find we're not under threat, and no one is hurt.

It may be the end of the longest day of our lives, and we may be dog tired after a sleepless night, but two days of collective adrenalin is still coursing through our veins.

This day of days has had enough trouble of its own.

What new crisis or disaster will we encounter tomorrow?

We don't know, but we leave it in God's hands, and let tomorrow worry about itself. As Jesus' words ring in our thoughts, we thank God for his mercy and goodness in bringing us this far, and look to tomorrow with the hope we surely need after this day of days. What we don't realise is that letting tomorrow worry about itself is exactly what any sensible Samoan would do. And so unwittingly, and perhaps unwillingly, we're making our first tottering steps to becoming a little bit Samoan.

Tossing and turning in the heat, the fan's white noise helps muffle the background clang and chatter. As we relax, the fog of sleep slowly drifts over our exhausted bodies and weary minds.

But the day is not over!

Suddenly, a pack of howling, barking dogs, erupts out of the darkness. Or so it seems; the noise is so close.

"What's that?" Heather calls out terrified.

The loud barking and howling subside to a growling noise at the window. Then it seems to move into the room as another frenzy of barking shatters the night. As I imagine savage, bare teeth, gnashing and salivating in the darkness, I realise they're under the floor.

Leaping out of bed, I bang the floorboards with my fist. As another frenzy of barking and yelping erupts, the noise moves towards the window. Peering out, I see a single dog run off in the moonlight, pursued by a larger pack.

> They're gone now.
> Heather groans and we lie down again.
> Is that all?
> We hold hands in the darkness,
>> hearing the ship's anchor chain,
>> "clang, clang,"
>> voices in nearby rooms,
>> laughter in the street,
>> and the rhythmic sound of the fan sweeping
>> back and forth in the sultry moonlight ...
> and
>> ... finally
>> ... we fall asleep.

3

APPEARANCES

*"Do not judge by appearances, but
judge with right judgement."*
John 7:24

I t's early morning when the sound of the ship's anchor chain drags us awake. The fan still blows, but the air feels clean and refreshing. Fresh floral fragrances now mix with the scent of freshly fallen rain.

I get up quietly to let Heather sleep longer. Poking my head out the door, I see Hannah emerge from the bathroom holding a bundle of clothes.

"Morning," she says smiling. "Grab the shower now if you like - we're having breakfast in the garden."

Quickly finding a towel and some clothes, I enter the empty bathroom and close the door. A six-inch gap separates the shower from the building, and I look through the gap into the backyard, where anyone can look in.

When I turn the shower's only tap, a torrent of cold water falls from the open pipe above me. No shower head. Or hot water. That's okay - we haven't stopped sweating since we got off the plane.

The cold water is bracing at first, but as I wash off the sweat and grime with soap, the baptism of cleansing water renews both body and soul. For the first time, I not only feel positive and hopeful, but also cool and refreshed.

True, the cool and refreshed feeling only lasts five minutes, but it's worth it.

Back in our room I find Heather pulling clothes from her suitcase. After telling her there's only cold water, and to mind the gap, I head to the garden.

I pass through a kitchen alive with activity and the enticing scent of coffee and toast. Three Samoan women cut up fruit, butter toast, and carry delectable dishes to waiting guests. Wearing matching colourful *puletasi* (traditional women's formal wear) like a uniform, the place looks like a proper hotel. Morning sunlight breaks through the leaves and flowers in the front garden, where guests eat breakfast.

I join Hannah sitting at a small table.

"Try this pawpaw and lime," she says. "It's great - they'll bring you some soon."

A little later, one of the Samoan servers puts a plate on the table; half a pawpaw, cut lime, and a spoon.

While the breakfast is enticing, I also smell oil and diesel fuel from ships at the nearby wharf, and occasionally the distinct odour of a nearby septic tank.

But Hannah's right - the pawpaw and lime are delicious. After toast topped with jam, we finish with orange juice and coffee. It feels wonderful. Heather joins us a little later, also looking like a new person.

After breakfast we clean our teeth once again, using water from the tap that Mick declared doesn't make him "sick much."

Erin arrives with Mick, who promised to walk us to the UNDP building for our first day of orientation. We soon set off wearing appropriate clothing

- cotton shirts, shorts, and thongs (flip-flops). Being sun-conscious Aussies, we also wear hats and sunglasses.

A few doors down from the Seaside Inn, we pass a dilapidated building. Decayed wooden steps lead to a door of peeling paint. Fungus covered walls shelter under a rusty iron roof, and uncontrolled vegetation grows up the side. A faded and peeling sign says, 'Ministry of Transport'.

"An abandoned building, Mick?"

"No," says Mick, indignant. "That's the Ministry of Transport."

"Really? Looks derelict."

A car pulls up and a Samoan man emerges carrying a briefcase. He wears a well ironed shirt and enters the building looking like how civil servants might look in Samoa. Maybe I should stop judging by appearance?

I dodge broken glass on the path, skirt a large hole, then trip on a lump of concrete. Is this a footpath or a minefield?

When three teenage boys standing by the roadside stare at us shamelessly, we feel unsettled.

Turning a corner, a battered red motorbike lies on the ground. Not far away, a small group of people gather around as a prone body raises a quivering leg.

"Hello, someone's come off their bike," says Mick.

"No helmet," observes Bruce.

"Yeah, nah they don't wear helmets 'ere. 'S too hot."

We stare, momentarily wondering if we can help when a battered green pickup stops next to the group. Two men climb out and confer with the people. They lift the victim onto the pickup and climb back up before the vehicle drives off.

"Samoan ambulance," says Mick without emotion. "Hopefully they'll take 'im to the hospital."

Mick's detached attitude is disconcerting, even if it's understandable. A stark reminder that life can be rough here.

"What about the motorbike?" asks Hannah. Hannah has a motorbike coming from Australia, and she's keen to make sure no one steals it.

"Someone'll come an' get it. Y' can't steal stuff like that 'ere."

"Why not?"

"Well, if ya take it 'ome to yer village it'll turn out to belong to your neighbour's cousin - or somethin' like that. They'll drag you outa ya *fale* and beat you up."

"Couldn't they hide it?"

"Ya can't hide anythin' in Samoa - everyone knows everythin' 'bout everyone. Ya know, people park their cars down there in front of Chan Mows and leave the keys in the ignition. It's not like you can drive it to Fiji and sell it."

We're in a busy road filled with Monday morning traffic. Hearing reggae music behind us growing louder, we see a colourful bus pass full of people. Painted bright yellow with red trim, there's a large sign on the side that reads 'Queen Maggie'.

Music blaring from loudspeakers smothers the engine noise, as a dusty cloud of black diesel smoke drifts over us. The others screw up their noses, but I don't mind. Diesel and dust take me back to my childhood driving a tractor on our family farm.

"Do they like reggae here Mick?" asks Bruce.

"They don't like it - they love it. Ya hear it all day, every day. 'Cept in church."

Erin groans. "I love music," she says, "but I can't stand that dink-a-dink-a reggae beat."

"Well, ya gonna have to get used to it 'ere," says Mick.

We cross the street and enter the air-conditioned UNDP building.

"Lovely," says Erin.

Doug and Jill Dalton are waiting for us and offer cool drinks. Teachers from Vaipo'uli on the island of Savai'i, we recall their faces from the barbeque yesterday. Jill wears a colourful but faded *ie solosolo* (a skirt made by wrapping one by two metre cloth around her waist).

"Before Elena comes," says Mick, "I thought ya might have some questions for us AVAs who've been here a while."

As we ply Doug and Jill with questions, we learn a 'palagi' is any European looking person - German, American, Italian, or Australian. Japanese are not palagi, and Chinese are called *saina*.

"What about black Americans?" asks Emma.

"Probably not," says Doug, looking at Mick for help. "Do we know any black Peace Corps?"

"Nope. But there's a Kenyan bloke at the UNDP. He's not palagi."

"Sounds a bit racist like," says Emma.

"Maybe," says Jill. "It's not normally derogative, but it can be. Anyway, that's just the way it is, so get used to it."

"Are there many Peace Corps Volunteers (PCVs) here?" asks Erin.

"Compared to AVAs (Australian Volunteers) there's heaps," says Jill. "You find 'em everywhere. Actually, rule number one is to make friends with a Peace Corps quick. PCVs are employees of the US Government, so they get lots of free stuff - and they like to share it."

"What sort of stuff?"

"Medication for a start - they've got a full-time nurse here to look after them. Last year a Peace Corps friend got me some cortisone cream."

"Seems mercenary," says Erin, who finds the idea of sponging off Americans distasteful.

Jill laughs. "Yeah, maybe, but all the volunteers help each other out, and sometimes you gotta get help from wherever."

While the Peace Corps have a full-time nurse and manager in the country, our support from the OSB is a reverse charges telephone call to Australia - if we can get to a phone. But while we're on our own, Judy points out while the Peace Corps have to obey US government rules and regulations, while "we have complete freedom."

While Heather and I will be living a bus ride away from Apia, Doug and Jill live on the more isolated island of Savai'i. Since Emma is also going to Savai'i, she listens keenly as Doug and Jill explain how they travel back to Apia every six weeks or so for supplies.

Says Jill, "The Lady Samoa ferry operates between Apia and Savai'i, but travel is pretty unpredictable. Sometimes it takes all day to get to Apia, and we often take a smaller ferry to Mulifanua - an hour drive from Apia. We then catch a bus or taxi, although taxis are expensive."

"What's expensive?"

"The bus fare from Mulifanua to Apia is about one *tala*, but a taxi costs twenty, a quarter of our weekly wage. And you gotta make sure the driver's not drunk, particularly at night."

"How do you tell?" asks Erin, looking shocked.

"If they slur their words or drive slowly, then get out and find another taxi."

"Will they fleece us?" asks Bruce.

"No, the fares are all laid out on a sheet of paper. There are only so many places you can go, and the Ministry of Transport has fixed the prices. It's a pretty simple system."

"They did a good job o' fleecin' that cruise ship last year," says Mick.

"What happened?" asks Emma, always keen on a juicy story.

"Well, this American cruise ship pulls into the harbour, and I don't think anyone's expectin' it. Western Samoa's not really on the cruise ship route, so it doesn't 'appen much.

"Anyway, it pulls up at the wharf and they all wanna go shoppin' - dunno what they were expectin' to buy at Chan Mows. Anyway, the yanks won't leg it to the shops cos it's too far, an' prob'ly too hot. So they start takin' taxis, an' the taxi drivers start chargin' the one *tala* fare from the Apia wharf to the clocktower. But the yanks 'ave never heard of *tala* - they've only got American dollars.

"They give taxi drivers a few bucks, but the taxis twig they can ask for more. They start chargin' ten bucks and yanks don't bat an eyelid. In the end they're chargin' twenty US dollars for a one-way trip to the shops, and the same t' come back. It was a gold mine - like all their Christmas's come at once.

"Anyway, the next day they all packed up and left - prob'ly had a good time. 'Course we don't want the taxi drivers getting' any funny ideas about charging all the palagi like that. But I reckon Yank tourists are fair game."

If anyone has moral reservations about Samoan taxi drivers fleecing American tourists, no one says so. Later, we discover that one such taxi fare would have covered a child's term school fees.

"Elena's 'ere from Immigration," announces Mick, as a smartly dressed Samoan lady appears at the door. She looks striking, in a brightly coloured *puletasi*, with a red flower pinned into her beautifully groomed hair.

"Visas can be tricky, so Elena's 'ere to talk to y'se about it."

Mick never uses surnames, or titles like Mr or Ms, and I wonder if Samoans have surnames?

Elena explains how we need to extend our six-week tourist visa for a three-month work visa and get an exit visa if we leave.

"Exit visa? What's that?"

"You can't leave the country without government approval," explains Elena.

We have to get permission to leave? Is this North Korea? Even more surprising, Elena says we need to get the local library to sign off on our exit visa - to make sure we return any borrowed books.

"Exit visas are pretty common," says Mick, as Elena leaves.

Outside, the rain buckets down in torrents. Soon after, a palagi woman appears at the door brushing rain off her clothes.

Mary Peters is from the Australian High Commission, but in contrast to the striking Elena, she has a very casual, almost frumpy look. She oversees the Australian aid programme to Samoa and tells us a little about current projects, including assistance to the AVA program.

"If you need help," she says, "you can make an appointment with the High Commissioner, Basil Teasey."

After Mary leaves, Mick says, "Ackshully Basil's not a bad bloke, but the best place to meet 'im is over a beer at Don't Drink the Water (popular bar), and you won't need to make an appointment."

The next speaker doesn't turn up, but Mick is not surprised. "Maybe tomorrow," he says.

As we finish up, Jill suggests we go to a nearby Chinese restaurant for lunch.

The rain has stopped, but as we step out of the air-conditioned room, it's like walking into a steam room.

A group of nearby loitering Samoans stare at us like we're aliens. Maybe we are.

The motorbike has gone.

Further along the road, we pass some children, who first stare and then wave vigorously calling out, "Palagi, palagi." We feel conspicuous and confused. Are we that unusual, or do they do this to every palagi?

"You get used to it," says Doug.

We pass Aggie Grey's Hotel, looking smart and beautiful against the surrounding decay.

Born to an English father and a Samoan mother, Aggie set up a small hotel in the thirties. American soldiers garrisoned Samoa during the Pacific war. Being an enterprising businesswoman, Aggie sold hamburgers to the soldiers and sailors, making her hotel very popular. After the war, returning soldiers provided a stream of guests, along with famous names like Marlon Brando and Gary Cooper. James Michener apparently modelled his South Pacific character 'Bloody Mary' on Aggie, forever immortalised in the 1958 musical film 'South Pacific'.

We heard Aggie may have sold more than hamburgers to the sailors and soldiers, but that was probably amusing gossip and tittle-tattle spread to take her down a notch. By the time Aggie passed away the year before we arrived in Samoa, she was a worldwide legend, recognised as the grand old lady of the south seas, a successful businesswoman, and a pillar of her community.

After passing the hotel, the smooth concrete footpath turns back into a minefield. Exposed jagged edges, sharp coral, or rusty iron, conspire to catch toes, cut feet, or trip the unwary, landing them flat on their faces in the dust and mud. Where streets intersect the main road, depressions fill with black mud, food wrappers, drink cans, plastic, and broken glass. Frequent heavy rain fills the depressions, forming dark pools several metres across and inches deep, successfully hiding booby traps.

We pass more children who call out, "Bye-bye", and then burst into hysterical laughter. Feeling like we're being ridiculed, we wonder what's funny. Are we beginning to feel annoyed? It's hard to tell.

I think good parents teach their children it's bad manners to call names and laugh at foreigners, but these parents suffer from no such inhibitions. Instead, they join in, laughing along with their merry children.

We stumble along, expecting the footpath to improve when we get to the shops. It gets worse.

Sure, there are proper drains, but the covers are missing, leaving randomly placed concrete pits, two feet deep - excellent traps for unwary pedestrians to fall into, break legs or injure themselves.

"Why don't they cover these holes up Mick?"

"They cover 'em up, but the covers keep walkin'. They make great shower bases, or a nice step in front of ya *fale*."

We regret wearing thongs on our casual saunter to the shops.

Next time, wear shoes.

Then, as I'm about to cross a road, a car appears from nowhere, missing me by inches. Where did that come from?

"The traffic closest to you is on your left!" says Doug.

"Try an' think like a Septic," adds Mick.

I feel shaken, but it's not the last time I'm almost run over.

While we're not dodging Khymer Rouge bullets or stepping on land mines, it seems there's no shortage of ways to injure or kill the unwary palagi.

Meanwhile, we're amazed to see Samoans saunter willy-nilly across the road at any place or time. Traffic politely slows or stops to let them cross. There's no horn honking, or road rage.

We arrive at the restaurant, which looks as familiar as Chinese restaurants everywhere. We order drinks as we scan a menu with over sixty numbered dishes.

The waiter soon serves me a glass of orange juice. With ice. Only days earlier, doctors warned us to avoid ice because it might be contaminated.

While I look at the glass doubtfully, wondering what evils might lurk within, everyone else is swashing down their iced drinks like drunken sailors.

Should I send it back?

Holding the cold glass, the delicious thought of imbibing the sweet liquid makes resistance futile. Certain I'm indulging in a guilty pleasure, for which I'll surely suffer when I'm caught, I sip the chilled, sweet beverage.

This time, I'll take the risk.

But I WILL be vigilant.

Next time.

After lunch, Doug and I walk to the grand sounding 'Chan Mow's Department Store', while others go to the market and Post Office.

Outside Chan Mow's stands a young palagi man wearing a faded red tee-shirt, a tattered blue *ie solosolo*, and well-worn thongs. He almost looks Samoan.

He nods to Doug, then looks at me and says, "Hi" with an American accent.

Returning the greeting, I ask Doug, "Who's that?"

"*Pisikoa* (Peace Corps) - prob'ly wondering who the new palagis are."

I see now why we get so much attention. We're clean, pale, and wear pristine clothing, while they're all brown and weathered, wearing faded and frayed clothing. As Jill explains later, everyone adds bleach to their laundry water to kill fungus that proliferates in the heat and humidity. The bleach, combined with dust, sun, and salt, beats, stains, and fades clothing into the weathered look we see everywhere. We stand out like unblemished and innocent lambs.

I feel envious of the young American. How long before I can blend in and feel at ease like him? More to the point, avoid children pointing at me and calling out, "Palagi, palagi."

Stepping into Chan Mow's, I think I've stepped back into 1930s rural Australia.

On my right are shelves stacked with saucepans, kerosene lamps, slabs of soap in different colours, and hand tools displayed in no particular order. Larger items sit on the concrete floor - coils of rope, nets, axes, spades, and machetes.

Picking up a machete, I find it's blunt and crudely cut.

"They sell 'em that way so you can sharpen it yourself," says Doug. "We call it a 'bush knife' here. Everyone has one. You should get one too, but lock it up, or it'll walk."

Doug also points to some hurricane lamps. "Power can be unreliable. Those lamps are a lot better than candles that blow out in the wind."

Stacked rectangular tins of kerosene sit beside foodstuffs in the 'supermarket' section. They were common in rural areas of Australia or America in the 1930s. Nearby are cube shaped tins of 'cabin biscuits' - the same biscuits that fed English sailors for centuries, also known as 'hard tack'. Next to the cabin biscuits are colourful tins of Hellaby's Corned Beef. Nineteenth century sailors introduced this food to the South Pacific and Samoans enthusiastically adopted it, calling it *pisupo* (pea-soup-o).

We catch up with the others on our way back to the Seaside Inn.

"We got a pumpkin and a loaf of bread," says Emma, visibly excited. "Cost us five *tala* - we can make soup for dinner."

"Did you haggle?" asks Erin. "I hate haggling."

"Me too," says Heather.

"Don't worry - no haggling here," says Jill.

We spend the afternoon relaxing on the hotel veranda. Another torrential downpour blots out the sun, and the noise on the roof is deafening. When it subsides, the sun comes out, and it feels even hotter.

Since the Germans have gone, Erin gets a room with us. Betty Moor's may have been nicer, but Erin seems happier in the company of friends.

Later, we migrate to the kitchen to prepare our pumpkin soup. We shoo away two mangy ginger cats sitting on the kitchen bench. Horrified and hygiene conscious, Erin searches for something to wipe the bench clean.

The kitchen appears devoid of utensils. We find one battered aluminium saucepan, and a frying pan with a cracked handle that's seen better days. There's a well-worn, wooden chopping board, but only one long, narrow knife, with half its handle missing. While it's unsuitable for cutting pumpkin, it's all we have. As I cut, the splintered handle digs into my soft hands.

As the others ransack the kitchen cupboards, they find odd pieces of cutlery, plates, bowls, and a few simple utensils.

"Where's all the stuff we saw at breakfast this morning?" asks Hannah.

"Prob'ly locked away so people can't steal it," says Emma.

"Here's some salt," says Erin, putting a small saltshaker on the bench.

"Can someone get rid of that bloody cat!" calls out Emma.

One of the ginger cats is back on the benchtop looking aggrieved. I yell, brandishing the knife, and the cat leaps off and scurries away.

"I get the feeling he lives here," I say.

"It's terrible having animals in a kitchen," says Erin, looking disgusted. She wipes the bench again.

"They might keep the rats away," suggests Bruce positively.

Hannah laughs, but Erin's face clouds at the idea rats also inhabit the kitchen.

"Don't worry," says Emma. "The soup'll be boiled so it should okay."

After a struggle, I put the chopped pumpkin in the saucepan, and the saucepan on the stove.

We're the only hotel guests using the kitchen. Is that a hint?

And the ginger cat is back on the bench, looking at us in the prim way cats do.

Emma swipes the cat away with her arm.

Scraping together enough plates, bowls, and odd pieces of cutlery, we eat our simple meal in good company.

God has been good to us today, giving us friends who are encouraging, tolerant, and able to laugh even in difficult circumstances. They're probably not the people we would have chosen, but God chose well. For life is more than food and clothing, it's also about building relationships, bonding in shared experience, and caring for those who share our journey.

Walking back past the kitchen, we see the two cats back on the kitchen bench. This time, even Erin leaves them alone. There's no point fighting battles we can't win.

That night, we lie in the darkness with the fan blowing, hearing dogs barking close by, and the noise of people in the street. This time, the screeching noise of ship scraping against ship, pierces the fearful hollow of our ears. But then the heavens open, and rain thunders down on the corrugated iron roof above our heads, drowning out everything - dogs, voices, fan and even screeching ships.

4

CULTURE

"So whatever you wish that others would
do to you, do also to them..."
Matthew 7: 12

The next day, we meet a movie star.

True, no one's seen the movie. Or heard of it.

But in 1953, Return to Paradise was a real Hollywood movie. And if Gary Cooper was its world-famous draw card, sixteen-year-old Moira MacDonald was its Samoan star.

She was working in the bank as a typist when the visiting Hollywood film producer walked through the doors. Getting his attention by making him wait at the counter (just like everyone else), the confident, charming, and beautiful teenager impressed him so much, he offered her a role in the film. Moira's strict and protective father initially opposed his young daughter mixing with wayward Hollywood actors and film directors. She would have stayed behind her typewriter if Aggie Grey hadn't pleaded on her behalf.

Mick has asked Moira to talk to us about the *fa'asamoa* (Samoan culture), and as she walks into the room, it's clear she has presence.

Her original surname being Macdonald (now Walker), Moira is obviously *afakasi*, which helps her bridge Samoan and palagi worlds. And having lived in New Zealand for many years, Moira's communication style resonates with palagis like us.

In truth, I thought I knew a little about Polynesian culture from my Auntie Anna, who came from the Tuamotu Islands near Tahiti. Soon after I was born, my mother became gravely ill, and I was nursed by my beautiful Tahitian aunt, newly arrived in Australia. Auntie Anna doted on all her nieces and nephews, and we thought she was cool; after all, who else amongst our friends had a Tahitian aunt? However, little of Auntie Anna's Polynesian culture rubbed off onto me, because it turns out I know almost nothing.

Moira begins by explaining the complex hierarchical nature of Samoan culture.

"An *aiga* (extended family) elects a *matai* to lead and represent them - it's very democratic. A *matai* has an ancient title that has an oral history extending into deep time. They're custodians of the family land and must make sure everyone has land to grow taro and feed their families. There's a hierarchy of titles, with some titles having authority over lesser titles. Below titles, there are other indicators of status, like age. Older children rank higher than younger children."

She talks about the importance of honour, shame, and face-saving.

"It's disrespectful to look someone in the eye when you talk to them. You need to look away, particularly if the person is more important than you."

Might be difficult.

"Samoans really appreciate you wearing their national dress," says Moira. She pulls an *ie solosolo* from her basket - a one by two metre piece of cloth. Wrapping it around Heather, she shows her how to tuck it in.

"Is that all they do to keep it there?" asks Heather.

"That's all - you'll be fine," says Moira with great confidence. But Heather can't help feeling insecure. What if it falls off?

Looking at Bruce and me, Moira adds, "You need to practise wearing one too."

She tells us to never wear shoes in a *fale*; don't point your feet at anyone, and say, *Tulou* (pronounced 'too-low') when you walk between people.

"Ladies, don't wear shorts in a village and definitely not bathers on a beach. Don't introduce people (how can it be rude to introduce someone?) and always sit down to discuss something important (how important?)"

Above all, Samoan culture revolves around gift giving - always bring a gift!

As we drink information like water from a fire hose, we discover that despite our best intentions, we might insult or offend someone in every interaction.

Not having lived in another culture, I'd always thought we can't go wrong treating people the way we'd like to be treated. Well, it seems we can go wrong, because it's more complicated when people are part of a different culture. Although, doing what we know, might be a good starting point.

"Don't worry," says Moira. "Samoans are very tolerant and accepting of people when they first arrive. They appreciate you making even a small effort to understand and fit in."

"An' after we've been 'ere a while?" asks Emma.

"They'll expect more of you then, but don't expect them to tell you. Face-saving is important, so to respect your dignity, they'll subtly try to suggest you do things differently."

"There's a Samoan way of doing things," goes on Moira, "the *fa'asamoa*, and there's a palagi way - we call that *fa'apalagi*. Sometimes these operate in parallel, but the more you do things within the *fa'asamoa* - the Samoan way - the easier it will be. In fact, it's wonderful to see what you can achieve when you make it work for you."

Like thirsty camels, we eagerly drink in Moira's advice. Of course, we'll be the culturally sensitive, non-patronising, non-paternalistic people we think we are. Obviously, we will do things the Samoan way. Because we want to fit in, and get things done. Don't we?

But to do things the Samoan way, we first need to understand Samoan culture, and then put it into practice.

This time we walk to the Treasure Garden (a 'better' Chinese restaurant) for lunch. This time I firmly tell the waiter I don't want ice in my orange juice. The drink turns up with ice, and I drink it, determined to be more vigilant next time.

Mick says our employers will meet us at the Seaside Inn after two in the afternoon but adds, "They may not turn up."

Nevertheless, we wait in hopeful expectation under the garden's shady trees, grateful for any zephyrs of cool breeze that waft our way.

We wait all afternoon, but no employers turn up, confirming Mick's low expectations.

Later, we clear three scrawny stray cats out of the kitchen, hoping to prepare dinner feline-free.

At Bruce's suggestion we make pineapple sandwiches - a Queensland delicacy, and very nutritious. Locally grown pineapples are a deep yellow colour, and deliciously sweet.

"Y'know," says Emma, "we've been here a couple-a-days and hardly seen a mozzie."

"I saw one in the bathroom last night," says Heather.

"You'd think after all they told us last week the air'd be thick with them," says Hannah. "Maybe they're worse in the villages?"

Nor have we become sick from drinking or cleaning our teeth with the water. Not yet.

We sleep well that night, buoyant and full of hope for the future.

I now look forward to the morning shower. It's refreshing and routine. And routine suggests stability. And stability suggests peace and serenity.

Stepping into the shower, I think about breakfast while working soap into a lather. Delicious pawpaw and lime, followed by fresh toasted bread, and the alluring aroma of coffee. Anticipation provokes pleasure.

Then the water stops.

Covered with soapsuds, I look up at the pipe, as the last few drops fall on my face.

I jiggle the tap handle. Left. Right.

Nothing.

Be patient. It'll come back.

I pace around the shower.

How can the water suddenly disappear?

It HAS to come back. I can't go through the day covered in soap.

I look up at the pipe pleading - like a dog begging for a treat.

Please.

Just enough to wash the soap off.

But no treat comes.

Thinking that the handbasin might have water, I turn those taps too.

Nothing.

There are torrential downpours in the morning, afternoon, and half the night, so why is there no water for my shower?

I give up, and resigning myself to a soap-sudded future, I wipe off as much residue as possible. Pulling clothes over my soapy skin, I head for breakfast.

Instead of showing sympathy, Hannah and Bruce think my predicament is hilarious.

"Mick said the water can be unpredictable here," says Hannah. "It can turn off for minutes or hours."

"Why? When there's so much rain?"

"No idea - but it happens in a lotta places. People sometimes keep a tub of water handy to use when the water goes off."

"Same with the power," adds Bruce, reaching for his coffee.

Adding insult to injury, Heather joins us later, having had a shower under abundant water.

It's a valuable lesson. Anything in Samoa can abruptly disappear for no apparent reason.

Be grateful when it's there.

Have quick showers.

It turns out our skin's so permanently wet with sweat, I don't notice the soap.

Entering the training room that morning, we're introduced to our professional language trainers, Jake and Fagalele.

"I love teaching people to speak my language," says Jake. "We call it *fa'asamoa'* - the same word as Samoan culture." His infectious enthusiasm creates a keen desire to learn. Although less exuberant, Fagalele oozes the same enjoyment teaching his native language.

I've always wanted to learn a new language, but it was difficult in 1970s rural Australia. But now I'm in Samoa, surrounded by Samoan speakers, it should be easy, right?

We've been told repeatedly, at the airport, in tourist brochures, and other official documents, that '*talofa*' is the way to greet a Samoan.

Straight off we learn '*talofa*' is just a formal first greeting.

"Use '*malo*', they tell us. It's more like 'hello' in English. People think you're a tourist if you say *talofa*."

Great. The only Samoan word we know turns out to be almost useless.

Over the next few days, Jake and Fagalele try to condense a six-week Peace Corps language course into four mornings.

The Peace Corps get six weeks of training living in a village? Our organisation, and hence the Australian Government, seem like miserly skinflints. Not for the first time, I get the impression Australia does things on the smell of an oily rag.

We later learn Samoan is an Austronesian language in the same family as Bahasa Malay - compelling evidence Polynesians came from South-East Asia.

Jake 'Samoanises' our names using a set of simple rules - separate all consonants with a vowel and end every word with a vowel. I become *Ieni*, and Heather becomes *Eta*.

We soon discover Samoan is a language of vowels sprinkled by the occasional consonant. A*e ia oe*? (what about you?) contains no consonants at all. While our enthusiasm is undiminished, we finish the morning with our heads exploding, and our tongues tangled with our vocal cords.

We eagerly set off for the market to practice our new language skills.

"*E fia o le tau?*" (what's the cost?), says Erin to a woman selling vegetables.

"*E a?*" (what?), says the woman, frowning at Erin.

No one understands us, and we don't understand them.

It's going to be a lot harder than we think.

The next day we take matters into our own hands and seek out our employer. Feilo Feleti is the Director of Education for the Congregational Church of Western Samoa.

We walk to the church offices in the John Williams building, which, at six stories high, is impressive and modern.

We're greeted in the ground-level reception by a young, bored-looking Samoan girl chewing gum.

She makes a phone call and directs us to the fourth floor via a cramped lift. As we wait, the cool, air-conditioned air is a welcome respite from the oppressive heat and humidity.

A tall, thin man approaches, wearing a formal business shirt, a tie, and a smart navy blue *ie faitaga*. Reaching out a hand, he thanks us for coming, and leads us to his office. We assume he must be Feilo but he doesn't introduce himself. We're not surprised, because thanks to Moira, we now know it's rude to introduce someone. How weird is that?

He directs us to sit in two chairs squeezed into a cramped office, while he sits behind a large desk.

Looking at the wall, he thanks us for coming to teach and mentions they've had AVAs before.

He's speaking to us, but why does he look at the wall?

"Did you have a smooth trip to Samoa?"

While Feilo speaks crisp English, he finishes his sentence with the Samoan intonation drop, signifying a question (we learned yesterday).

"We had no trouble," I say. It might be misleading, but I don't want to mention our passport debacle - it might make us look foolish on our first meeting.

"We're staying at the Seaside Inn for the moment," says Heather. "But we're wondering when we can go to the school?"

Feilo turns in his seat and looks past us towards the door. Thinking someone's at the door, I glance behind but there's no one there. Why doesn't he give us his attention?

He tells us our house is being painted but will be ready by Sunday.

"We have some unaccompanied baggage at the airport," I say. "But we're unsure how to pick it up, or whether we'll have to pay Customs duties."

"Oh, don't worry," says Feilo, turning to look out the window. "My cousin works at the airport - we'll get your baggage."

Then I remember Moira saying it's rude to look someone in the eye! Is Feilo being polite and showing us respect? Are we being rude looking at him?

"What address did you give?" he asks.

"We addressed it to you," I say, forcing myself to look away from Feilo. It feels uncomfortable, because my mind says I'm being culturally correct, but my instinct says otherwise.

"Good," says Feilo. "Don't worry about duties - my cousin will sort that out."

We have the distinct feeling Feilo's cousin might cut a few corners to avoid paying duties. Is that corruption? Or just doing things the Samoan way, as Moira said? Since Feilo's getting the baggage and not us, does it matter?

"I'll pick you up from the Seaside Inn after church on Sunday morning," says Feilo.

"Fa'afetai lava" (thank you very much), says Heather, trying hard to articulate her best Samoan vowels.

"Fa'afetai fo'i" (thank you also), replies Feilo, smiling and looking pleased.

We leave Feilo's office feeling buoyant with certainty. In a few days we'll be moving into our own home, which we hope will be free of stray cats, barking dogs, screeching anchor chains and sewerage smells. We will be out of Apia's shabby decay, in the clean countryside, by a tranquil lagoon surrounded by coconut palms enchanting as the tranquil villages we saw on our first morning in Samoa. Sure, arrival was a shock. But now everything's falling into place, and the future is bright.

We should know by now things rarely 'fall into place' in Samoa the way we expect. But we haven't learned that lesson.

Not yet.

5

RUMOURS OF WAR

*"Behold, I am sending you out as sheep in the midst of
wolves, so be wise as serpents and innocent as doves."*
Matthew 10:16

To mix with locals on Friday evening, we all go to Otto's Reef - a popular bar frequented by Samoans and expats.

Reggae greets us as we enter under a pergola festooned with coloured lights. Bright coloured benches, tables, chairs, and stools, adorn a bare concrete floor stained brown by spilt beer.

We get drinks from the typical bar at the back and sit down. The condensation drips from the cold glass, and the warm evening air is pleasant.

A Samoan man called Tavai engages us in polite conversation. The conversation turns from sickness in his family, to his financial difficulties, and then he asks for help.

Moira told us generosity is a strongly held cultural value; that Samoans give to anyone in need. We want to be culturally sensitive, but this doesn't seem right, and we only just met the guy. We're in a bar, not a village, and we're palagis, not Samoans.

We feel uncomfortable, but suddenly, a young palagi woman wearing a pretty blue dress intervenes.

"Go away Tavai," she says dismissively with an American accent. "You're not getting any money."

Tavai backs away, like he got caught with his hand in a cookie jar.

"Ignore him," she says sitting down. "He's a local conman. I'm Helen Schaeffer."

While we're a little shocked to see a young palagi woman dismiss an older Samoan like a child, we're glad to be rid of him.

Short, with shoulder-length blonde hair, Helen looks better dressed than everyone around us.

"We've been looking forward to meeting you guys," she says with characteristic American fervour. "We heard you were coming."

"Oh?" I say, intrigued.

"Tammy and I are PCVs teaching at Leulumoega Fou. Obviously, you're from Australia - I detect a certain accent."

"We're from Melbourne," says Heather. "I'm an English teacher. Ian's an engineer, but he's going to teach maths and science."

"What's the school like?" I ask eagerly.

"Where do I start?" says Helen, rolling her eyes. "Last year was tough. We were the only palagis on staff, so it's great to have you guys."

She says this like lack of palagis caused all their problems.

"Why was that?"

"For a start, the *pule* - that's the principal - he was hopeless; a pastor who couldn't run a school for nuts. He made the most bizarre decisions - seemed like it to us anyway, and the teachers ran rings around him. It was chaos."

"Why? What happened?"

"Sometimes Samoan teachers are too drunk or too lazy to turn up. If they do, they often don't teach. They get the class captain to write stuff on the blackboard, so the kids copy it into their books. Then they smoke with their friends or sleep somewhere."

"Sleep?" asks Heather, shocked.

"Sure - Samoans can sleep anywhere," she says, like it's an established fact.

"But don't they care about their students?" asks Heather, incredulous at the idea of drunk teachers.

"No, they don't give a damn - it's terrible, but pretty common here," says Helen with surprising candour.

"At home, a teacher would be dismissed," says Heather.

"Yeah, same in the US, but welcome to Samoa guys. They're often connected to someone with influence in the church. They might get a reprimand, but they still get paid. It's hopeless."

"Can't the principal do something?" asks Heather.

"I don't think our *pule* was high enough up the social strata. We'd have a staff meeting every morning. He gave directions, but the teachers did whatever they liked and lied about it - the hypocrisy in this place is terrible. The teachers can be violent too. Some teachers beat kids for getting wrong answers."

"Beat?"

"Hit them with a stick - or over the head with their hand."

We'd heard corporal punishment was alive and well in the Pacific, but beating students who give wrong answers seems harsh and unreasonable.

Helen says, "Last year a teacher pushed me off the school truck while it was moving. Of course, they all denied it later and said it was an accident," she adds, rolling her eyes. "But I KNOW I was pushed."

The implied animosity towards Helen alarms us. Will that spill onto us because we're palagi too? Are we entering a war zone? Or is this something Helen stirred up because she's a young, outspoken American?

Ostensibly, we're in Samoa because the country doesn't have enough qualified secondary school teachers. But if the real problem is that local teachers don't turn up to work, or turn up but don't teach, then what's the point of our help?

Are these problems pervasive across the country, or just at our school?

"We're hoping the new principal will be better, but we'll have to wait and see," says Helen.

"Who's the new principal?" asks Heather.

"Tavita Amosa - he's from Samoa College."

"What did you do before the Peace Corps?" I ask, changing the subject and hoping to learn more about her.

"College in Cleveland. I signed up before I finished so I could travel and see a bit of the world. It's my first full-time job, and it's been quite the learning curve." Helen laughs adding "Believe me!"

She's very confident for a twenty-two-year-old. Is she an 'over the top' American? Or did she grow up a lot last year?

"It'll be great to have a REAL English teacher at the school," she says.

"I thought they have English teachers?" asks Heather, surprised.

"Sure, we do - sorta," says Helen vaguely. "Kale's in charge of English, but a lotta the kids don't understand much. I don't think they teach it very well."

"Who's Kale?"

"Probably one of the brighter Samoan teachers - he's a 'faff'."

"A what?"

"A *fa'afafine* - a man who dresses and acts like a woman. They're pretty common here." Helen pauses. "Sounds like you don't know about that yet?"

"Know about what?"

"Depending on who you talk to, some boys get brought up as girls. Let's say a couple has four boys but no girl, so they bring up the last boy as a girl.

They dress him like a girl, and he does all the girl things in the family. Later they turn into normal men, but some go on living like women. They're called *fa'afafine* - which means 'womanly'. Apparently, it's pretty common in Polynesian cultures - it's sort of accepted, but no one talks about it. To be honest, Kale gives me the creeps, and I don't think he likes me much either. At least his English is pretty good."

"We have to teach in English don't we?"

"We do, but a lot of Samoan teachers don't. They're not confident, so they teach in Samoan - so what hope do the kids have?"

"What do you teach?" I ask.

"Commerce, bookkeeping, business. Tammy teaches chemistry and biology. To be honest guys, I nearly gave up when I went home for a break in December. I decided to stick it out for another year because I heard you guys were coming, and the new principal."

Hearing she stayed on because she heard we were coming makes us feel special. But she knows almost nothing about us, except we're palagis from Australia. Is she that desperate? Or is there a line between warring camps, and Helen assumes we'll be in her camp? Whatever that is.

We think that if we're going to be in any camp, we want to be in the Samoan camp - not with some young, ignorant, American. Maybe we should keep some distance between us and Helen? Until we've formed our own views.

"Hey, Tammy," Helen suddenly calls out over the noise. "Come over here and meet Ian and Heather."

A tall, thin, redhead walks towards us with a daypack hanging off her shoulder. Tammy Lind looks bookish with large round glasses and a pale but friendly face.

"Welcome to Samoa," she says warmly in a quiet voice that's hard to hear over the noise. "When are you arriving at the school?"

"Sunday - Feilo said he'd take us there in the morning."

"That's great."

"Are you guys doing any language training?" asks Helen, getting up to leave.

"Yes, some Peace Corps trainers are teaching us," says Heather.

"Oh good, have they told you about K language yet?"

"What's K language?"

"Surprise!" says Helen.

Tammy smiles like they belong to a secret club. "They teach you T language because that's the 'proper' language," she says. "But everyone speaks K - it's different from what you're learning."

"What? How different?"

"They swap 'k' for 't', and 'ng' for 'n' in words. No one writes K language, but everyone speaks it, except in church and school."

"Ask Fagalele about it," adds Helen as they leave.

"Take care, we'll see you on Sunday," says Tammy kindly.

Why are Jake and Fagalele teaching us a language no one speaks? No wonder we couldn't understand the people in the market.

"She seems pretty full on," says Hannah as we walk back.

"Very American," adds Erin, and we all know what she means.

"But it does seem like there are some big problems at our school," I say.

"Like there's a war going on and we don't know which side is which," adds Heather.

"I wouldn't worry," says Hannah. "Wait till you get there and decide for yourself."

"She was way over the top," says Erin. "With her attitude, she probably made things worse."

"Possible - she's young," I say. "Straight from college to Samoa."

"If I was a Samoan teacher, I wouldn't want some wet-behind-the-ears American telling me what to do," says Erin. "Who does she think she is?"

Our heads spin as we drift off to sleep that night. Is Helen just an overzealous young, cultural imperialist American? And being young and headstrong, is she going to be difficult to work with? If the situation is that bad, what should we do? And what was all that *fa'afafine* business? Men behaving like women. While we want to be wise as serpents, we're very naïve. Does that make us as innocent as doves?

Every new layer we uncover brings curiosity and trouble in equal measure. Certainty and serenity seem as elusive as soap in a bath.

In our final language class, being a teacher, Emma insists Jake and Fagalele teach us to recognise Samoan student swear words; a small investment of effort that later pays huge dividends.

Afterwards, we spend Saturday afternoon in Moira's backyard making an *umu* (traditional Samoan oven).

We first build a fire around some large stones, which, it turns out, have never been in a fire before. Trapped moisture in the stones soon turns to steam, causing them to explode violently. Red-hot rocks and burning embers shoot randomly in all directions, occasionally hitting me and others. Moira and her Samoan friends seem blissfully unconcerned, as the mini-Vesuvius showers rocks and sparks down on us and her house. Fortunately, no one dies, nor are they maimed or disfigured.

We de-husk coconuts (harder than we thought), cut them open (easy when you know how), scrape out coconut flesh, and squeeze out coconut cream.

We're surprised to find Samoans discard the juice of mature (brown) coconuts as undrinkable rubbish. Instead, Moira gives us all *niu* (green coconuts) to drink. A little sweet, they feel slightly carbonated, and are very refreshing.

We use the coconut cream to make *palusami* (a Samoan delicacy), peel taro and breadfruit, prepare fish, and wrap foods in banana and breadfruit leaves.

While the *umu* bakes, we raise our concerns about the school with Moira.

"I'd talk to the Samoan teachers about it, or the new principal," she says. "It's true, things can seem very chaotic, and drunkenness is a problem. But outspoken young Americans build resentment and make things worse."

The *umu* baked food is delicious, and later that evening, some of us *siva* (dance) to music and beautiful Samoan singing.

Moira's advice and the *fiafia* experience is a positive end to our first week in Samoa. We're pleased to be moving to our new home tomorrow, but after meeting Helen, we're apprehensive about what we'll find.

6

SPIDERS AND CENTIPEDES

"For I was hungry, and you gave me food,
I was thirsty and you gave me drink, I was
a stranger and you welcomed me..."
Matthew 25:35

To our surprise and delight, Feilo picks us up from the Seaside Inn on Sunday morning as planned.

As we farewell our friends, we realise how close and dependent we've become in just a short time. Feilo drives back down the road towards the airport, through the same enchanting villages we passed a week earlier. Somehow, they don't seem so enchanting now - perhaps we're settling in.

After half-an-hour, Feilo turns off the road. He follows wheel tracks through a swamp overshadowed by trees, to a wide expanse of grass topped with a few houses. He stops behind a bright blue concrete brick home near an enormous mango tree. In the distance is a rugby field, and long school buildings.

Feilo unlocks the door and hands me the keys.

"Your luggage is here," he says, pointing to boxes stacked neatly on the floor. I also see a new electric stove and refrigerator still in their packaging.

"An electrician will wire the stove tomorrow, and Leaula will see you later today," says Feilo.

"Who's Leaula?" I ask.

"The principal."

"Isn't that Tavita Amosa?"

"Yes, but he just became a *matai*, so now we call him Leaula." Feilo points with his chin to the neighbouring house and adds, "The American girls live there."

As he drives away, we explore the house, finding it more spacious than we expected. Leading off a large living area is a galley kitchen, a bathroom and two bedrooms. The front doors open onto a concrete patio facing the grassy slope to the swamp, the road, and the lagoon. A corrugated iron lean to roof covers the back door like a carport.

Opening our boxed baggage, we rediscover items we packed a month earlier. It's like opening presents on Christmas morning. We unpack the fridge, plug it in, and start setting up our new home.

"There's a giant cockroach in the kitchen," says Heather.

It's about three inches long. I kill it and throw it outside.

Then she finds another, and another. Then we realise they're everywhere, and the 'giant' is a normal cockroach here.

In the bedroom I find a black, hairy spider, the size of my hand, sucking the life out of a cockroach. Sensing Heather's discomfort with the idea of cohabiting with a tribe of large, hairy spiders, poisonous or not, I quietly remove it. But it's not long before there's a shriek from the other bedroom where Heather points to a similar spider.

The house is full of living creatures. In the drawers, cupboards, and shelves we find beetles, ants, termites, and bright green lizards.

A voice calls out and we find Helen Schaeffer on our doorstep.

"Welcome to LFC," she says, smiling. She invites us to dinner because "you're settling in, and it'll be easier."

"She seems kind," says Heather, after Helen leaves.

In addition to the menagerie inside our home, we find other creatures outside. A group of chooks scratch around the back door, and then some cattle wander past. Why are there cattle at a school?

In the afternoon, a grey Landcruiser stops by our back door. A moustachioed Samoan man with a round, friendly face, leans out the car window.

"My name is Leaula Tavita Amosa," he says.

He declines our invitation to come in saying, "Sorry, I finished my tattoo last week, and it's very painful. Do you have everything you need?"

"We'd like to get some food," says Heather.

"I'm on my way home to Afega now. If you like, I can drop you at the *falealoa* (store) in Saleimoa?"

Gathering some money and a bag, we climb into the Landcruiser. Sitting in the front seat, I notice he wears a bright yellow *ie solosolo* tucked above his knees, revealing dark swirling patterns on his upper legs.

"You're lucky you're palagi and don't need to get a tattoo," he says smiling. "It's an important part of our Samoan tradition, but I tell you, it's painful!"

"When does school term start?" asks Heather, concerned it could be in a few days.

"Oh, classes don't start till next week. You have time to settle in."

Not far away then, I think.

A few minutes later we stop by a store.

"I'll see you later in the week," says Tavita, before driving off.

In the shop, a bored looking Samoan woman stands behind a long counter fanning herself with an *ili* (Samoan fan). Cans sit stacked in pyramids on shelves behind her, alongside soap, powdered milk, vegetables, and bread.

I point to the bread and ask, "*E fia le tau*" (what's the cost?)

She smiles (amusement or pleasure, it's hard to tell) and responds in perfect English with a New Zealand accent. At least she understands me.

As we walk back along the road through Saleimoa, we see a village up close for the first time. People sit in the shade of their *fales*, and laundry hangs on lines strung through neat and pretty gardens. It seems Samoan people are house proud too.

Teenage girls who loiter under a tree wave and smile. We wave back - perhaps we'll see them in our class next week? Other people stare curiously as we pass. Children approach carrying kettles and pans, calling out something we don't understand.

"*Malo*," we say, and they burst into laughter.

We pass a long white fence with a sign that says, 'Malua Theological College' opposite a vast expanse of a shallow lagoon. Further on, there's a rectangular pool fringed with coconut palms on our left. Looking into the water, a dark round shape rises, and a scaly face breaks the surface.

"A turtle," says Heather.

So it is. About one metre wide, the turtle turns and sinks slowly back into the water.

Large shady trees line the road near our school, but the tide is out, leaving the lagoon full of murky mud and coral giving off an unpleasant odour. The swamp smells strongly of methane, and swarms with insect life that probably includes deadly mosquitos.

The sun sets as Helen welcomes us into their house. It has a similar layout to our own, but smaller.

A beige coloured mongrel dog lies in one corner, and a skinny ginger cat in the other.

Peter, whom we met briefly last week at the Seaside Inn, sits at the table. Tall, cheerful, and friendly, he arrived in Samoa a week before us. Having recently finished an arts degree in New Zealand, he saw a teaching job advertised in a newspaper, and thinks a year in Samoa will be good experience.

"Meet Leua," says Peter, turning to a Samoan woman in her mid-twenties.

"*Malo lava*," says Leua smiling. She has a bright, friendly face, and dark close-cropped hair.

"How's the newly painted house?" asks Tammy, putting a salad on the table.

"Okay," I say. "The paint job looks rough though. They put a single coat over the mould on the walls, without cleaning it first. And one door frame's painted on one side but not the other."

"Welcome to Samoa," laughs Helen. "They painted around a calendar hanging on our wall," she adds, pointing to a green square on her blue wall.

Leua laughs. "The workmen were probably told not to disturb anything - so they didn't."

While Tammy and Helen's house was painted only last year, it already looks shabby.

"They've given us a new stove and fridge," says Heather. "And there's a new kitchen table, couch and armchairs."

"Wow," says Helen. "They must really want you."

"The stove still needs to be wired up though," I add.

"Good luck with that," says Helen, putting another dish on the table. "Let's hope they do it before school starts."

"I'd love a new stove," says Peter. "Mine barely works."

"Tell me about it," says Helen. "I can't bake because our oven doesn't work."

"You can use our oven," says Heather, keen to be neighbourly.

"Why thank you, I'd like that."

"Is that your dog?" I ask Helen.

"That's Pe'a. I adopted her last year, or she adopted me."

"What about the cat?"

"That's Alex, Tammy looks after him; she's more of a cat person."

I notice Leua's accent is more Australian than New Zealand.

"Did you grow up in Samoa?" I ask her.

"Yes and no. Saleimoa is our home village, but mum and dad were missionaries in PNG, so I grew up there too. Dad's now a *faife'au* - that's a pastor - in a village on Savai'i."

Since Samoans have been Christian for more than one-hundred and sixty years, it made sense they were sending out missionaries. We later discover they sent missionaries to other Pacific Islands in the 19th Century.

Helen bustles about like a mother, placing a simple but tasty meal on their old wooden table. She uses an *ie solosolo* to make a colourful tablecloth. The plastic plates are from a picnic set, and no two pieces of cutlery are the same style. As we later discover, many departing volunteers pass on their possessions to new arrivals.

"Water anyone?" asks Helen, filling a glass.

"Is the water okay to drink?" I ask.

"Seems okay, but we add Clorox to make sure."

"What's Clorox?"

"Bleach - chlorine. We add it to our laundry to kill fungus on our clothes, and a few drops in water kills bugs."

Drinking from my glass, I sense a slight chlorine taste, like swallowing water at a swimming pool.

"Is it rainwater?"

"No, it's from a spring at Malua," says Tammy. "We open a faucet under our tank to fill it."

"The water's the least of your worries," says Helen. "There's worse."

"Like cockroaches?" suggests Heather.

"No," says Helen. "They're a fact of life. It's the rats you should worry about."

"Rats?" says Heather in surprise.

"I found one in my house yesterday," says Peter, looking indignant. "It ran out the door."

"You should kill them," says Leua, "otherwise they come back."

"Have you been up to the school yet?" asks Helen, changing the subject.

"No," I say. "We've been unpacking - maybe tomorrow?"

Helen and Tammy appear warm and welcoming neighbours, and gracious hosts. But Helen is the most vocal and seems to take charge - like Tammy is a willing helper, but not a decision maker. Our first impression of Helen hasn't diminished. But while she might be a bossy, over the top American, she can also be thoughtful and kind.

Returning to our house that evening, I suggest we should check what Leua thinks of Helen and the school.

"She could give us a Samoan perspective," agrees Heather.

Adding rats to our list of feared fauna, we check our food containers are rat proof, and put everything we can into the fridge. Curiously, the house is now filled with a fine mist of tiny insects that cover kitchen benches with a dark film. Since our window screens look intact, they must be small enough to pass through the mesh. We light some mosquito coils in our bedroom, hoping to discourage their presence.

With a wetland only two hundred metres from our house, we anticipate a nightly assault by squadrons of vicious mosquitos. When we install our mosquito net, we realise it also keeps us safe from beetles, cockroaches, spiders, and any other life-forms we haven't encountered yet.

We're beginning to put some order into our lives.

God has been good to us this day. We've arrived with all our luggage into a home we can make our own. We have welcoming friends, and kind neighbours who have shared their food and home. Maybe there are rats hoping to eat our food, scary spiders, and disgusting cockroaches, but there's also beauty and tranquillity. For the first time we hear the soothing sound of ocean waves crashing on the distant reef, and water foaming over broken coral. Soft and comforting, we sense the eternal rhythm of the ocean - the earth's lullaby and hum of a mother sending her baby to sleep. Sensing a oneness with nature, I feel like I've reached out and touched the wondrous beauty of the world God created for us all.

Later that the night, our slumbering celebration of God's creation is broken by the sound of grunting noises a few feet away in the darkness.

I grew up on a farm.

I know that sound.

Pigs.

I know God created pigs.

But why?

Neither wondrous nor beautiful, their stench penetrates any nostril within half a mile, and even further down wind.

Realising they're not going away, I slip on my thongs, and cautiously creep outside in the darkness. Under our bedroom window, I see their dark shapes rooting around in the ground. Hurling rocks and insults at the porcine malingerers, they run off squealing towards Utuali'i village.

The next morning I'm up first and walk into the kitchen. There are two cockroaches staring at me from the kitchen sink, and another on the bench. Feeling a squish under foot, I realise I just stepped on another.

And there's a pool of water on the floor. The roof leaks! Should we tell Tavita and get it fixed?

Later, as I use the shower for the first time, a centipede drops on my foot from behind the shower wall. About twelve centimetres (five inches) long, it's as thick as my finger. According to Mick, who has experience, the pain of a centipede bite is excruciating. I need to use a hammer to kill it.

Our conventional wisdom, absorbed by osmosis from our culture, warns us that rats and cockroaches are the very worst harbingers of disease. Wasn't it rats that brought the black death?

Given that threat, we unilaterally declare war, and I add insect surface spray to our growing shopping list.

And a rat trap.

Besides the cows and chooks, we now notice underfed dogs and cats circling our house, much like vultures, or starving beggars.

After breakfast two workmen appear on the doorstep wearing thongs, dirty singlets and *ie solosolos*. They don't look like my idea of electricians, but they wire up the stove and it works. Feilo's word is good. Or he has clout.

Peter joins us later when we walk up to the school; he's keen to hear Heather's opinion.

There are five blocks of classrooms and an assembly hall. Louvre windows cover most of the walls facing the sea and plantation.

"The windows let the sea breeze blow through," says Peter.

Many windowpanes are gone, and those that remain are very dirty. There's a broken pinboard covered with ugly graffiti at one end of each classroom, and a blackboard at the other. One classroom has fresh cow pats on the floor, while some have no doors, and only a few desks. While they all look shabby and dirty compared to an Australian school, they seem functional.

"Leua says an Australian aid project built the school around 1967," says Peter.

Makes sense. Despite obvious wear and tear, the buildings and connecting pathways look solidly built with steel frames and 'real' concrete - not the scruffy stuff we see in Apia. However, they've probably not seen any maintenance in the twenty-three years since. Does it matter if it's dirty and needs a paint job? Probably not. And since Samoans live in unwalled houses, they probably don't care if half the windows are missing.

The assembly hall is a vast, empty building, except for an enormous mosaic on the stage depicting a Samoan mother holding a child in a village setting. Beautiful. A little haunting perhaps. Such beauty seems so out of place in this shabby building. But maybe that's Samoa - stunning beauty alongside weathered decay.

"Apparently the art school did that," says Peter.

"Art school?"

"Helen tells me an Italian artist runs it - it's kind of separate from the school." Peter nods towards an isolated group of classrooms. A mural decorates the end wall depicting a man carving an outrigger canoe.

"What do you think?" says Peter to Heather as we walk back home.

"Not many desks, but we can teach using the blackboards."

"Helen said kids sit on the floor."

"We'll need more than a blackboard to teach science," I say.

Later, Tammy tells me there's a science lab, but not much equipment. "There's some test tubes, but not enough for class experiments in groups."

How will we teach Form Six I wonder?

Returning from the school, Heather is alarmed by bees hovering near the back door. I follow a bee and see it enter the house through a crack around the water pipe. Inside the house, I put my ear to the dividing wall between kitchen and bathroom and hear the hum of busy bees. There's a beehive literally inside our house.

While that sounds alarming, I think cohabitation with bees is possible with mutual respect - if we don't bother them, and they don't venture into our part of the house.

Then again, maybe Tavita can have the bees removed?

As we unpack and set up our home, we make a long list of things to buy in Apia tomorrow. I do repairs and improvements using the small set of tools I packed, along with a can of WD40. We discover no mirror in the house, but we brought one the size of a cigarette packet - a step up from the shard at the Seaside Inn. There are many large louvre windows around the house to catch the sea breeze, but some rusted window frames are stuck open.

"It's so hot," says Heather. "Maybe they're better open?"

7

VIOLENCE

"You are the salt of the earth .... You
are the light of the world."
Matthew 5:13

We're up early next morning and wait for a bus by the roadside. Waves lap the rocks nearby, as we stand in the shade of a large tree watching traffic from Utuali'i. Our eyes light up when we see a bus approach, but it's full of people and drives past. Eventually a bus marked 'Nofoali'' slows and stops beside us.

Climbing the steep, wooden steps, we peer down the aisle. The bus is so crowded people sit on each other's knees. Curiously though, there is one vacant seat. Letting Heather sit down, I stand in the aisle. But a teenage girl quickly gets out of her seat, sits on a man's knee, and gestures to say, "You sit here." When I hesitate, she insists, and I sit beside an elderly woman.

Without knowing it, we've just encountered Samoan bus culture. Before the bus stopped, a passenger had vacated their seat so I could sit with Heather on my knee. Being palagi, I let Heather take the seat. But it's not right that a lower ranking teenage girl should sit while I stand.

So she offers me her seat, graciously accommodating the ignorance of obvious newcomers. Would people in Australia be so gracious to new immigrants? I think not.

When the driver picks up two more people in Saleimoa, the passengers shuffle to create another vacant seat.

The wooden seat, being hard and cramped, digs into my bony frame. Every bump on the rough road bangs my knees into the next seat back, close to a protruding steel bolt. But a cooling breeze streams through the open windows while a UB40 song plays through loudspeakers. Although basic, it's a pleasant journey.

When the driver considers the bus to be full, he stops taking passengers and heads straight to Apia. When he stops at the market, I'm jostled towards the doorway as everyone exits the bus together. I toss our sixty *sene* (cents) bus fares into the tin beside the driver (like Tammy told us), and Heather follows.

"I sat on a man's knee," she says laughing. "A fellow tapped me on the shoulder and said he was too heavy for his friend. It was more comfortable than the wooden seat!"

I initially question the motives of a man who wants my pretty wife sitting on his knee, but later Tammy says it's what people do. We want to fit in, don't we?

After shopping at Chan Mow's, Heather goes to MacKenzies' Supermarket (expensive but air-conditioned), while I walk to a hardware store to buy the rat trap and other items. There's no surface spray there, so I walk to a pharmacy Doug suggested. The palagi chemist reaches under the counter and hands me a paintbrush and jam jar filled with brown liquid.

"Paint this on the floor around the edges of each room," he says. "It'll kill insects for a week or two. Do it again if they haven't gone."

Wonderful. A chemical weapon of mass destruction. Looking forward to the insect free future that awaits us, I wonder if the small jar is sufficient to defeat our house's vast invasion horde.

Following Moira's advice, we buy some *ie lavalava* (clothes) at Carruthers' store. After choosing colourful *ie solosolos*, the shop assistant fits me with a formal blue *ie faitaga* to wear to school. Finally, we buy fruit and vegetables at the market, before waiting for a bus to return.

When the afternoon rainstorm breaks, everyone dashes for cover under the market roof. For ten minutes we watch buses come and go as pools of muddy water grow. Then a red and white bus labelled 'Leulumoega Fou' arrives.

Ignoring the falling rain, everyone crowds around the bus doorway. When the last passenger gets off, they all scramble on at once, jostling and elbowing their way up the steps. Wanting to be polite, we hang back from the melee, not realising queueing is cultural and Samoans don't queue. Finally getting to our seats, we wonder why everyone fought to get on a half empty bus.

We're about to leave, when an elderly woman hurries from the market towards the bus, shopping bags in each hand. When she trips and falls face first into a muddy pool, Heather puts her hand to her mouth in shock, while everyone else bursts into hysterical laughter.

We're horrified.

Picking herself and her bags out of the mud, the poor woman sheepishly climbs into the bus, while a few people still laugh and giggle.

Don't Samoans respect age? Or are they laughing because they're embarrassed, like Moira said? Maybe we should ask Leua?

Visibility is poor under the dark clouds when the driver departs. He flicks on the headlights, but they don't work. Using one hand to navigate around pedestrians and vehicles, he uses the other hand to change the fuse. As the lights come on, I feel relieved no one died.

Picking up speed, people raise windows to prevent rain blowing into the bus. The windows are loose Perspex sheets that passengers lift to rest on the window ledge. As the cabin fogs up and becomes unbearably humid, people lower some windows, and more rain comes in.

We first stop at a large village store. The driver passes some money to a teenage boy, who returns minutes later with a bottle of beer. Turning back into the traffic, the driver grips the cap with his teeth to pull it off, then proceeds to drink and drive. Raising our concept of 'driving under the influence' to a whole new level, he holds the beer in one hand and steers with the other.

By the time we get to Saleimoa, he drops a passenger at one *fale*, then drives twenty metres to the next to provide a door-to-door service. The rain has stopped when we finally get off. We feel relieved; not only are we alive, but we also feel like we're learning to participate in Samoan life and culture at a basic level.

We use our newly purchased kettle to boil drinking water, let it cool, and store it in the fridge. With clean water sorted, we feel safe from gastroenteritis and diarrhoea.

That evening, we eagerly paint our floor as the chemist instructed. We sleep soundly, confident the tide of war has turned decisively in our favour.

But the next morning we find our living room has become a field of battle covered with the carcasses of a multitude of lifeforms. Dead centipedes up to fourteen centimetres long, enormous hairy spiders, large and small beetles, cockroaches, and some lifeforms we didn't know exist. Yesterday they were a distasteful inconvenience; today our lives feel threatened.

Not wanting to wake to visceral reminders of our mortality each morning, we unilaterally declare a ceasefire with respect to chemical warfare. Ignorance really can be bliss, and so is a verbal treaty for peaceful co-existence with the enemy. And while I'm no lawyer, I think verbal treaties are enforceable, and enforce it we do.

The lizards are our wartime allies - they eat insects, are decoratively green, and don't share our food.

While we're sympathetic to the spiders because they eat cockroaches, they're visually threatening. They can roam at night provided they don't walk on us.

Rodents inside the house are verboten, but ignored outside the house, provided they don't bother us.

We respond to treaty violations without mercy. A low-level guerrilla war of daily skirmishes persists, with transgressing insects executed on the spot, without trial, and swept outside.

Cockroaches become the most frequent treaty violators, and we often feel a crunch underfoot as cockroach wings and entrails squish up between our toes. Every morning two or three glare at us defiantly from the kitchen sink. During our second year, my younger brother stayed with us for a while and woke one night to find cockroaches on his face. We thought it was hilarious.

The ants and termites ignore the treaty, and lay siege to everything made of wood, slowly turning it to dust - including the house's roof beams. We just hope they last two more years.

While to their credit, the ants cart away dead cockroaches, they also attack food with industrious vigour. Sitting down to dinner one evening, we find ants carting food off our plates before we've even finished our meal. We put food in ziplock bags brought from Australia, but ants eat through the plastic. Tupperware becomes the only reliable way to protect food. And while rats can gnaw their way through Tupperware, experienced volunteers assure us it slows them down.

We spend the rest of the week making home improvements so we're better prepared when school starts on Monday. We make insect infiltration difficult by sealing cracks in our kitchen cupboards using acrylic sealant I bought in Apia. After stringing a wire between two coconut trees, we dry our laundry in the sun. Taken off the line the clothes feel dry but turn moist again when we bring them inside.

On Sunday, Leua invites us to *to'ona'i* (Sunday lunch) where we meet her brother Latu, and sister Anita. Latu has just finished high school but is unsure what to do next. Anita is twelve.

There's a newly arrived American teacher named Ramon. With short, black hair and a round, friendly face, he looks vaguely Polynesian.

"I'm Hawaiian-Japanese come American," he says. "I was born and raised in Hawaii but lived in California the last few years."

He thinks he's teaching history and geography but is unsure.

After Latu sees two palagis walking up from the road, we recognise them as Hannah and Bruce, who've come to visit us. Leua quickly invites them to lunch too.

Sitting around her table, or cross-legged on the floor, we help ourselves to roasted taro, *palusami*, breadfruit, and chicken followed by fresh pawpaw and bananas. Ramon claims he's vegan, but how will he fit into Samoan culture if he doesn't eat pork, seafood, *pisupo*, or chicken?

We share with Leua how the bus crowd laughed at the old woman falling in the mud.

She smiles. "You're right, they laugh because it's embarrassing. But we also laugh at troubles to hide our pain - a kind of black humour."

Being Australian, black humour is something we understand.

"But she might have been hurt," says Heather.

"Someone would have helped if she was hurt, but people get hurt all the time. They just put up with it."

Seems harsh, but perhaps understandable.

After lunch we show Bruce and Hannah the school and our house. They're unimpressed by the school, but like our spacious home.

Bruce says he's about to move in with a Japanese volunteer in Alafua.

"What about you, Hannah?" asks Heather.

"Still at the Seaside Inn, but I've started work."

"Great - what are you doing?"

"Nothing, mostly reading the paper. Hopefully, I'll start something 'real' this week."

Later that afternoon we walk them to the road and wave goodbye as they board a bus to Apia. We've only known them two weeks, but they feel like long-lost relatives.

As the bus takes off, an ancient pickup wheezes to a stop behind it. A palagi man and woman climb out. A little brown and weather-beaten, they look slightly Samoan wearing *ie solosolos*. They cross the road carrying a red suitcase, as the pickup wheezes its way towards Apia.

"*Malo lava,*" says the tall man. "I'm John. This is Zoe."

"Are you visiting someone?" I ask.

"John's moving here, but I'm on my way to Apia," says Zoe, with a New Zealand accent. "We've come from Tuisivi."

"I'm sharing a house with Peter," says John. "Apparently, your *pule* (principal) wants me, and I'm not needed at Tuisivi."

"He means he's not wanted," adds Zoe.

"Not needed, not wanted, same thing in Samoa," says John.

"What do you teach?" I ask.

"Science, maths, chemistry - whatever."

"I thought they were crying out for science teachers here?"

"They are," says Zoe. "But they don't like troublemakers."

"John's a troublemaker?" I ask, intrigued.

"Anyone the *pule* doesn't like is a troublemaker," says John. "He doesn't like me, and he's got a new Australian teacher now."

"That's probably Emma - she arrived with us last week."

"We like her," says Zoe. "But she seems to speak her mind like John."

Peter is surprised to see John, who he'd last seen at university, and even more surprised to find they're now sharing a house together. Obviously, Tavita hadn't communicated the new arrangement, but Peter seems pleased to have company.

When we invite them all to dinner, Helen and Tammy join us. Helen knew John was coming because she keeps her ear firmly plugged into the volunteer gossip grapevine.

John says he's been at Tuisivi for eight months, after applying for a job advertised in New Zealand. Pulling out a packet of loose tobacco, he rolls a cigarette.

"I studied linguistics," he says. "I thought teaching here might give me some practical experience."

"I heard Tuisivi is tough," says Helen.

"Teaching was fun, but the standard's very low. Most of the kids fail."

Says Zoe, "It was a lunatic asylum run by a psychopath with public beatings for the misbehaved."

"True, discipline was pretty arbitrary," says John. "Some kids got away with anything, and others were beaten for some minor infraction. Then the principal broke a kid's arm - they took him to the hospital."

Heather is speechless with shock, while Helen and Tammy seem unsurprised.

"Didn't the parents complain?" asks Heather.

John smiles at Heather's naivete as he searches for a box of matches. "No, they apologised, ashamed their son had done something so bad the principal had to break his arm."

"What!" Heather's jaw drops.

"Why am I not surprised?" asks Helen.

"He isn't a teacher," adds Zoe. "He's a pastor."

"Apparently no village wants him," adds John.

Talking late into the evening, we enjoy the company of our new neighbours. Helen appears negative about everything Samoan as much as Tammy seems reserved. John's stories seem even worse than those Helen told us. Maybe she has a point?

We both go to bed wondering how we're going to cope if we have to witness such violence. Centipedes, spiders and even rats seem trivial compared to breaking kids' arms. We wonder how we can be salt and light in the darkness of such violence directed at children. Does God expect us to respond by proactively trying to prevent it, or by setting a better example?

The next day Zoe catches a bus to Apia.

Meanwhile, we attend our first staff meeting. I count thirty teachers sitting around the room - equal numbers of men and women. Most are obviously Samoan; the women, beautifully dressed in colourful *puletasi*; the men wear short-sleeved dress shirts, and *ie faitaga* in dark colours. There's Arjun from Burma, who according to Tammy, is the Science Department Head. A few men and women smoke, so John pulls out his tobacco pouch to roll a cigarette. While we wait for Tavita, everyone sits in stony silence, or they whisper to each other.

Tavita emerges from his office and welcomes all the newcomers. Besides the new palagi teachers, half the local teachers are also new. It looks like Tavita's making a fresh start.

"School starts Friday," he says, passing around copies of the Congregational Church Teacher's Handbook. "There will be a staff meeting every morning, and I expect every teacher to be here. Teachers must attend to teaching their classes. Turning up disorderly, or missing classes, will not be tolerated," he says with firm authority.

I might have found the statement odd if Helen hadn't told us about last year's problems.

After the meeting, Arjun approaches and asks if I teach Physics.

"Sure, I'd like that," I respond.

"Very good, we haven't had a physics teacher for years."

We emerge from the meeting with the knowledge school begins in three days, but with no idea what we'll do on the first day, or what classes we'll teach. Except I might teach physics.

"What will happen Friday?" I ask Helen later over lunch.

"Oh, who knows? Sorting kids into classes maybe. It'll be chaotic whatever we do."

"What do we do before then?"

"Just relax Ian," says John. "*Fiafia, aua le popole*" (don't worry, be happy).

If we were Samoan, we would relax, but being palagi, we feel compelled to work. Preferring a clean kitchen floor, we scrub the vinyl, one square at a time. It's heavy work, and as sweat drips into our eyes, it's hard to see.

I heard an incandescent globe in a cupboard lowers the humidity and prevents clothes going mouldy. Buying electrical components in the hardware shop, I wire bulbs into the bottom of our wardrobe. Helen asks if I can install one in her wardrobe, and I do that, to be neighbourly.

Meanwhile, each day dawns with the early sun breaking over the sea, reflecting off bright orange flowers falling from the *tamalini* trees, and the stirring scent of nearby frangipani flowers. We walk down the road under large, shady trees, and gaze across the azure blue lagoon, while little waves lap the white coral beach. The sunsets are short but beautiful, and after two weeks in Samoa, we finally begin to feel settled and peaceful.

While the stories of violence, school political infighting, and chaos make us apprehensive, our home gives us a sense of safety and stability. Home is a haven we can fall back to; something to call our own, even if we share it with a menagerie of alien and threatening creatures. While political storms rage, we think our home is a roof over our heads - somewhere we'll always be safe.

But as we're about to find out, we are very, very wrong.

8

DISASTER

*"Therefore I tell you, do not be anxious about your
life, what you will eat or what you will drink, nor
about your body, what you will put on. Is not life
more than food, and the body more than clothing?"*
Matthew 6:25

The next day, as the soft sea breeze slowly turns into a strong north wind, we wonder if a storm's brewing. That's not unusual, in the wet season there's thunder, lightning, and heavy rain almost every day.

But late in the afternoon, Arjun appears at our back door.

He cheerfully tells us he just heard on the radio Cyclone Ofa is coming - like it's an unexpected treat. "It's passed Tokelau and will hit us tonight."

"A cyclone?" says Heather frowning, as Arjun walks off to warn others. "That doesn't sound good."

Australia has cyclones that damage power lines, cause flooding, and destroy buildings that aren't cyclone-proof. We recall images of Darwin destroyed by Cyclone Tracy in 1975. In a single night it levelled entire city blocks. Is that destruction coming our way?

"Do you think our roof could blow off?" asks Heather. Our termite ridden roof beams don't look like lasting our two years in Samoa, let alone a cyclone.

"We're going to get wet if it does."

The walls look strong - solid brick on a concrete slab.

"The louvre windows might break, and I don't think they'll keep the rain out," I say. "Putting stuff in cupboards and drawers might help keep them dry."

Having spent the last ten days unpacking, we now pack everything up again. Books come off shelves and into kitchen cupboards. All dry food goes into the fridge. We pack clothes, and electrical appliances into cupboards and drawers.

I feel pleased I sealed our cupboards; the effort might pay off by keeping things dry. Worried the wind might blow cupboard doors open, I nail them shut.

When it rains, water blows through the north-facing windows. Closing as many louvres as possible (some are jammed open), I nail curtains across to catch any flying glass. We work feverishly into the night 'battening down hatches' as best we can.

Tammy and Helen aren't home. Perhaps they're stuck in Apia, or making their way back?

"Maybe we should put their stuff away too?" suggests Heather.

"But we don't know them well, and it seems rude to rearrange their house."

About ten-thirty the lights briefly flicker and go out as power lines blow down somewhere. Ominously, it reminds me of the lights going out on the Titanic before it sank.

Fortunately, we have our hurricane lamp purchased from Chan Mow's a week earlier. And now we are literally in a hurricane. To preserve batteries, we try to avoid using our only battery powered torch.

While our frantic preparations give us a sense of doing something, the wind strength rises to a constant roar, and the real possibility we're experiencing a major disaster sinks into our consciousness. We recall international disasters reported on our evening news at home; images of wind and rain sweeping away buildings and people being pulled from raging torrents.

Is that what's coming our way?

We want to be optimistic, but we've only been in the country two weeks, and our imagination suggests anything is possible.

If our roof blows off, we decide to seek shelter in the school buildings - made of strong steel frames and trusses. Since we might be out of house and home for a while, we pack a suitcase of clothes.

When we finally get to bed, everything is wet or very damp, including our clothes and bedding. Rain blows horizontally through windows, drips down through the ceiling, and pools are on the floor in every room.

Fortunately, we have a dividing wall sheltering our bed, and we don't feel cold. The air's still very humid, and the temperature hasn't dropped.

But with a howling wind constantly rattling and shaking the roof and walls, sleep seems impossible. Frequent gusts punctuate the constant roar, like a freight train running through the house; everything shakes, rattles, and bangs even louder. In the darkness, the noise seems even more frightening.

We pray, perhaps more earnestly than before, asking God to keep us safe, regardless of what happens. We pray for the safety of Samoan people who must be hunkering down in their villages in distress.

A loud bang and crack of splintering wood pierces the darkness. Fearing the worst, I get up and shine a torch around each room. Everything seems okay. I guess the tree near our bedroom is disintegrating. Lying down again, I close my eyes.

Another scary crash, and I'm up again. The ceiling is still there, and everything appears okay. But we can't check the roof - we're not foolish enough to go outside where flying debris might injure or kill us.

"What if the roof blows off over our heads?" asks Heather.

Frightened by every crash and bang in the dark, we feel alone, anxious, and fearful of spending a sleepless night in the barrage of noise. But sometime after one in the morning, we fall asleep.

When we wake around five, it's still dark. The wind howls, and gusts shake and rattle the house, but the ceiling is still there. Water an inch deep floods our living area. In the past, the concrete foundation must have cracked, and the front sank down a little, so water forms a deep pool against the north wall. To prevent it from growing deeper and flowing into other rooms, we scoop the water into a bucket and remove it.

When the light grows stronger, I risk walking outside to check the roof. The wind pushes me sideways and stings my eyes, but everything looks intact. Debris lies everywhere, including leaves, tree branches, coconuts, timber, and roofing iron. Our two papaya trees lie flat on the ground. The two coconut trees near the house bend in the wind but look strong.

When the wind subsides a little, I feel buoyant. We've survived the cyclone and all we have to do is clean up!

"Is it over?" asks Heather.

"Well, Arjun said it was hitting last night, and the wind seems to be dying down."

"Power's still out," says Heather, flicking a light switch. "Maybe school will start today after all?"

Around eight, Tammy appears at our door to check if we're okay.

"We're fine," says Heather. "What about you?"

"Good, we got back about eleven by taxi, with Liam, Duane and Zoe from Tuisivi. The Lady Samoa didn't leave Apia, so they're trying to get to Mulifanua."

After the long, fearful night, talking with Tammy brings a sense of normality.

Tammy wants to use our radio to listen for news. Fetching it from a cupboard, we sit around our table while she tunes into 2AP - the local AM station. After some Samoan language announcements, the announcer swaps to English.

"*All government schools are closed today...,*" followed by a long silence before, "*That's that. And this is this...*" as a UB40 song starts playing.

"If government schools are closed, so are church schools," says Tammy.

"That's a relief," I say.

"I'll let the others know," says Tammy. "You could come over and meet Duane and Liam."

"Thanks, we'd better get this water out first."

Streaming through windows, and falling from the ceiling, the water keeps building up.

A little later Tavita appears at our door looking wet but cheerful. It's comforting to know people are concerned about us.

"We hear there's no school today," I say.

"No, not till after the cyclone."

"Wasn't the cyclone last night?"

He laughs. "No, only the start. It's hitting tonight - this is just a lull."

Our hearts sink, realising the previous night's horror is just a prelude of worse to come. Will our roof survive that long?

Cyclones in Australia only last a day or so, quickly dissipating when they hit the continental land mass. But in the Pacific, a cyclone can build up over the warm ocean into unrestrained ferocity, its path unpredictable as it batters little islands for days. All we can do is hope and pray it eventually moves away.

After Tavita leaves and we walk next door, a bus full of people drives past us heading towards Utuali'i. While passengers stare curiously from the windows, we look back equally astonished. Why is a bus driving through the school? Then we see cars following behind, and more crowded buses.

With no north-facing windows, Helen and Tammy's living area is more sheltered than ours. We find everyone huddled around the table and meet Duane and Liam - PCVs in their early twenties teaching at Tuisivi.

Chatting to them, we wonder how Emma and our other friends are faring. I imagine Mick's rickety flat disintegrating, and Hannah abandoning the Seaside Inn as its rusty iron roof blows away.

Helen's dog lies in one corner, while John sits in another corner reading a book.

"Bit of a bummer Ian," he says sympathetically. "A cyclone comes just after you arrive."

"Well, our roof's still on ... for the moment. What's with the buses and cars going by?"

"Road's gone."

"Really?"

"All washed into the sea. Kaput. And the trees. There's boulders and coral everywhere."

"Looks like people are getting home before the worst comes tonight," says Duane.

Peter appears at the door carrying tins of food, puffing and wet after running through the rain. Ramon, Peter, and John have relocated to Tammy and Helen's because their houses face north and are completely awash.

"Great, thanks," says Helen, taking the food.

"We spent the night here on the floor with all our earthly possessions," says John, pointing to his red suitcase in the corner.

By late morning the ferocity of wind and rain increases. No more vehicles pass by.

"Hey, what's the difference between a hurricane and a cyclone?" asks Liam. "We have hurricanes. I never heard of a cyclone."

"I think they're an Aussie thing," says Duane.

Tammy consults her dictionary and informs us hurricanes occur in the northern hemisphere while cyclones are in the south. "Otherwise, they're the same thing, except they rotate in different directions."

"Like water going down the plughole in a bath," says John. "Clockwise in the southern hemisphere - anticlockwise in the north."

Says Tammy, "If Cyclone Ofa is rotating clockwise, and the wind is coming from the north-east, the eye might be over Savai'i."

"Or further west," says John. "Near the Wallis Islands maybe."

We're in a major disaster but using a dictionary to work out what's happening.

"I heard the wind is most intense near the eye, but it's calm and quiet inside," says John. "Then the wind swings from the opposite direction."

"Well, the eye ain't here, that's for sure," says Helen, looking out the window. "I'm getting lunch - you guys can eat with us if you like," she says looking at Heather, who offers to bring food.

"Whatever you've got'll be welcome. I'm making 'hurricane stew' - a new recipe!"

To cook Helen's stew, Duane and I light a fire on the concrete floor of their lean-to garage, which is sheltered from the wind.

While we work, John watches the canteen roof lurch up and down in the wind.

"That roof's going for sure," says John. "Give it another hour."

"Nah - it'll last longer," says Duane.

"Want to make it interesting?"

"Sure."

"Five bucks it's gone by two."

"Five bucks it is."

Arjun walks towards us in the wind and rain but leaps sideways when a breadfruit tree crashes down beside him. Arjun says his house, an old concrete and wooden structure, is faring well. When Helen invites him to lunch, he politely declines. We guess he prefers more appetising Indian food to 'hurricane stew', whatever that is. Probably wise.

When Helen brings out a battered cauldron full of water and chopped ingredients, we position it on rocks over the fire.

"Looking good guys," she says, handing me a wooden spoon. "Can you stir it?"

"Where'd you get the pot?" I ask Helen.

"John found it on the rubbish heap and cleaned it up."

While it sounds dodgy, Duane assures me, "We only die once, but we won't die hungry."

As we stir the pot, we dodge the sparks and smoke blowing into our eyes. It's worth the effort. Helen's hurricane stew is hot, tasty, and there's plenty left over for dinner.

After two, John says he thinks the canteen roof's about to go. As though applauding an athlete approaching the finishing line, some of us shelter in the garage to watch and cheer it on.

A roof corner repeatedly rises a few feet in the air before slamming back down. Eventually, it lifts higher and keeps going, as the entire roof tears away. It flies fifty feet through the air before crashing in a heap of timber and twisted metal. It's an awesome sight, and although we're a safe distance away, the thought that might happen to our house roof is sobering.

"Here y'are mate," says John, handing Duane five *tala*.

During the afternoon the walls of the canteen collapse into a heap, while we bail accumulating water out of our house.

By nightfall the wind blows from due north, suggesting the eye is near Savai'i - moving closer and growing stronger.

Duane and I stoke the fire back into life to reheat the hurricane stew. When I call out to Helen that we're ready, there's a loud flash-bang as the fire blows up in our faces.

"Hell!" yells Duane, staring at the smoky embers glowing in the darkness.

Tammy and others appear at the doorway, asking what happened.

"The fire exploded," says Duane, sounding shaken in the dark. "I think my hand's burnt."

Duane goes inside the house as Peter shines a torch on the fire. A lump of blackened concrete pokes up through red coals.

"I think the concrete exploded," I say.

"Really? How?"

"There must be moisture trapped in the concrete - it can turn to steam and explode under pressure."

"Well, that's just great," says Peter. "We're sheltering from a cyclone and the floor explodes!"

Guessing any trapped moisture has gone, I stoke up the fire again and soon have another pot of hurricane stew ready.

When I carry the pot inside, Duane sits in a chair as Heather shines a torch on him. With his left hand bandaged, Tammy gently applies cream to the burns on his neck.

"How's the walking wounded?" I ask.

"The doctor says I'll live," says Duane.

"We have a doctor?"

"Tammy teaches biology - it's close."

"Actually, I studied biochemistry," says Tammy. "But I found this tube in the Peace Corps first aid kit that says, 'apply to burns.'"

When Duane flinches Tammy pulls her hand away.

"Sorry," she says, distressed that she might have hurt him. As she finishes, she adds, "It says to 'keep the wound clean and dry.'"

"Hah!" calls out John. "I wouldn't mind being clean and dry right now!"

As we all eagerly huddle around the candle-lit table, Helen dishes out stew like Oliver Twist's workhouse master. In the dim light we can't see what we're eating, but it tastes good. It seems Helen has a talent for making tasty meals out of anything.

But after dinner Heather frowns when Helen lets her mangy dog lick out the dishes.

"I hope they're washed properly," she whispers to me.

But later Helen washes the dishes in partial darkness and cold water, using no detergent, and leaving them on the drainer. Knowing we'll eat off those dishes tomorrow, we don't want to get sick.

Despite Duane's injury and the surrounding destruction, we're ending the day much as we started; we're wet, but our roofs are still holding up. However, knowing the cyclone 'hits' tonight, we're apprehensive. How much worse will it be? We want information, but all we have is Tavita's comment and what we see through our windows - wind, rain, and flying building debris.

Attempting to hear some news or a forecast, John tunes our radio into 2AP.

"What are you hearing?" asks Liam.

"There's a cyclone called Ofa," says John. "Keep sheltered ... places are closed."

When 2AP starts playing music, Duane suggests trying shortwave. "We might get news from Pago (American Samoa)."

With his ear close to the radio John slowly turns the dial until he finds a New Zealand station. We all lean in trying to hear over the static and roaring wind. Eventually we hear "... *after passing Tokelau, Cyclone Ofa is continuing to batter the small island nation of Western Samoa and the Wallis Islands. The cyclone is slowly moving in the direction of Tonga ...*".

Not much help. We'd worked that out ourselves. For the first time in our lives, we're at the centre of a growing national disaster knowing almost nothing. But unlike the previous night, we're now suffering in the company of people who depend on each other. Somehow, hardship, uncertainty, and danger seem less severe when they're mutually shared - even with people we barely know.

While we return to our house to sleep, everyone else sleeps on Helen and Tammy's living room floor, lined up like sardines. Except Peter, who sleeps at our house to relieve the crowding.

While we sense the wind is stronger, the second night passes much like the first. The roaring wind and freight train gusts shake and rattle, while rain blows in through the windows, drips down through the ceiling, and forms pools on the floor. I get up to check the roof is still there, and scoop water out of the house.

Waking in the dark early next morning, there's no respite from the noise, wind or rain, and the cyclone seems as ferocious as ever.

As the light grows, we see a coconut tree has blown down, narrowly missing Helen's room.

Peter claims he slept, but his sagging eyelids and drowned rat-like appearance suggest it wasn't much. Out of all of us, Peter seems emotionally downcast, different to his usual cheerful self.

When we join the others for breakfast, Helen is as cheerful and bossy as ever, despite limited sleep and sharing her house with seven unplanned guests. It seems Helen loves mothering others in her home. I suspect having people around her, even if they're subdued and weary, helps her endure the disaster. When she instructs Tammy to butter the last few slices of bread, we wonder whose house it is. Choosing compliance instead of conflict, Tammy says nothing as she reaches for the butter, but we feel tension in the air.

Seeing yesterday's dishes on the drainer covered with ants, Heather picks up a dish and finds a dead cockroach underneath. Not good. There's no need to add further health risks to an already unfolding disaster. We need to find a way to wash Helen's dishes better.

After breakfast we play cards, tell stories and resort to black humour, as the combined monotony of dim light, roaring wind, and rain, soaks further into our emotional fabric.

Looking at all the food we've pooled together, Helen and Heather conclude we're running out. Apart from a small bag of rice, a few lentils, and some tinned food, everything is perishable, and must be eaten in a day or two. Unfortunately, we didn't stock up in case of a national disaster and a bunch of unplanned guests. With the road destroyed, and without knowing when the cyclone will end, we consider rationing food.

We sadly watch nearby breadfruit trees blow down. They're nice, shady trees, and breadfruit is tasty, healthy, and cheap. Keeping a watchful eye for jagged sheets of iron flying randomly through the air, a few of us cautiously venture into the wind and rain to retrieve downed breadfruit and coconuts. Apart from drowning, being hit by flying debris is a significant cause of death in cyclones. We might be wet and windblown, but just doing something active helps raise our spirits to endure the wet, miserable monotony.

At midday, Heather says the toilet in our house won't flush. It turns out our water tank is empty. When I open the tap to fill the tank, no water appears because there's no power to the electric pump at Malua. I feel frustrated and annoyed with myself, because we should have filled our water tank while we still had power.

"Don't worry guys," says Helen kindly. "You can share our water."

"Thanks, but how long's it going to last?"

"A week normally," says Tammy.

But with seven people drinking and flushing the toilet, their tank will soon empty. To conserve water, we agree to use water collected off our roofs and flush the toilet by tipping a bucket into the bowl.

Fortunately, no one showers, so that saves water. We're already wet, and if any odours appear, there's plenty of ventilation.

"What if your tank runs dry?" asks Heather.

"When the cyclone finishes, we can carry water from the spring at Malua," says Tammy, "until the power is back."

"That could be months away," says Helen. "We better go easy on the water."

We now keep some water in a bucket and our wash tub. But we only have one bucket, and it takes a full bucket to flush the toilet. If we'd known, we would have bought more buckets last week.

Come lunchtime, Helen makes "hurrie burgers" by combining any foodstuffs that stick together long enough to fry. By midday, the wind has moved due west, and we need to relocate the fire.

I also heat a kettle of water on the fire. After lunch we collect the dishes, including those licked out by Helen's dog, and I wash them in the hot water with detergent. Seeing Heather dry the dishes and put them away, Helen doesn't complain, but the look on her face says she's annoyed, and the tension screws turn.

After lunch, Tavita's roof peels away piece by piece. The roofing iron tumbles and flies past towards Malua, where we see a large house collapse into a heap. We hope no one was hurt.

Seeing the fallen breadfruit trees, Tammy comments sadly, "Some families depend on their breadfruit crop, and the season was just starting."

"Taro crops will be damaged too," says John. "It'll be hard."

The thought of dwindling food and fresh water looms large in our thoughts. Will the heavy rain and floods contaminate water sources - potentially causing cholera, typhoid, and other outbreaks of life-threatening diseases? Or will the stagnant flood water breed mosquitos and increase our risk of dengue fever?

We now understand how disasters are different in developing countries. There's no flood of rolling news or emergency services taking action to protect people and property. Samoa doesn't even have a defence force. While there's some news on 2AP, our Samoan language skills are too poor to understand it. We're on our own, and with no end in sight, we're frustrated and depressed. How much longer can it last?

By evening, the wind blows from the south-west. Knowing cyclones rotate clockwise, it seems to be moving away from us.

After dinner ("don't ask what's in it guys," says Helen), we huddle around the shortwave radio again. We hear the cyclone is indeed moving towards Tonga.

Our spirits rise a little knowing the end is near, and our roof hasn't blown off. Not yet.

But with the change in wind direction, our bedroom is now awash. We sleep where it's more sheltered, settling down for a third long night of howling wind and rain. Peter sleeps on our floor again, and I rise in the night to scoop water off the floor.

When we wake on the fourth day, the rain has stopped, and the wind has slowed. As it continues to abate throughout the day, our world becomes strangely quiet and peaceful.

However, it's a new world, recognisable - but completely transformed from the beautiful, lush, green place we enjoyed a few days earlier. All trees, shrubs and other vegetation either lies on the ground, or is stripped of leaves and branches. The landscape has a ghostly appearance as bare, broken trees, raise lifeless limbs to the clearing sky. Fallen trees block the flooded school laneway.

After lunch, we wander through Malua to the airport road. Even the remaining coconut trees look ragged and stripped bare. The ground is covered with pieces of timber and roofing iron, mixed with other scattered debris. Tanks lie on the grass, dented, and crushed. We walk under severed wires dangling from a power pole at an angle, with corrugated iron wrapped around the cross beam. It looks like a crucifix.

At least two hundred metres of the road in front of the school has disappeared - washed into the sea. Gone too are all the shady trees that once lined the roadway. The road near Malua is strewn with boulders a metre high and blocked by uprooted trees - roots splayed out like branches. The road is impassable to any vehicles except a bulldozer.

We walk on to Saleimoa, where the road seems intact and free of boulders. *Fales* and other buildings have lost roofs or been turned into splintered heaps of wreckage. Bare frames and poles stand on foundations where iron roofs have peeled away. House poles that once supported a roof lean over at strange angles.

The same scattered debris lies everywhere, and many people appear homeless. While some clean up, others just sit, as though dazed and wondering what to do; perhaps pondering the sad truth that with coconut, banana and breadfruit trees lying on the ground, there'll be less food and income in the coming months. This doesn't stop children we meet calling out, "Palagi, palagi," followed by peals of laughter. Some things don't change, even after a national disaster.

Arriving back at our house, we too start cleaning up. When we get together for dinner that night, we're in high spirits.

"We need to get more food from Apia," says Helen, serving up the last of her bean and breadfruit soup.

"I can't see any buses running on that road," says Peter.

"Maybe Tavita can take us?" says Tammy.

"If he can get here," says Helen. "If the road's cut here, it's probably cut elsewhere."

"We might learn something from 2AP," says John, reaching for the radio.

This time we hear no music and a lot of announcements, including some in English. We hear the airport road is "being opened", "offices will be open" tomorrow, and the Australian and New Zealand governments have offered help.

"What does that mean?" asks Peter. "Are they sending money or the army?"

"Money won't help us right now," says Helen.

"But the army could be handy," I say. I began my engineering career working for the Army, and I know they often help with disaster recovery. But they won't be here tomorrow.

"I vote we see if Tavita turns up in the morning," says John. "Maybe he can drive us to Apia and let's hope the shops are open."

Since no one objects, this becomes the consensus decision. Although nothing is said explicitly, there's a strong mutual feeling that we'll do things together, keep sharing our homes and food, and looking out for each other.

While it's only three weeks since we stepped off a plane from Australia, it feels like a lifetime ago. Only a few days earlier, like the diligent and enthusiastic palagi we are, our primary concern was starting school. Our cunning plans are now gone with the wind, along with everything else dependent on power and transport - our food, refrigeration, electric stove, and fresh water. As our food and water supplies rapidly dwindle, our world is now stripped down to basic survival skills - seeking food, water, and shelter. The roof over our heads is now a luxury because thousands of Samoans have no roof.

We're mindful of Jesus' words not to be anxious about what we'll eat and drink, but we still need to work hard to find food and water. But we thank God for his goodness and grace, for keeping us safe, for keeping our roof on, and the gift of good friends and neighbours. Saying grace before each meal now takes on new meaning. While we're uncertain about many things, we have a sense of peace and confidence, knowing one way or another, God will meet our needs.

However, at this point we're unaware of the full impact of a natural disaster on a small country, and the very long shadow Cyclone Ofa will cast over our future in Samoa.

9

FAMINE

*"Therefore do not be anxious, saying, 'What shall
we eat?' or 'What shall we drink?' …your heavenly
Father knows that you need them all."*
Matthew 6:31-32

"Our tank ran dry this morning," says Helen, as we meet for a simple breakfast of leftovers. "There's some drinking water in a bucket, but we'll have to get water from the Malua pool."

Our fresh water source is six hundred metres away - a traditional village freshwater bathing pool used by the Malua Theological College.

But fetching water will have to wait. Our focus is on getting food and filling the information vacuum. Being the only proper town in the country, Apia is our only source of food and news. We wonder about our friends on Savai'i and want to inform our families in Australia we're okay - assuming Australia has even heard of Cyclone Ofa.

"Tavita's here," announces Tammy, walking through the door. "He thinks the road is open and he'll take us to Apia."

While we make up a combined shopping list, we decide who'll buy each item to avoid doubling up.

We hope the shops are open, but will there be food to buy? Unless the shops had back-up generators, refrigerated or frozen food will have perished in the four days since the power disappeared, and if roofs blew off, food could be water-damaged. Worse, if the other thirty thousand people in Apia decide to restock their pantries today, there might be a run on the shops, leaving us with empty shelves.

We need to get cash (credit cards do not exist in Samoa) so I offer to go to the bank.

Meanwhile Zoe, Liam, and Duane decide to travel to the wharf at Mulifanua, where they hope to take a ferry to Savai'i.

"Why not come with us?" asks Helen. "The Lady Samoa might be operating again."

They decline the offer. If the ferry's not operating from Mulifanua, they'll try a plane to Salelologa.

"At least we know the airport's open," says Zoe.

Gathering stuff into their daypacks, they wish everyone goodbye and set off walking through the debris-strewn grass. With our laneway blocked by trees and floodwater, they cut across to Utuali'i village, where they hope to hitch a ride to Mulifanua, or the airport.

A little later, we're sitting or standing on the back of the truck outside Tavita's house, surveying a dramatically transformed landscape. It looks like a giant lawnmower passed through, cutting, slashing, and scattering debris everywhere. Vegetation turns brown as life drains out of fallen branches and broken trees. Bare branches stand skeletal against the blue sky.

Near the lagoon, a bulldozer is working to re-build the road.

"That looks promising," says Heather.

Tavita emerges from his roofless house and climbs into the cabin. Arjun and some Samoan teachers from Malua climb onto the tray with us, sitting cross-legged around the edge like they do in a *fale*.

"You need to get used to travelling on the back of trucks and pickups," says Tammy. "It's cool once we get going but watch out for bumps!"

Having grown up on a sheep farm I'm used to travelling on the back of a truck or ute (pickup). But I also remember the people killed after being thrown from the back in a minor accident.

Avoiding the flooded laneway, Tavita navigates the truck through Malua, and heads down the road towards Apia.

The morning sun beats down, the humidity rises, and the sea breeze is back; signs of returning normality.

We pass the Saleimoa store, looking severely damaged but still standing. Situated close to the lagoon, it was unprotected from the waves.

Villages that had so enchanted us on arrival only three weeks earlier are now devastated and ruined. We pass primary schools without roofs and other collapsed buildings. Breadfruit and banana trees lie flattened near skeletal and roofless *fale* frames. Scattered everywhere are parts of buildings, roofing iron and timber frames, branches, iron tanks, and household belongings. Pieces of roofing iron wrap around poles and tree trunks, while power poles lean or lie on the ground, and severed wires blow lifeless in the wind.

But every village is also a hive of activity as everyone works to clean up and start rebuilding. People hammer roofs back on frames using scavenged roofing iron and timber. Others construct makeshift houses using pieces blown from destroyed buildings. Children pick up leaves and branches, sweep their yards clean, and dry wet clothes and bedding. Others cut up fallen trees with axes and bush knives. Some use chainsaws, wearing thongs - no boots or any protective clothing. New roofs appear as entire villages work to get homes back to a functional level. They heap fallen branches ready to burn, and stack sheets of iron, or anything else of value, ready for re-use.

Bulldozers have reconstructed the damaged road and added gravel. While it allows traffic to flow, the softer gravel road will soon be full of muddy potholes.

Entering Beach Road in Apia, we see a large, blue ship, sitting high and dry on the reclaimed land, a stone's throw from the main street. The words LADY SAMOA in white capital letters grace the stern. The cyclone drove the ferry aground, where it stays for the next eighteen months. There is no direct service between Apia and Savai'i while we're in Samoa.

Tavita parks the truck in front of Chan Mow's. Clambering over the side onto the pavement, we immediately bump into Matt.

"Hey, I lost my house," he says laughing. "I moved in on Thursday, and Friday the roof blew off!"

"Was anyone hurt?" asks Heather.

"No, but we got wet. The roof started peeling off Friday morning, and by the afternoon it was gone."

"What did you do?"

"We wandered down the road and asked the High Commissioner for help. Basil and Elizabeth were really nice, they put us up for two nights sleeping on the floor in their hallway, along with a bunch of Aussies and others like Akira."

"What about your stuff?"

"Oh, we didn't have much. Anyway, the house is kaput - after the roof went, it collapsed in a heap. I'm staying with Mick until I find something else."

"Mick's house survived then."

"Yeah - who'd a-thought, eh?"

"Might be hard finding a place with all the buildings destroyed."

"Maybe. I can always go back to the Seaside Inn," he laughs.

"So it's still there?"

"Yeah, and Hannah's fine, but I haven't heard from anyone else."

Apart from blowing down shady trees, there's surprisingly little damage to the buildings in Apia's centre.

While Heather walks to the High Commission, I go to the bank. There are no ATMs in Samoa, and the only way to get cash is to queue up with a passbook.

The bank is closed.

Oh no! I'll have to come back another day, but there's nothing to indicate when it will open.

Sitting down on the pavement, I carefully count out the remaining notes and coins. We'll need to spend it wisely today. I'd never thought about banks being important in a disaster.

Going on to MacKenzies Supermarket, it's open and not busy - there's no evidence of a supermarket run yet.

I buy all I can within my means, and as I'm paying the cashier, Heather arrives.

"The High Commission is closed," she says.

Great. "We're here to help," they said. But when we need them, they're closed.

We could call home from the Post Office, but there are queues stretching out the door and down the street; and a call will use the cash we need for food.

The market is closed. Everyone's probably too busy rebuilding homes and villages to think about selling produce. Instead, people crowd the hardware shops buying the limited timber, roofing iron, and nails available. Helen buys two loaves of fresh bread from a bakery.

A little later we all clamber back onto Tavita's truck. Curiously, he seems to shepherd me into the front passenger seat for the drive home. I sense he wants to talk, and as we travel down the road, he shares his concerns.

"I had a meeting with the Congregational Church. Taro crops and plantations have been wiped out, along with breadfruit trees. The wharf broke and a lot of food containers fell in the sea. The food is spoiled, and ships can't unload at the wharf."

He pauses before going on with deep feeling; "I really fear for my people. Prices will skyrocket and we'll have to import food. Many won't be able to afford it, and the church is worried about famine, disease, and rats."

Rats? I don't understand how famine will bring rats. But who knows, maybe? After all, what do I know about Pacific Island public health?

Tavita then asks if we, the palagi teachers, are okay?

"We're good," I say, wondering why he's singled me out to exchange thoughts. After all, others have more Samoan experience - I only just arrived.

"We've got enough food for a few days, and we all cook together on a fire," I add. "We've run out of water, but we can carry it from Malua."

"It could be weeks or months before we have power again," says Tavita. "We'll need water to open the school. I'll see what I can do."

"When do you think classes can start?"

"I don't know. Maybe in a few weeks? I've called a staff meeting for tomorrow morning to decide what to do."

As we travel along the road seeing people mend or rebuild their homes, Tavita says, "It's marvellous the way Samoans pull together in a crisis; something most palagis don't seem to understand or appreciate."

True, during the short time we were shopping in Apia, the progress is impressive. Based on what I know, which isn't much, Samoan villages and culture seem well equipped to cope with disasters like this.

Living a simpler and more self-reliant lifestyle, they're more resilient, and less dependent on government-built infrastructure. Rebuilding a home in Australia could take over twelve months (if we're lucky), but Samoan families can fix their homes in a day or two.

Perhaps a thousand years of trial and error navigating disasters like this have been built into traditional cultural mechanisms for cooperation in troubled times. In the way palagi cultures look to faceless government authorities to rebuild, Samoan villagers look first to their immediate family, neighbours and community. And unlike us, the *fa'asamoa* operates a cashless, gift economy, where food and shelter are always shared with the needy.

Tavita drops us at the school, before returning to Afega and his many *matai* responsibilities.

Getting together at our house for a late lunch, I share Tavita's concerns with the others, avoiding the prospective rat plague (I think the fear of rats is overblown and unnecessary).

"Who knows what will happen?" says Helen. "It could all be rumours."

"With crops damaged, taro prices WILL rise," says John.

"But famine? I find that hard to believe."

"Countries have promised aid," says Peter hopefully. "Surely New Zealand will bring food."

"That might take a while," says Tammy.

"Whatever happens, we have to go back tomorrow and buy whatever we can," says Helen.

"We won't be able to buy anything without cash," I say.

John claims many shops accept Australian, New Zealand and US currencies. We agree to pool our Aussie, Kiwi and US cash reserves if the banks are closed again.

Meanwhile, Peter is unhappy hearing containers fell in the sea. He worries they contain his belongings shipped from New Zealand.

"They might have gone to Pago," says Tammy positively. "I heard they're diverting ships there until the wharf is fixed."

"Could be a long time then," says Peter looking despondent. "If it's not already at the bottom of the sea."

We've done no laundry or had a shower for five days, so we head to the Malua pool. As Tammy and Heather walk off with buckets and soap, I gather our dirty laundry and carry it Samoan style, wrapped in an *ie solosolo*.

Situated beyond the turtle pool between the road and lagoon, the Malua pool is a circle of black rocks cemented together. Cold, fresh spring water bubbles into the pool at one end and overflows into the sea at the other. We sit on a concrete ledge and look through crystal clear water to a stony bottom.

A young Samoan woman stands waist deep in the water washing clothes, while her two children splash in the pool. Beating the wet clothes on a rock, she says she's from New Zealand and her husband is training to be a pastor.

Watching her work, I think of the pictures I've seen of poor women and children beating laundry and washing in streams in India and other countries. Now that's us.

Gathering her belongings, she loads the children up with wet laundry, and they all walk back to Malua.

There's no shade, and it's the hottest part of the day, so we jump in the pool in our clothes. Meanwhile, Tammy gives us a lesson in Samoan bathing. She wraps an *ie solosolo* around herself, grabs a bar of soap and washes in the pool.

"Aren't men and women supposed to bathe separately in a village pool?" I ask Tammy.

"They are, but don't worry," says Tammy. "They'll just think we're ignorant palagis."

Heather watches Tammy carefully to learn how we'll have to bathe when we visit a village family. Tammy makes it look easy, discretely moving in the water, and changing her clothes under another *ie*.

"I think I'll need to practise more," says Heather, embarrassed by feeling clumsy.

"You'll soon pick it up," laughs Tammy. "It's a lot easier for men," she says to me, "but you should practice too. You'll need to dress in a *fale* using an *ie*."

Heather feels daunted by the prospect of doing this in a village with women and children laughing at her. It could be a humbling experience.

"You can practise at home in the shower," says Tammy.

Unfortunately, there's no spin dryer at the Malua pool, and the sodden laundry is heavy as we carry it home. We hang it out to dry on our newly repaired clothesline.

Returning to the pool later, I fill two buckets with fresh water. As I carry the heavy buckets six hundred metres back home, the wire handles cut into my hands.

Putting a bucket on Helen's kitchen bench, she thanks me kindly.

When I put the other bucket in our kitchen, Heather says the toilet needs flushing. Our steady supply of flushing water vanished when the rain stopped.

"I'll get some seawater," I say. Provided I can cut through the laneway of fallen trees in the swamp, the lagoon will be much closer than the Malua pool.

Peter joins me to help carry the seawater, and I promise to buy more buckets - if there's any left in Apia.

With the flood water subsiding, the ground is muddy and covered with fallen trees, but a group of men and boys have cleared a path to the sea. The bulldozers have finished reconstructing the road, which is mostly red gravel. As we fill our buckets, a passing bus stirs up a cloud of red dust.

We carry the two buckets of seawater back and tip one down the toilet. It's not enough to flush it clean so I tip the other one down too. The toilet is flushed, but now the buckets are empty, and we need more seawater. Then as we leave, Heather calls out, "Make sure to get some for Tammy and Helen - they'll need it now their tank is empty."

Peter and I have become village water carriers.

I really don't want to make another two trips to the lagoon, but we do; because sanitation is important for life and health, and because the stench of unflushed waste builds up, and festers in the tropical heat.

It's hot work. Sweat runs into our eyes and down our arms, making the bucket handles slippery. The bright sunlight reflecting off the lagoon water is so intense it almost hurts. I now understand why living far from a source of fresh water, can be so debilitating and demanding. Carrying water every day makes us use it sparingly. No more unnecessary washing or showering.

Returning to the lagoon the third time, I detour to some damaged water tanks lying on the grass near Malua. The tops are missing, and one has a gash that looks difficult to repair. But one tank looks intact except for a missing plug at the bottom.

"Maybe we can collect rainwater in it?" I say.

"We'd need to plug it somehow," says Peter.

"We could bang a wooden bung in that tank. But the other'll be harder to fix."

"But the houses don't have any guttering."

"No, but we could put it under the valley where the two sections join. The rain's always heavy, so we might catch enough water to help."

"But can we just take them?" asks Peter. "Maybe they belong to someone?"

"Finders-keepers I'd say - no one's claimed them yet."

When it's time to cook dinner, Peter and I pull timber from the canteen wreckage and chop it into firewood with our bush knife. We light a fire, and Helen cooks dinner in their lean-to shed.

The sun sinks quickly, and we're soon eating a simple candlelit dinner - a pancake-come-frittata with boiled rice. It's tasty, even if we're not sure what's in it.

"We're nearly out of rice," says Helen. "Do you guys have any?"

"No," says Heather. "We brought all ours here."

"I didn't see any in the shops today," says Helen. "We'll need to get some tomorrow - it might be difficult getting taro now."

"The ants are getting worse," says Tammy, looking down at the trail of insects on the table.

"Yes, we noticed that," says Heather. "They're getting into everything."

For some reason the ant population appears to be growing to plague proportions. While we eat dinner, ants quickly form a line to our plates, carrying off food before we've finished.

Besides the ants, Helen's less than satisfactory dishwashing, means we sometimes find our plates contaminated by food remnants from the previous meal.

While our divergent food hygiene practices add relationship tension, Helen's bossy and opinionated attitude adds fuel to the fire. We cooperate, but Helen implicitly behaves like she's in charge. Understandable, when we're guests in her home. Except that it's also Tammy's home, yet Tammy seems to passively 'go with the flow' of Helen's decisions, rather than express her own opinion. Tammy seems more willing to suffer, or mutter, in silence than risk confrontation.

To make sure the dishes are washed clean, I heat another kettle of water, and use it to wash dishes using our detergent.

Helen comments, "We don't bother with that," as though I shouldn't bother either.

"I think the hot water cleans better," I say.

No one says anything, but the tension is there.

"Leave the bowl," says Helen, pointing to the pancake mix in the dim light. "I'm going to scrape it out."

The short-term cyclone danger may be over, but now we face long-term threats that may be more harmful. Toilets can't be flushed every time they're used, and waste attracts disease carrying flies. The surrounding, stagnant, flood water promises to breed dengue carrying mosquitos. Then there's the growing ant plague, the cockroaches we find underneath Helen's washed dishes, and Tavita's potential rat plague. In these circumstances, we need to be vigilant about basic cleanliness and hygiene; and being more organised and ship-shape will add routine, stability, and certainty, to our chaotic lives. With the basic tasks of living now taking so much time and effort, the prospect of soon adding teaching time on top, is doubly daunting.

Heather brings a clean tea towel from our house. While Helen looks on, Heather dries the dishes and puts them in the cupboards. Our actions are an unspoken rebuke, and Helen knows it.

And we know she knows it.

The emotional screws tighten, and the tension rises; threatening to boil over from a pot of simmering irritation and frustration, into a fire of angry words and resentment.

Meanwhile, Peter and Ramon seem oblivious to the whole situation, but John looks on knowingly and smiles.

Heather suggests we have breakfast at our house tomorrow - to share the load.

"I'll cook some porridge," I say.

Helen raises her eyebrows and says, "Okay, thanks guys, that'll be nice."

At least then we'll be able to control what we cook, and when we eat, and how we clean up.

We think Helen should be relieved to get everyone out of her house. But looking back, despite her apparent self-confidence, it's possible having people in her home was an emotional support in troubled times.

After washing up, John and I sit outside by the fire's glowing ashes. John rolls a cigarette, running the edge of the paper over his tongue, before patting his pockets in search of matches.

"Coming home in the truck today it seemed like Tavita wanted to tell me about his worries," I say. "Like he singled me out."

"Probably because you're the oldest palagi and you're married," says John. "In the *fa'asamoa*, you're the one Tavita should talk to."

I've only known John for a week, but after experiencing the cyclone together I already feel like he's a trusted friend.

"Tavita's worried about a rat plague," I say.

"Really? There's already a plague of rats if you ask me."

"We haven't seen any in our house."

"Well, I hope it stays that way - hopefully the cyclone's drowned a few and pruned the population back."

"How does Tavita call a staff meeting when the teachers aren't at the school? How will they know to come tomorrow?"

"He'll announce it on 2AP," says John. "People use the radio for all sorts of announcements. Even if the teacher isn't listening, their child, relative, neighbour or someone else will hear it and pass it on."

A piercing shriek emanates from the house.

Rushing inside, we find Helen in the kitchen spitting and spluttering into the sink.

"Oh, God," she says.

"What happened Helen?" asks Heather.

Helen points to the wooden spoon she used to mix the pancake batter, now completely covered in ants.

"… put the spoon in my mouth…didn't see the ants in the dark."

"That's terrible," says Heather putting, her arm around her. Meanwhile Tammy takes the spoon outside to knock the ants off.

"Oh God, those ants," says Helen, looking at us in the flickering candlelight with tears running down her face.

John thinks it's hilarious and can't contain himself laughing. I think it's funny too, but diplomatically turn my smile to the darkness. Perhaps uncharitably, I also think it will teach Helen to clean up better. Maybe she won't leave dirty dishes around for ants and cockroaches to crawl all over them.

Or rats.

When we return to our house, Heather wants to write a letter to her parents. I put our kerosene lamp on the table, lift the glass and light the wick. She labours writing in the flickering yellow light but stops without finishing the letter. She can feel the dim light straining her eyes.

"I'll finish it in the morning," she says.

Everything seems so much harder by firelight or candlelight.

We go to bed early because there's nothing else to do except sit in the darkness and talk. Peter sleeps at our house while their house dries out. He seems to welcome the company, and we don't mind.

As we lie in the darkness, Heather asks, "Do you think we'll run out of food?"

"I don't know. I've never heard of famine on a Pacific Island, but Tavita is worried."

Talking about it alone, with just the two of us in the darkness, I feel a sense of rising panic. Maybe there will be a famine, and we won't have enough to eat? We went shopping today, but only have enough for the next few days, and we've spent all our cash. Until the bank opens, we can't buy more food. What if we catch dengue fever? Or become ill?

Despite all our effort, we end the day with more questions than when we started. We pray for courage, because we need courage to do what's right and good, knowing we may well suffer harm or loss. We all want courage to succeed, but true courage demands we go on, knowing we face pain, suffering, and possible failure. And we don't want our lack of courage to limit our opportunities to serve or miss the narrow gate that leads to life.

While clean water is a priority, we're unconcerned about lack of power, which now seems like a trivial luxury. The world is silent without power. There are no lights, radios, or parties. Lying in the darkness, we hear nothing but the eternal, rhythmic roar of the distant ocean waves crashing on the reef. Hearing those waves brings comfort - knowing that even after a great natural disaster, some things never change.

And since God is also changeless, we pray earnestly for many things. For food to avert famine in Samoa, for our health and safety, for good relationships with our friends, for the health and wellbeing of the people we've come to serve, and courage to face tomorrow.

10

IMMERSION

"Truly, I say to you, unless you turn and become like children, you will never enter the kingdom of heaven."
Matthew 18:3

n antiquity, by awesome deeds, it was possible to become a god.

By conquering the known world, Alexander the Great joined the august company of the gods. Starting with Caesar Augustus, Roman emperors were declared divine, and commanded worship from their subjects. Whether all Romans and Greeks believed in the divinity of their emperor or king, is beside the point. The point is, if you were one of the greatest men on earth, by your mighty deeds you might become a god. For everyone else, women and children especially, there was fat chance of anything so exalted in this life, or the next.

But Christians claimed God did the reverse. God became a man in the person of Jesus Christ - a step called incarnation. To the Greco-Roman world that was weird and unbelievable. Why would a god possibly do such a thing?

What was even more weird, was that Christians claimed Jesus lived as the poorest of the poor. He kept company, not with gods or princes, but with beggars, prostitutes, and other outcasts. Worse, he suffered the indignity and agony of death by crucifixion, as a slave or common criminal.

The whole idea was obscene.

But Christians said by becoming human, their God knew what it was to be truly human by lived experience. Their God was tempted, felt hunger and cold, slept rough, lost loved ones, suffered terrible injustice, and died an agonising death on our behalf. Wherever we are in our lives they said, our God has been there before us, shares in our suffering, and even suffers with us.

It's only when we become someone else that we truly walk in their shoes. When Jesus said, *"Unless you become like children..."* he was referring to the childlike humility and trust we need to exercise to become a child of the kingdom of God. Following Jesus' example, incarnation has been a model for Christian service since the very beginning. *"I became all things to all men so that I might save some,"* said Paul.

The two-thousand-year history of Christian work is littered with stories of people who chose this pathway. St Francis of Assisi, and Mother Teresa in Calcutta, are perhaps well-known examples.

To us, incarnation means becoming Samoan. But while that's an inspiring idea, it's also an impossible goal. Without being born again as Samoans, no matter how hard we try, we can never truly become Samoans, and certainly not in a two-year volunteer stint.

The best we can hope for is immersion, where we do our best to engage in Samoan culture and adopt whatever we can. But to really engage with Samoan culture, we must first cross a difficult barrier - we must think like Samoans. For the moment, while we take part in contemporary Samoan society, and its struggles, we still think palagi thoughts, in our palagi language, and try to make sense of the unpredictable world around us, in palagi terms.

And while it's true that incarnation might be an unreachable goal, on the journey from immersion to incarnation, we can head in that direction, even if we know we'll never arrive. We learn a lot by climbing a mountain, even if we never reach the summit.

The next morning we're up with the sun. I soon have a fire burning outside our back door and I cook porridge for breakfast. It might seem odd to be eating porridge in the tropics, but with an open fire, it's an easy and nourishing meal to prepare for seven people. After breakfast, we walk to the school for Tavita's staff meeting.

Looking around the staff room, it's obvious half the teachers are missing. Tavita explains that many are still on Savai'i or repairing homes and villages. Leua is here. She weathered the cyclone with her family in Saleimoa.

"I want to open the school as soon as possible," announces Tavita. "But we won't have water or power for weeks or months. What do the staff think we can do?"

Iosefa (vice principal) thinks we should wait until we have water, and Mele (headmistress) agrees.

Helen pipes up saying, "We don't need power, but we should start soon, because the students are missing out on classes, and it'll be hard to catch up."

Sitting next to Mele is Kale, the *fa'afafine* Helen had spoken about. Kale visibly stiffens when Helen speaks, showing it takes more than a holiday break, and a national disaster, to soften resentment towards her.

Kale thinks we could start with a few classes a day, with or without water. Others point out that the school needs to be cleaned up first.

We say nothing and listen. Lacking experience, we feel contributing would be presumptuous.

Tavita concludes the meeting by announcing he'll call students to help clean up on Friday. Meanwhile, he'll talk to the church about opening in a partial capacity.

"If anyone wants to go to Apia they should meet at my house in fifteen minutes," he adds.

Returning to our house we grab our packs. With a feeling of déjà vu, we're soon back on the school truck.

As we sit on the tray waiting for Tavita, we hear the distinct chop-chop noise of a helicopter. A small military chopper flies by, low enough to identify it with the New Zealand Air Force.

"The Kiwis have arrived," I say.

"Great," says Peter smiling, his spirits rising. "They got here quick. I wonder if the Aussies have arrived too?"

As Tavita drives the truck down the laneway to the road, the denuded, browning, and broken branches remind me of a bushfire aftermath. Although not blackened or burnt, they look equally dead.

Heather sits scribbling a letter to her parents as the truck bumps over the rough road. Although visually damaged, the villages on the road to Apia now look neat and tidy. Just two days after the wind stops blowing, village life appears to have rapidly recovered.

Arriving in Apia, Heather heads to the High Commission while I go to the bank. There's only one teller, no queue, and everyone appears to be withdrawing cash. To avoid being caught out again by a closed bank, I withdraw more than we'll ever need for the next few weeks. We're still drawing on savings brought from Australia because the church hasn't paid us yet. I feel nervous carrying such a thick wad of cash and think I should hide it somewhere at home.

"Hide it in a book," says Helen later. "Samoans don't read, so they'll never look in a book."

This time, unrestrained by the cash in my pocket, I buy as much food as I think we can carry - particularly preserved foods like tinned fish, vegetables, and fruit. Unfortunately, all the rice has sold out.

"I saw Hannah," says Heather when we meet at MacKenzies. "She spent the cyclone at the Seaside Inn. She says Erin's okay but hasn't heard from Emma."

Heather also wrote our names on a list at the High Commission, so they can contact our families to let them know we're okay.

With packs full of heavy tinned food, we stagger back to Chan Mow's, finding Tammy waiting, but the school truck gone.

Why did Tavita abandon us? Now we'll have to carry everything to the market and catch a bus.

As we head off, we bump into Leua, Latu and Anita.

"We heard there's rice being sold off the back of a truck in Fugalei Street," says Leua. "We're going there now."

Since we need rice too, we all walk there together.

Turning the corner into Fugalei Street, a crowd gathers around a truck stacked high with rice sacks. I see a man pass a sack down to someone in the waiting crowd.

Leua makes enquiries and discovers the sacks only cost ten *tala*, but we must buy a ticket from a nearby office.

"We should get one," I say to Heather and Tammy. "We can share it."

"Sure," says Tammy.

As Leua walks off to buy tickets, we stand watching the truck. As the crowd mills around, I'm reminded of images on the TV news. A crowd mobs a truck delivering international aid to famine stricken, or war-torn countries in Africa and sometimes riots ensue.

Now that's us - hoping for a simple sack of rice because it satisfies a basic need for food. Maybe Tavita's right and we really are heading for famine? Otherwise, why would this truck be delivering rice like this? It can't have come by ship - there's been no time for that.

After Leua returns and gives us our ticket, Latu and I approach the truck. We're in Samoa so there's no discernible queue. Latu pushes his way to the front, and I follow in his wake.

He hands his ticket up, and after someone puts a sack on his shoulder, he turns and walks away. I hand my ticket up, a man dumps a sack of rice on my shoulder, and my knees buckle. Staggering under the load, I re-shoulder the heavy sack to be more comfortable, and regain my balance. Carefully, I trudge back to the others.

"Let's go," I say, eager to get to a bus before the heavy sack topples me over.

Arriving at the bus stop, I rest the sack on the ground. It says it contains twenty-five kilograms of PNG rice. Was it flown into Samoa as aid by some government - Australia, New Zealand or maybe PNG?

Who knows? But really, who cares? The fact is, we are the proud owners of twenty-five kilograms of rice. Even if we share it with everyone else, it should keep us alive. And if we add some vegetables, fish, and other protein, we can be healthy and well fed for some time.

How long does twenty-five kilograms of rice last? We don't know, but we're more than happy to find out.

We catch the Malua bus which drops us off at the Malua entrance gate, so we have to walk the rest of the way home. To walk, I balance the rice sack in my arms in front with the pack on my back full other heavy food.

"Are you okay?" asks Heather.

"I think so," I say, but I really don't know, because with every step I feel like a post being hammered into the ground. After two hundred meters, I rest the sack on a fence post before walking on to Leua's house. Then Latu kindly drops his sack and carries ours home.

We put the rice on the bench in our kitchen, where it stays for many months. The bag of rice, and the assurance that God will provide, gives us valuable peace of mind.

Of course, after a few weeks, we tire of boiled rice and tinned herring, garnished with a few vegetables. Months later, while we're still eating our way through the sack, a grey scum forms on the boiled rice.

"Weevils," says Tammy. "Don't worry, they're safe to eat, and they'll add protein to our diet."

Added protein or not, we skim off the layer of boiled weevil carcasses before serving the rice. But the weevils multiply, and when we see them moving about in the uncooked grains, we discard the remaining rice. We're not that desperate!

Over the coming months bananas and breadfruit are non-existent. Taro is always available, but the price quickly triples, and inflation hits everything else too. Our bus fare to Apia doubles.

But despite the growing hardship inflicted by the cyclone, we never hear of any Samoan who lacks sufficient food. An important foundation of Samoan culture is the strong social obligation to help someone in need. If you or your family are without food, your neighbour or relative must share their food with you. Not helping someone in need is worse than socially unacceptable - it's unthinkable. Refusing would make one a social outcast. That's the sort of behaviour you expect from selfish palagis - not Samoans.

Such a deeply rooted cultural obligation helped families survive hardship and troubled times in a way that's unfathomable to a European culture. It goes far beyond charity as we understand it. The *fa'asamoa* provides a cultural social security system that ensures everyone starves or prospers together.

When it rains that afternoon, we use all the bowls and containers we can muster to collect water off our roof. Every litre of water is a litre I don't have to carry six hundred metres from the Malua pool.

After the rain, Helen appears at our door with news: "Tavita got hold of some kerosene stoves - there's one for us, and another for Kale and Mele."

"Really? He disappeared in Apia."

"Yeah, he heard about these stoves, and had to grab them quick."

We don't know when school starts, but we know that living like we do now, we're going to struggle to prepare lessons, teach for a day, and correct homework. A stove will free up valuable time from preparing meals.

Meanwhile, Peter and I carry more drinking water from Malua, and seawater to flush the toilets. Then it's time to collect firewood, light a fire and cook dinner.

It's dark and difficult to see when we all sit around a single flickering candle eating a dinner of rice, tinned herring, and vegetables. We can only wonder at what the crunchy bits are that stick in our teeth, as we swap stories in the dim light.

"I heard three people died at the hospital," says Tammy. "Their life support systems stopped when the power cut."

"How sad," says Helen.

"You'd think they'd have a back-up generator at the main hospital," comments John.

"You'd think," says Helen.

"Apparently, the Yanks and Aussies arrived yesterday," says John. "The Yanks landed in a humongous plane and got out in camouflage gear with weapons ready. I dunno what they were expecting, but they ran around the airport and surrounded the runway."

"It was probably a C17," I say. "And they were most likely making sure the runway was clear of debris before their other planes land or take off."

"Good old US of A," Helen says proudly, and John rolls his eyes at me.

"Are they staying in tents somewhere?" I ask.

"I heard they're at the Tusi and Aggies," says John.

"Oh, how hard that must be," says Helen, quickly exchanging patriotism for sarcasm. "It's great to know our army's toughing it out in the best hotels."

While we're merely threatened by food and water shortage, we're starved for news. Word of mouth, from Tavita or the volunteer grapevine, has rapidly replaced proper news sources.

We've given up listening on short wave to Australian or New Zealand radio; the news is high level and useless for Australians trying to survive in cyclone ravaged Samoa. We struggle to understand Samoan news on the local radio. The Samoa Observer (the local English language paper) only comes out weekly, and there's been no issue since the cyclone.

Like John's story of the US Army's arrival, word-of-mouth information is local, relevant, definitely embellished, probably inaccurate, and possibly untrue. It might be hard to distinguish fact from fiction, but because it's all we have, we devour every scrap of real, compromised, or imaginary news like ravenous animals. And it's using the information we know, or think we know, that we make daily decisions that impact our lives at a very basic level.

The next morning, we all breakfast together, and then head to the Malua pool to bathe, and bring back fresh water for the day.

Tavita delivers the kerosene camping stove, and we soon have it set up in our kitchen.

We share the stove on a roster system - two days at our house and two days at Tammy and Helen's. Peter and John are happy to contribute by preparing meals and cleaning up. Their house is further away, and they don't have plates, cutlery and other things needed for seven people. While sharing the stove forces us to work together, and share meals, if we're not careful it could be a source of additional tension and disagreement. Sometimes the very thing that draws us together can also force us apart.

Meanwhile, Peter and I scavenge a water tank - rolling it several hundred metres to place it under Tammy and Helen's roof. It's tempting to put it under our roof, but it doesn't seem right to take it for ourselves. Besides, we'll share the water and it's only twenty metres from our house.

Using my pocket-knife, I carve a tapered wooden bung, then hammer it into the hole at the bottom to make a plug.

"Will that hold water?" asks Helen, standing on the doorstep as I climb out of the tank.

"It should, if there aren't other leaks."

Was that a tear I saw in her eye? Maybe, for all her apparent confidence, Helen feels more vulnerable than she's letting on? Somehow, the tension seems to relax a little.

Meanwhile, the growing pungent odour in our bathrooms says it's time to get seawater from the lagoon.

That afternoon it rains as expected, leaving a foot of water in the tank, representing a hundred buckets of water we won't carry from Malua.

"We've got water," I call out.

"Woo-hoo," says Helen, her eyes lighting up with delight.

Then she sees plant debris floating on top, and the unsightly rusty wall of the tank.

"Is it clean?"

"Sure - we'll wait for the dirt to sink to the bottom."

"What about the stuff floating on top?"

"Just skim it off - it's harmless. It rains every day so we should have plenty of water."

"What about insects and germs in the water?"

"We can strain out the insects - it's just clean rainwater, straight out of the sky. I grew up drinking rainwater."

"Yeah, but this water ran off our roof, and look at it," says Helen, pointing to the discoloured, green-grey fungus covered roof.

"We can treat it with Clorox," says Tammy, unfazed by Helen's concerns.

"Okay, I guess," says Helen doubtfully, walking inside.

"Is the asbestos roof a problem?" I ask Tammy quietly.

"Is it asbestos?"

"If it was built in the 1960s, it's sure to be asbestos. Will that kill us? After all, you're the biology teacher."

Tammy laughs. "I don't know, ask John, he's the chemistry teacher. But I know it's great having water by our back door."

I think I'll ask John later, but I'm not sure I should mention it to anyone else. I don't want to unnecessarily alarm them by suggesting they'll die thirty years after drinking our water.

That evening we cook a meal for the first time using the kerosene stove. It certainly frees up time gathering wood and lighting fires, but the soot spreads like an infectious disease, contaminating the bench tops, dishes, dishcloths, our hands, faces, and clothing. The stove rapidly burns through the small kerosene bottle Tavita gave us, and there's a shortage of kerosene.

"Apparently because the cyclone silted up the harbour," says John. "They can't get ships to the wharf."

"I thought the wharf was damaged?" I say.

"That too."

"Well, we'd better be careful with the kerosene," says Helen.

When I heat a kettle of water to wash the dishes, she says, "it's a waste" and we should save the kerosene.

We ignore her, and she doesn't enjoy being ignored. The tension screws turn back up another notch.

When the others go to the Malua pool to cool off in the moonlight, John and I talk in the darkness, illuminated only by the red glow of John's roll-your-own cigarette.

"Do you think there's a problem collecting rainwater off the asbestos roof?" I ask John.

"You mean from fibres in the water?"

"Yeah - like, I know breathing asbestos fibres causes mesothelioma, but what happens if you drink it?"

"I dunno, Ian. I reckon any fibres have washed off long ago. But look at it this way - you try your luck with asbestos in the tank or weed killer at Malua?"

"Weed killer?"

"They spray weed killer on the plantations up there in the hills, and probably ends up in the spring water we drink at Malua."

Fear grips me as I think about John's claim. Are we spending the next two years drinking poison? Shortening our lives by succumbing to cancer, or something else?

"But then rocks and soil filter water, don't they?" I venture. "Basalt must be a good filter, and it rains so much the water must dilute it."

"Probably, but really, who knows? A lotta things can kill us, Ian. Like I said, take your pick - asbestos or weed killer."

"Those rollies'll kill you one day, if you keep smoking."

"Probably," says John, tapping his cigarette into an empty tin. "But increasing my risk from smoking, dilutes my risk of dying from asbestos and weed killer."

The next morning, Peter and I roll the other abandoned corrugated iron tank to our house and put it under the roof on the concrete front porch. There's a long gash torn in the side and some rivets have popped.

I patch the holes and gashes with discarded fly screen soaked in the acrylic sealant I used to seal our cupboards. I hope it will form a composite material that will bond to the rough mineralised surface inside the tank. It's oppressively hot inside the enclosed tank. Sweat runs in my eyes making it difficult to see, and down my arms making the tools slippery. As I climb out soaked in sweat, I hope it all cures before the next rain shower and that it holds against the water pressure.

Against all expectations, it doesn't rain that day, and the sealant cures nicely.

But it doesn't rain the next day either.

Or the next.

Day after day, there's no rain. But it's the wet season in Samoa when it's supposed to rain three times every day. Are we in a drought? Maybe it has something to do with the cyclone disrupting weather patterns?

All we know is that the very day we put up our tank to collect rainwater, it stops raining. It's hard to believe and impossible to understand. Our tank remains as dry as dust.

Meanwhile, we do our best to conserve the small amount of precious water we have in the tank at Tammy and Helen's place. We only use the tank water for drinking and cooking, continuing the daily grind of carrying seawater to flush toilets. We do our laundry and bathing at Malua.

Meanwhile leaves, twigs and insects blow into the tank, first floating on the surface, before sinking to the bottom to form a dark layer of organic matter. It doesn't do much for Helen's confidence but doesn't bother Tammy or me. Having grown up on farms, we're familiar with the layer of mud that sits in the bottom of every rainwater tank. Leua needs water too, and more teachers arrive with their families. The precious water dwindles dangerously close to the murky bottom, while not a drop of rain falls.

We see more army helicopters going back and forth, often with loads slung underneath, timber, perhaps a generator, or building materials. I wonder if they're from the Australian Army, but they're too far away to tell.

We're busy with the mundane but necessary tasks of simply living. In fact, simple living turns out to be a lot more complex than we thought. We gain new skills - mostly by trial and error. Time and hard physical work replace leisure and everything else we took for granted. Flicking a switch to light a room, or turning a tap for water are simple. Living by candlelight and carrying water demands thinking, planning, and hard physical sweat and toil.

Then, every afternoon we seem to be struck down by sleeping sickness; our bodies force us into a siesta lifestyle in response to the tropical climate. We feel tired after lunch, so we lie down, only to wake up three hours later, when we wander around in a stupor for a while before living life returns. Now we understand why Samoans sleep all afternoon in the shade of their *fales* in the sea breeze. They're being sensible, not lazy.

A few students turn up on Friday to clean up the school. They cut some grass and clear up some cyclone debris, but it's a token gesture. Clearly, most families can't yet spare hardworking teenagers to help get the school ready. Although there's no water at the school, Tavita decides to open next Tuesday - for a few hours a day, maybe a few days a week, and then see how things go.

That's just three days away.

In three weeks, we transitioned from being Australians living in a major city, in one of the world's wealthiest countries, to living much like millions of the world's poor. Seen through palagi eyes, it's a descent into a valley of chaos, hardship, and a return to a more primitive way of life. But for us, it's a positive step forward. It reminds us that God has not only provided a bag of rice, but also a crash course in Samoan living, and surrounded us with the right people for the moment.

Because living like Samoans is an important step towards becoming Samoan.

Now we know, through hard experience, how important it is to have ready access to fresh water. How hard it is to carry water a long distance to home, as millions do throughout the world. And why people use such water sparingly.

Now we know what it means to gather firewood every day to cook meals in a pot cradled on three rocks and preserve food without a refrigerator - keeping the rats, ants, cockroaches, and other enemies at bay.

Now we understand the fragility of our modern world. Our fridge, stove, running water, and home conveniences, can vanish in a moment.

Now we understand that the more time we spend securing essentials like food, water, shelter, and sleep, the less time we have for anything else. And why we rise before dawn to work in the cooler parts of the day, and tell stories sitting in the dark around a campfire, because that's our leisure time, and telling stories is all we can do in the dark.

Now we know a natural disaster's devastation, but also how resourceful and resilient the world's poorest people can be in the most appalling circumstances.

And why, in the absence of any information, we depend on unreliable stories, rumours, and gossip.

Now we know the value of lost life skills, the skills poor people depend upon to live day by day. Including learning to live in community with others, with all the tensions and disagreements that always arise when even a few people cooperate. That cooperation is not possible without sacrifice, and that patience and tolerance can be painful. Perhaps, real tolerance is always painful.

Now we know the strongest bonds are those formed in the cauldron of shared suffering. That suffering can be an enriching experience because it teaches us things we can never hope to learn otherwise. Perhaps it's only then that we truly know one another, when all the sheltering walls of pretence have blown away, and who we truly are, is no longer something we can hide.

Finally, it's giving us an insight and appreciation for Samoa because living in community is the very fabric of Samoan culture and village life. The fact that they've lived here successfully for several thousand years, means they have a thing or two to teach us about living in cooperation and community on a tropical island.

Sharing our food, water, possessions, and homes, lights more than a fire in the darkness. It opens a door in our minds to the idea that there are excellent reasons for the things we find most perplexing and alien in Samoan culture. And that changes our perception of the world, ourselves, and the fabric of our deepest thoughts.

Learning all this by lived experience is a gift of wisdom we've carried with us in the decades since that time.

The deep impact of the cyclone on our personal lives is to immerse us up to our necks and possibly over our heads. But while true incarnation may be impossible, and immersion is difficult, we can all learn to identify with others.

Now, in a small way, we identify with the people in our adopted country. We've been through the same disaster together and now we live much like them. By getting the school running again, we work alongside them to recover and rebuild.

We're beginning to understand what it truly means to walk beside someone, to tread the same rocky physical and emotional journey, share the same fears and good fortune, even if it's impossible to truly walk in their shoes.

While everyone has their own cyclone story, we now have a common shared experience with all our students, their families, and their villages. We'll always have something to talk about - something we've shared together.

While there is no greater respect we can give to a culture than to adopt it as our own, incarnation brings more than we realise. At this stage, we think adopting culture is about adopting cultural practices. But by changing how we think, it's going to change our values.

And that, is a fearful thing.

11

ESCAPE

*"Everyone then who hears these words of mine and
does them will be like a wise man who built his house
on a rock. And the rain fell, and the floods came, and
the winds blew and beat on that house, but it did not
fall, because it had been founded on the rock."*
Matthew 7:24-25

One Saturday afternoon finds us standing by the dusty, red gravel
roadside, waiting for a bus. We need food again, and bus trips into
Apia are becoming more routine. The afternoon sun beats down;
there's no shade after the cyclone blew away the trees.

When a bus stops and we climb aboard, a ghostly cloud of diesel and
dust coats us and all the passengers. But the trip to Apia is pleasant, as a
cool breeze blows through the windows, and Bob Marley sings through the
loudspeakers.

The bus stops at the market where we get off and walk towards Chan
Mow's. As Apia returns to the dusty, muddy, and falling down place it was,
navigating the ubiquitous hazards on the non-existent footpath is becoming

part of our subconscious reality. There are some permanent changes, like the fire station that looks like a Samoan Leaning Tower of Pisa after the cyclone pushed it over; and the Lady Samoa, sitting high and dry nearby on the reclaimed land. For the next two years they remain permanent, visual reminders of the disaster.

We're delighted when we see Erin approaching in the street. We've not seen her in three weeks, and she's equally excited to see us. As we swap cyclone stories, we hear how she and Norah sheltered in their house at Alafua without losing their roof.

"We're having dinner at the Treasure Garden later," she says. "Why don't you join us?"

"Have they got any food?" I ask.

"Let's hope so," laughs Erin. "It's open, so they must have something."

With boiled rice and tinned herring already becoming monotonous, dinner at a restaurant is a welcome change.

After shopping, Peter joins us as we make our way down Fugalei Street towards the Treasure Garden Restaurant, where we meet Mick, Matt, Hannah, and Erin.

It's the first gathering of volunteers since we waved goodbye outside the Seaside Inn weeks earlier. Also joining us are Norah (Erin's housemate, and UK student) and Kevin, a Kiwi friend of Peter's.

Kevin is an economist by trade, but he's recently taken a teaching position at Maluafou - another smaller Congregational Church high school in Apia. Escaping a bitter divorce, it seems Kevin took the job for some adventure and a fresh start. Heather and I hadn't warmed to Kevin when we met three weeks earlier at the Seaside Inn - he seemed opinionated, intense, and complained easily.

Having just opened for the evening, we're the first guests. Walking inside, it seems little has changed since we ate there nearly four weeks earlier. After we sit down at a large round table, the waiter distributes the menu of over eighty dishes - all numbered for easy reference - typical of many Chinese restaurants in Australia.

We start by ordering drinks from the five-page menu. But we're told they have no alcoholic or non-alcoholic beverages, except Supa-Banana and tap water. Not even Coca-Cola.

"Because of the cyclone," says the waiter.

Locally manufactured soft drinks, Supa-Banana and other 'Supa' beverages, combine reduced life expectancy with saturation bombing of the human sensory system. Drinking any Supa beverage is to imbibe liquid sugar with a heavy dose of artificial flavours. Guaranteed to either cause diabetes or permanently cure the hypoglycaemic, the artificial flavouring could also be carcinogenic. Of the available flavours, Supa-Banana is the most lethal.

"They've got Supa-Banana because no one wants to drink the stuff," says Hannah.

"The shop across the road sells Coke and Fanta," says Bruce hopefully.

'Shop is closed.'

A few order Supa-Banana - those whose endocrine systems can manage the glucose overload or are happy to play Russian roulette with the artificial flavours. But the more cautious stick with tap water.

Although the menu has over eighty dishes listed, by a painful process of trial and error, we discover they have no beef, pork, or chicken.

"Because of the cyclone," says the waiter.

"But there are chickens everywhere," protests Erin.

While we don't want to complain, we wonder why the waiter didn't save us and himself a lot of trouble, by telling us they only have two dishes at the outset.

"I feel like I'm in an episode of Fawlty Towers," says Erin.

Since there are plenty of beef cattle, pigs, and chickens in Samoa, we suspect Cyclone Ofa is being unjustly charged with crimes it did not commit.

We order multiple plates of the sole dishes available - fried rice with vegetables, and fried noodles with vegetables.

Kevin opens a copy of the Samoa Observer, the first issue since the cyclone, and reads out snippets of interest.

"According to this, entire villages disappeared on the north coast of Savai'i," he says.

"How do you mean 'disappeared'?" I ask.

"Apparently everything washed into the sea - there's just lumps of concrete left in the sand. The people moved to higher ground and took their belongings with them."

Wow, that sounds bad, it makes our troubles seem trivial.

"And some patients died at Tuisivi Hospital when part of the hospital fell in the sea," adds Kevin.

"Really? Surely, they'd move the patients?"

"Who knows? It also says they've run out of petrol at Asau."

While the reports of disaster on Savai'i seem catastrophic, we also hear from Hannah that Emma and our fellow volunteer friends are okay.

"How's your house?" asks Kevin, turning to me.

"Well, we've got no power or water, but the roof stayed on."

"Did Feilo give you everything he promised?"

"Sure. We weren't expecting much, but we've got nothing to complain about."

"He promised me a furnished house, but I still don't have a pillow."

"A pillow?" I ask, puzzled.

"I've asked Feilo for a pillow three times now. A pillow is part of a furnished house. There are sheets but no pillow."

"You could buy a pillow at Carruthers," suggests Erin.

"The Congregational Church," says Kevin, ignoring her, "is enticing people here on false pretences."

I think he must be joking - as if the offer of a pillow would entice anyone to move to Samoa? But the look on his face suggests he's serious. Then Peter says what we're all thinking.

"The country's just gone through a disaster. People have lost their homes - maybe Feilo's got more important stuff to worry about than a pillow."

"It's the principle - he should do what he said," says Kevin, unrepentant.

Since the cyclone, Peter has been subdued, but now he seems quite cheerful - positively buoyant. It's like he's risen above the squalid turmoil of his existence and can see a bright future ahead.

By contrast, Kevin finds a dark cloud in every silver lining. I wonder how he can cope living in Samoa for any length of time. While we haven't been in the country very long, we've learned enough to know that standing on principle is unpleasant and pointless. Feilo probably thinks Kevin is another painful palagi who can't fit in, or cope with a minor inconvenience.

We're also conscious that Kevin's behaviour rubs off onto the reputation of other palagis like us. It seems many Samoans view palagis the way many palagis view Samoans - they're all the same. But we aren't all the same - are we?

While the Samoa Observer brings us our first reported news that isn't word-of-mouth hearsay, the news travelling down the gossip grapevine is more interesting. Mick and Hannah share a steady stream of juicy stories they heard through their connections to people at the Australian High Commission.

"The cyclone damaged Mary Peters' hot water system," says Hannah, "so she had a new one flown in from Australia."

"What?" says Heather.

"Prob'ly part of the deal for a posting here," says Mick.

"Maybe," admits Hannah. "A cold shower must be considered a hardship."

The story might be a rumour, but it still grates on us. Mary's hot water system will take precious air freight space and displace something more desperately needed elsewhere in Samoa. It feels selfish to expect hot showers, when entire villages are homeless on Savai'i, and hospital patients died.

Hannah describes other rumoured scandals, possible illicit romances, and whispers of sexual exploits. We're gratified to know that none of the rumours involve Basil, the High Commissioner, or his wife, Elizabeth. Apparently, there's a widely held consensus that Basil is 'a good bloke', which gives us some hope our country isn't entirely represented by a bunch of selfish, sexually deviant fruit bats.

"How are you getting on with those American neighbours of yours?" asks Hannah.

"Pretty good," I say. "They've been a great help, but we notice Helen's always got to say something in staff meetings, and the other teachers seem to resent it."

"I'm sure she means well," says Hannah. "Americans can be great people - if they'd only learn to shut up. I'm sharing with a Peace Corps woman in Motootua now. I finally got out of the Seaside Inn today."

"Conveniently close to the hospital if you need it," says Bruce.

"Yeah! I'm right next to the Ambulance Station, and the funeral parlour."

"An ambulance station next to a funeral parlour?" says Heather, incredulous.

"Convenient if the patient's dead-on-arrival," jokes Bruce.

By the time we leave the restaurant it's late, and since there's a risk of getting a drunk taxi driver, Hannah suggests we stay the night at Mick's.

"I'd offer my place, but I only moved in today, and don't want to push my luck."

Mick is unbothered that Hannah just offered his place to sleep overnight. He acts like it happens every other week - because it probably does.

Walking to Mick's flat in the darkness, and climbing his steps, I realise it's four weeks since we spent our first day there, sweltering in Samoa. At the time we thought his place was a decrepit hovel, but now it seems like a luxury suite. The only thing that's changed is us.

"You'se are lucky - just got the power back on today," says Mick, as he flicks a switch. Not only that, Mick also has running water.

"Prob'ly best if youse sleep on the floor," says Mick. "Take some cushions off the chair if ya want a pillow."

We sleep on the floor in our clothes. It's hot, so sheets and blankets are unnecessary, and while it feels uncomfortable at first, we're learning to sleep in all circumstances. It's a habit that serves us well in Samoa. We just hope we're not sharing the floor with gangs of malevolent cockroaches or centipedes.

Bruce, meanwhile, who's still looking for new digs, sleeps on the couch, now minus a few cushions.

We wake late next morning as Hiruki, Mick's Japanese flatmate, gingerly steps over our prostrate forms on his way out the door. Being Sunday, we suspect Mick and Bruce anticipate a lazy morning. After a cold shower, we rummage around in Mick's kitchen finding food for breakfast - toast topped with jam and vegemite, followed by tea.

Four weeks earlier, I couldn't have imagined helping ourselves to someone's house like this. But we've discovered the international volunteer community live in and out of each other's houses, in ways that are alien in their own cultures. The host may not be home, or even know visitors are coming, but it doesn't stop visitors making themselves at home overnight, or for a few days. We'd do the same for Mick, or any other volunteers that needed a place to crash for a while.

Leaving Mick and Bruce, we walk to the market and take a bus back to Leulumoega Fou.

We feel surprisingly refreshed after spending time with Australians. While being with Samoans teaches us a lot, there's a cloud of communication uncertainty hanging over us that makes it difficult to relax and be ourselves. And although Tammy and Helen both speak English, there are subtle communication gaps that trip us up. Americans have different meanings for the same words, joke in different ways, and laugh at different things. We've already had the experience of having to explain jokes, and once a joke needs explanation, it's no longer funny. We better understand now why Tammy and Helen visit Peace Corps friends on the weekends.

It's Monday morning and school starts tomorrow.

On the roster system, we have the kerosene stove, and expect everyone to come for breakfast around seven-thirty. There's still no rain, and with only a few inches of water left in the tank at Tammy and Helen's, we're back carrying water from Malua. Despite the difficulties, life is more stable now.

As I stir the porridge, John walks in, quickly followed by Tammy and Helen.

"Has Peter slept in?" asks Helen, sprinkling sugar over her porridge.

"I thought he was here," says John.

"Maybe he went for a walk?" suggests Heather.

"Well, if he doesn't turn up soon, I'm eating his porridge," I say, "otherwise it'll go hard."

Later in the morning John is back, breathless with news.

"I just talked to Keola - he saw Peter at the airport this morning."

"Really? What's he doing there?"

"I think he's done a runner. I checked his room, and his suitcase is gone."

"He can't have," says Heather reluctantly. "Can he?"

"Looks like he's taken off somewhere," says John. "If Keola saw him at the airport, I reckon he's gone home - he's probably in New Zealand by now. Couldn't hack it I suppose."

"But he said nothing to us," says Heather, feeling betrayed.

"He must have bought a ticket on the weekend," says John.

"He did seem cheery on Saturday night."

Tammy wanders in to ask if we have some powdered milk because they've run out.

"Peter's scarpered," says John.

"What do you mean?"

"Gone - skedaddled back home."

Tammy looks at John dumfounded, as Helen walks through the door.

"I overheard from my room guys. Peter's gone, hey?"

"Looks like he's done a runner," says John.

"Well, Tavita IS NOT going to be happy."

"I guess we didn't know how he was really feeling," says Tammy, always ready to sympathise first and ask questions later. "He said nothing about leaving."

"Prob'ly too scared," says John.

Just when we think life is improving, we've suddenly lost a friend and teacher. Somehow, life is going to be more difficult.

Emotionally we feel abandoned.

Then we feel betrayed.

"He must have bought his ticket home on Saturday, while we were shopping," I say.

That's why he was so buoyant at the Treasure Garden on Saturday night. He knew he was going home. And he knew if he'd talked to us, we'd have done our utmost to convince him to stay - after all, we need him here. Without him it's going to be harder for all of us. Escaping like a thief in the night was better than having us tug every heartstring we could find, piling guilt on his fragile conscience. No hard conversations. No emotional farewells.

Did he leave because the reality of Samoan life is harsher than he expected? But what, exactly, did Peter expect?

Today it's easy to see travel blogs on YouTube posted by tourists in Samoa. From the comfort of a lounge chair on another continent, we can saunter through the streets of Apia, check out the shops, and food for sale in the market.

Before we went to Samoa, we scoured books in our local library, often published decades earlier. They showed Samoans dancing in picturesque villages, thatched *fales* backgrounded by white sand beaches, and coconut palms, often in black and white photographs. That meagre information fed our imagination enough to develop a vision of our future life in Samoa; living in a house by the sea; on a tropical island, and teaching students eager to learn. While that idealised Samoa was a pale shadow of reality, it was based on that vision that we plucked up the courage to come here.

But nothing could convey the experience we're living in Samoa, or the daunting prospect of teaching in the shadow of stories of violence and chaos

Helen shared with Peter. If we'd known ahead of time what would happen in our first four weeks in Samoa, we'd probably have stayed in Australia. Peter's job description didn't include chasing rats around his kitchen or enduring a cyclone and its aftermath. Like us, he'd spent the last five weeks re-aligning his romantic vision with the real world.

While Peter's courage might limit his opportunities, perhaps he wasn't ready for this particular opportunity. While we're embracing and adapting to the challenges thrown at us, perhaps Peter was feeling overwhelmed? Did the daunting prospect of meeting students, and teaching, finally tip the scales? Whatever the reason, Peter's "I made a commitment", at some point became "I made a mistake". Maybe he found comfort knowing that the struggle, and the daily burden of uncertainty we all live with, would evaporate the moment he left.

Perhaps our sense of betrayal arose because we thought we'd made an unspoken commitment to each other. After all, the idea that we "look after our mates" is a strongly held Australian cultural value. And in the recent past, we had looked after each other through a cyclone and its aftermath.

What's true is that we're all here for different reasons, and therefore have diverse reasons for staying. Nietzsche was right when he said, *"He who has a why to live for, can bear almost any how."*

Heather and I see our commitment to living and teaching in Samoa, as part of our purpose in God's bigger plan. We have a 'why' that transcends the sacrifice we make when storms descend upon us.

It doesn't mean we won't falter or feel fearful in the face of threats to our safety, or even fail to meet some commitments. For if we're honest, we all fail to meet commitments, particularly as we grow older and take on more responsibility. We make commitments to God, family, friends, employers, and employees, only to find them in conflict, or beyond our well-intentioned ability to achieve. Sometimes we're unprepared to risk our health or the wellbeing of people we love. Sometimes we underestimate our own fragility. Sometimes we just stuff up.

Peter's disappearance teaches us we never really know what people are thinking, and that we all respond differently when the reality steamroller flattens our fantasies and confronts us with harsh realities. When confronted with the suffering that sacrifice and commitment often demand, some rise with courage, and even revel in the moment, while others wither and run away.

No one enjoys suffering, but a purposeful life demands commitment, suffering and sacrifice. We can't truly commit ourselves to anything worthwhile, without at least the sacrifice of what we might otherwise do with our lives. To keep a commitment is to shoulder responsibility and demonstrate the willingness to be accountable. And being responsible and accountable gives meaning to the suffering that results from commitment and sacrifice. And when we do what's meaningful, we make an investment in our soul. We build something permanent; something no one can ever take away. For while we're busy making commitments, it's our commitments that make us into the people we become.

When Tavita drops by in the school truck that afternoon, Helen, and I relay the news. He sits in the driver's seat, passively listening with his elbow on the windowsill.

Then his face clouds.

He swears in Samoan, and then in English for good measure and our benefit. He clearly received no resignation letter, and now he has to either find a replacement at short notice, or somehow fill the gap.

Because as Tavita loses a teacher, the enrolment numbers grow. Culturally, it's very difficult for Tavita to reject students who've already enrolled, or whose important parents, or pastor, want their children to attend school.

Tavita also knows that to refuse a student means some children miss out on a high school education - potentially depriving them of a life changing opportunity in one of the world's poorest countries.

He can still accept students if he spreads the same number across a smaller set of classes - further stretching meagre resources. That means already bulging classes become even larger, making them more difficult to teach, and increasing the teacher's workload.

Alternatively, some teachers can take on Peter's classes besides their own full teaching load. For teachers committed or foolish enough to accept that load, it means more class time, and less time to do preparation, correction, and administration, adding to the workload while reducing the time available to do the work.

We all feel pressure to take on an extra class to give more students the chance to learn. The stress, exhaustion and chaos of the previous year has left Helen gun shy about doing extra work. But Tammy's sacrificial soft heart, and willingness to help, means she can't say no. And since we haven't actually taught in Samoa, we're too naïve to know what we're signing up for. Sure, we'll do what's difficult, and burn our candle at both ends. Living without power, it isn't long before we realise extra classes literally means burning candles at night to complete the work.

In the short term, Peter's departure reflects poorly on us and other palagi teachers. It's confirmation to our Samoan critics that palagis are weak, 'lily livered, and have no staying power, or strength of commitment. While we feel indignant about such criticism, it's too often quite valid.

While we liked Peter and enjoyed his company, he left us with Kevin, who is proving to be the painful person we thought he was. Since he complains about every little thing, we expect he'll quickly follow Peter back to New Zealand. But when I share my thoughts with Hannah later, she disagrees:

"I've seen people like him before - they complain a lot, but they also hang around."

"Why doesn't he go home if he doesn't like it?"

"He probably complains and whinges about everything in New Zealand too. It's a way of life for people like Kevin. I bet he'll still be here in ten years."

"I hope he's got his pillow by then."

"If he hasn't, he'll still be complaining."

The experience helps us better understand the Samoan view of palagis. Too frequently, the flotsam and jetsam of palagi society floats into Apia harbour, complaining about everything from the get-go, and sometimes hanging around for years like a bad smell.

With that background experience, the question in Tavita's mind is whether we too are going to scarper?

I don't think the thought even occurred to us. Why go home when we're surrounded by urgent needs everywhere? Every day that passes, our students are missing out on much needed education. And getting the school operating again is our contribution to reconstruction.

After discussion with the other palagi teachers that evening, Helen walks to Tavita's house to assure him we're all committed to stay.

In fact, we've never felt more alive. We're finding purpose and fulfilment in the most mundane and simple daily activities - like getting clean water, cooking our food, ensuring appropriate sanitation, and avoiding illness. Sure, basic living is hard work, but if the experiences are frequently unexpected, surprising, and sometimes scary, they're also unforgettable. We're forming strong, deep relationships, and learning life lessons that will endure.

But we also have the firm conviction that God has placed us in Samoa now, for this purpose. Doing the will of God is a rock on which we can build with confidence, knowing it will stand whatever storms come our way. To run away now would be to ignore that purpose and betray our faith in God. We have the 'why' that enables us to bear almost any 'how'.

So, unless we're medevac'd out on a stretcher, we're not going anywhere.

12
SCHOOL OPENS

"Look at the birds of the air: they neither sow nor reap
nor gather into barns, and yet your heavenly Father
feeds them. Are you not of more value than they?"
Matthew 6:26

W aking in the darkness, the alarm shatters my dreams. Fumbling, I turn it off. As I lie staring at the mosquito net, I hear the clock's monotonous ticking in the morning stillness. I had set the alarm for six - I must remember to wind the clock.

As I shave in the semi-darkness, my mind races ahead thinking about the coming day. Ever since we signed up as volunteers five months earlier, we've been working steadily towards this very day, and it's finally arrived.

While I look forward to meeting students for the first time, I'm also apprehensive and nervous. I wonder if they'll like me, whether they'll be well behaved, and if they'll understand me. After all, I'm not a trained teacher, and I'm in a foreign country teaching in English, which is not their first language.

While Heather is an experienced teacher, the cloud of uncertainty makes her apprehensive too. We really don't know what's going to happen, or what we're supposed to do.

I hear John call out as he walks into our kitchen to start mixing pancake batter. Rostered on to prepare the communal breakfast, John treats our kitchen like his own.

Well dressed, as a Samoan teacher should be, he wears an ironed shirt, an *ie faitaga*, and *se'e vae* (thongs) on his feet. The *se'e vae* are unnecessary, as bare feet are quite acceptable for a teacher or student. I have an *ie faitaga* but decide to play it safe on my first day by wearing cotton trousers. I'm still getting used to wearing a wrap-around skirt, and I don't want to make any faux pas in front of my students on the first day.

It's nearly seven o'clock when John scrapes off the first pancake onto a plate. Helen and Tammy soon join us from next door, bringing honey and coconut cream.

"What's going to happen today?" I ask the group, hoping for some comforting clarity.

"We don't know," says Tammy, "but hopefully we'll find out at the staff meeting. If we get classes, write down the kids' names."

Record their names; I should be able to do that.

"But they might change classes," adds Helen, "so don't worry too much."

"We'll just have to play it by ear," says John, dumping another pancake on my plate.

Helen looks out the window and sees the school truck approaching.

"Tavita's here guys," she says, "I gotta grab him before school starts." She leaves, holding a rolled-up pancake to finish her breakfast on the run.

Tammy leaves a little later, as we clean up and wash the dishes. We then walk to the staff room, where I'm about to become a high school teacher for the first time.

The staff room is reverently quiet as we walk in and sit down. Tavita enters the room from his office and sits at the long table in the centre of the room. He welcomes everyone back, and after making some administrative announcements, begins reading the names of each class and their allocated form teacher. Heather is given 'Upper Five D2' while my form class is 'Upper Five D1'.

"All form teachers should now go to their class and record the students' names," he says.

As teachers get up to leave, Heather asks Helen; "Where do we go?"

"We're D block," says Helen, pointing to the classrooms behind us. "I've got D3, so you and Ian'll be the last two rooms in the block."

As the form teachers all head off in different directions, we walk together towards D block. I wonder how the students know where to go and why Tavita hasn't given us class rolls. How will we know whether we've got the right students in our class?

"We should record the name of each student's village too," says Tammy.

"Good idea, make sure you do that," says Helen, wagging an instructional finger at us. "It can be helpful later on."

"What do we do after that?" I ask. "That won't take all day, will it?"

"It'll be harder than you think," says Helen.

As I approach classroom D1, I see a crowd of teenage girls around the doorway watching me curiously. Around seventeen years old, they're all in uniform - white blouse, maroon skirt and *se'e vae*. I don't know it yet, but Samoan students actually want to wear a uniform - like it's a special privilege.

As I nervously walk into the classroom, I tell them to come in and sit down. While they crowd into the room and find seats, I clean the blackboard and carefully write my name in white chalk - 'Mr Reilly'. As

I'm cleaning and writing, I hear the noise of banging desks, scraping chairs and voices behind me, dissipating as the students all settle down.

But when I turn around, the room is empty except for a single girl sitting near the door. She smiles, revealing a set of crooked teeth.

"They go to assembly," she says looking a little embarrassed. "I go now," she adds, then walks out leaving me alone and bewildered.

How do they know to go to assembly when I don't?

While I'm confused, I'm also encouraged that one student had the presence of mind to stay behind and let me know.

Perhaps they allocate students to classes at the school assembly? I wonder if those girls are my class after all. Expecting my actual class to appear soon, I wait patiently.

Patience is rewarded when another crowd of girls comes trooping into the classroom. I don't know if they're the same group as before, but I recognise the girl with the crooked teeth sitting up front.

Just when I think girls make up my entire class, a single boy walks in.

When students find there aren't enough desks or chairs, they take matters into their own hands and pilfer furniture from other classrooms. I later discover they took Heather's class furniture leaving some of her students sitting on the floor. They might have thieved furniture from Helen's classroom, had she not expected the problem, and vigilantly guarded her domain like Fort Knox.

By the time everyone settles down, I count one boy and thirty-five girls. A large class I think to myself, not realising that thirty-six is a small class in Samoa.

"My name is Mr Reilly," I announce, pointing to my name on the blackboard. "I come from *Ausetalia,*" using the Samoan pronunciation.

Everyone stares in silence.

How quiet and respectful, I think to myself; almost like they're scared of me, wondering what I'll do next. I glance at the girl with the crooked teeth, and when she smiles briefly, I feel reassured.

Suddenly a boy walks into the room and hands me a note, which I read out to the students.

"There is to be no normal school tomorrow. Boys must come with bush knives (machetes), and girls must bring rags and brooms for cleaning."

A sea of blank faces stares back at me with incomprehension, while a few glance nervously at their friends. The boy who gave me the note says a few words in Samoan, and the confusion vanishes. Then he turns and walks out.

The note also says not to dismiss the students until ten o'clock. Looking at my watch I see it's already nine. Mercifully, it's going to be a short day, but I still have an hour to go.

"I need to record your name and the name of your village," I announce.

Stunned stares and deathly silence.

I turn to the girl with crooked teeth but friendly smile and ask her name.

"Avele," she says, and I write that down, spelling it phonetically.

"What village are you from?"

"Paia."

While I've heard of the village, I don't know where it is. Later I hear Paia is associated with a well-known Samoan legend on Savai'i.

I turn to the girl beside Avele, but when she says her name, all I hear is a jumble of sounds.

"Pardon?"

She repeats her name more loudly, but again the sounds are unintelligible.

"Can you say that more slowly?"

"Maluima'auga," she says.

"Malui …?"

"Malu-ima -a- uga," she says, beginning to articulate the syllables.

"Maluima'uga," I say mispronouncing it, and the entire class erupts in laughter. I probably just insulted her, or said something highly amusing in Samoan, but at least the ice has broken. And while Helen's right, recording names won't be easy, the little language training we did a few weeks ago now proves a lifesaver. At least I know how to pronounce the sounds theoretically, even if they're not yet intelligible to the average Samoan. At this stage of our journey, we still can't pronounce Leulumoega Fou properly.

Eventually I spell out her name and move onto the next girl.

"Mutini," she says.

"Mutini," I repeat, and she smiles, looking as relieved as I feel.

Mutini lives at *Le'auva'a,* a village on the road to Apia.

Then as I struggle to pronounce *Fia'alua'e,* and the class erupts into loud laughter again. When I can't understand the name of her village either, Avele comes to my rescue and spells it out for me.

"Near the airport," she says.

Some names are simple and easy to pronounce, like *Fuli,* who has a beaming smile. Then there's *Pelopia* and *Violeta,* sounding like romantic European names.

Others, like *Fa'aao,* are simple but unpronounceable. I wonder how I'll teach when I can't even pronounce their names.

Then there's a girl who says her name is *Valu,* which I understand is the Samoan word for 'eight'.

"Are you eight?" I ask in English, thinking I might have mis-heard.

"Yes," she says smiling, and a few students laugh. I wonder why a parent would name their daughter 'eight'?

When the boy claims his name is *Lua* (two), I think he might be joking, but that's his real name.

Another girl has the name *Tausaga*, which I'm pretty sure is the Samoan word for 'year'.

Eventually I have the list of students, and just when I feel pleased with myself, Heather appears at the classroom door to hand me a note also given to her. I follow the instructions and write on the board, 'Students can go to the hall to change options'.

One girl abruptly gets up and leaves the room.

A little later three boys and three girls walk in. I add the new names to my list and now have four boys and thirty-seven girls. Why so few boys I wonder?

Since we're all left staring at each other in deathly silence, I walk to the next room to find out what Heather's doing.

"Ask them to tell you something they like doing, and something they don't like doing."

Returning to my class, I choose an easy-to-pronounce name off the list.

"Mutini, tell me something you like doing."

Looking up, I find Mutini in the sea of faces.

She looks like one who's just received a death sentence.

First, she looks out the window, then at the ceiling, hoping it will fall on her, and then turns in fearful desperation to her friends. They laugh at her, like she's more amusing than the palagi teacher mis-pronouncing their names.

She looks back at me and then out the window, perhaps desperately hoping the world will end and swallow her up. Anything to save her from torture and death at the hands of this merciless palagi teacher. Turning angrily back to her friends, a vigorous Samoan discussion ensues before relief floods her face. As though discovering she'll not be shot at dawn after all, she calmly says, "I like *volipolo* (volleyball)."

I feel equally relieved to see the torture end.

"And what is something you don't like?" I ask.

She gives me a deer in the headlights look, as though suddenly realising she was deceived all along, and now she's going to be executed after all. Open-eyed, she stares defiantly at the firing squad as they aim their weapons and says, there is nothing she doesn't like. She likes everything.

Given the absurdity of the response and her obvious psychological suffering, I decide to leave Mutini alone and move on to someone else. No use starting the year by inflicting painful, psychological torture on an innocent student.

Avele. She seems to be a mature and intelligent girl.

Suddenly, another older male student bursts through the door and without talking to me, begins speaking in Samoan to the class. Then he simply turns and walks out. When I call him back, he looks like I rudely interrupted him from his most important mission in life.

"What did you say to the students?" I ask.

"There is to be an assembly of all boys in the hall after class."

Since my watch says the time is nine-fifty, I have ten minutes to go. However, everyone suddenly gets up, and starts exiting the classroom. When I call them back, they hurriedly return to their seats looking anxious. While it's not ten o'clock, I see all the students in C block leaving their classrooms.

I'm confused again.

Maybe C block finished early? But walking to the door, I see all the students in D block leaving too. Guessing something else unexpected has happened, I dismiss the class and they quickly leave.

I feel relieved, but probably not as relieved as students like Mutini, quaking in fear I might randomly ask them a question.

Leaving the classroom, I meet Helen.

"I thought classes were finishing at ten o'clock," I say.

"They did."

"No, we finished at nine-fifty."

When we compare watches, mine is ten minutes slower than hers. My watch must be wrong.

"My class just got up and began walking out," I say.

"You can't let them do that," says Helen emphatically, wagging her finger at me again as though I were a student. "They can't go until you dismiss them - if you let 'em do that they'll soon walk all over you."

While I fear they might have already walked all over me, I'm relieved to have played-it-by-ear without catastrophe. However, the reality is that I follow instructions, while still guessing the underlying reasons for those instructions. I hope that will change soon.

As we walk back home, it rains.

At last.

As the rain becomes a torrential downpour, we dash for the shelter of our house. Heather puts every dish, jug and bucket we have under the eaves to catch the rain pouring off the roof. Checking the tank I put there five days ago, I see it filling rapidly; and all my patches and plugs are holding well.

I never imagined feeling so happy about a shower of rain. Sure, it's not water coming out of a tap, but it's literally on our doorstep, which to us is nearly the same thing. After so much effort carrying water from Malua, we now feel immensely wealthy. Henceforth we're going to live like royalty in unimagined luxury.

By the time the rain stops fifteen minutes later, our tank is one third full. Since all that water fell from just a tiny fraction of our roof, I realise a Samoan rain shower can be very heavy.

Checking the tank at Tammy and Helen's, I'm pleased to see it half full, and without leaks.

"Woo-hoo," calls out Helen through the window, equally excited.

The rain stops, and when the sun appears again, the air is hot and humid.

"We should do the washing," says Heather. "I think I'll go to Malua; I don't want to waste our precious water here."

"We should let it settle in the tank first anyway," I add. "Let the dirt fall to the bottom."

While Heather takes our dirty laundry to Malua with plastic buckets and bars of soap, I rig up a makeshift gutter to catch even more water in the tank the next time it rains.

Later, Tammy and Helen join us for a lunch of bread and whatever toppings we can find, including vegemite, which Tammy likes, despite being American.

"Some of my students seem to be named after numbers," I say. "One's named Valu and the other Lua."

"That's pretty common," says Tammy. "I have a Fitu (seven) in my form class. Actually, those aren't strange as far as Samoan names go. Last year I had a girl named Asoleaga, which means 'bad day'."

"Why would you call your daughter 'bad day'?" asks Heather, visibly shocked.

"Who knows?" says Helen. "Could be something bad happened the day she was born. They can be a lot worse than that. I'm not sure anyone understands it, but you could talk to Leua about it."

"A girl in my class is named Vaiaso," says Heather, looking at her list. "Isn't that the Samoan word for week?"

"That's right. I had a boy named Sigaleti in my class last year. That's Samoan for cigarette. I see he's in Form Six this year."

"Why would you call your son cigarette?" I ask.

"Maybe his mother enjoyed smoking?" ventures Tammy.

We don't know it, but this was an introduction to feeling both shock and admiration for Samoans' highly creative approach to naming children.

"I heard of a baby in a village on Savai'i named *Taemoa*," says Helen. "It means 'chicken shit'. I can't imagine it was a great start in life."

"Stinky pig was another I heard," says Tammy.

While Heather and I can't believe our ears, they're clearly not joking.

While we're eating, Ramon appears at the doorway saying he's locked out of his house, and thinks he lost his key in Apia. Ramon may be very well educated and intelligent, but I'm still mystified by how challenged he seems by anything remotely practical.

I agree to help him break into his house by taking out some louvre windows. He's unlikely to be robbed because his house is empty except for a few clothes and books. He's the closest person I've met to a vegan hermit. In the meantime, he joins us for lunch, but eats only a plain slice of bread. As an American there's no way he's touching vegemite.

After walking to Ramon's house and breaking in, I return to help carry the kerosene stove to Tammy and Helen's home, where they'll prepare the communal meals for the next two days.

"Can you help me chop up this up?" asks Tammy, struggling with a knife and a pumpkin. "I'm making pumpkin soup for dinner tonight."

As I finish cutting up the pumpkin, Keola appears at the door. He thinks he has a portable generator that could power the water pump but needs help to connect it up. I walk with him to the pump house at Malua and discover it's a three-phase pump. Unfortunately, Keola's generator is only single-phase.

Nice try.

By the time we sort all that out, it's late afternoon, and I realise anyone with any sense is having an afternoon siesta by now - except the crazy palagis and Keola who are still working.

Later, we come together for an early pumpkin soup dinner at Tammy and Helen's. We're learning to eat early before the light fades, which makes it easier to prepare and clean up. In fact, we're now governing our daily routine by the movement of the sun rather than clocks. We rise before sunrise, and then try to get everything done before darkness falls. The phases of the moon are also proving important. When the moon is near full, it's easier walking around at night without a torch or lantern - saving precious kerosene and batteries.

As twilight falls, we walk to the Malua pool to wash and relax.

Sitting down on the concrete step of the pool with my legs in the cool water, Helen, Tammy and Heather, float, and splash about in the semidarkness. John sits atop the black rocks, his form silhouetted against the soft glow of the sun's remnant light illuminating the peaceful lagoon. The red glow of his cigarette glows bright in the shadows.

The balmy evening air is warm and comforting, as we discuss the day's events, and soak in the cool water. Soon the stars come out, and the near full moon rises spectacularly from the wine-dark sea, bathing the lagoon in a soft, iridescent light, with a beauty no words can describe.

God has been good to us this day. With water on our doorstep, food in our cupboards, and purpose in our hearts, we're not only happy, we also feel immensely privileged.

Today, I met my class of Samoan teenagers and became a teacher. True, I need to find out how to avoid torturing them, but we've looked each other in the eye and seen that we are real people.

We enjoy God's provision of rainfall and good friends to share our journey. We've also acquired the knowledge we can live happily without electricity, or even running water.

We wonder how those poor people in Australia can possibly be happy in their comfortable houses, with their running water, gas stoves, and electric lights. Where they spend an hour or more a day safely driving their comfortable cars through organised traffic, so they can work in clean air-conditioned offices, where everything is predictable and organised, and where they are well paid.

Those poor sods.

And to think they're probably feeling sorry for us - as though it's we who are suffering, living in this cyclone ravaged country, with cockroaches, centipedes, and mosquitos.

At this moment, there is no place in the world we would rather be. The moon is bright, the starlight shines from the heavens, and in this moment, our world is the most wonderful place. God has returned us to Eden, where our hearts and souls belong.

But not for long.

13

CHALK AND TALK

*"Heaven and earth will pass away, but
my words will not pass away."*
Matthew 24:35

We're told that in the beginning, when God created the world, one of his first actions was to call the dry land into form from the water.

And so Samoa formed in deep time, when great forces from the earth's hot depths punched through the crust, moulding mountain peaks over two thousand metres high, in the largest and deepest expanse of water on earth. After the sweet dew of heaven cooled the hot lava, it left a paradise of awesome beauty for all God's wondrous creatures, both great and small.

But there were other great forces at work. The falling water and crashing waves tore the rock into smaller fragments, then pebbles, then sand, and finally washed its constituent elements back into the vast ocean. As the sun, wind, and rain, cracked the rock, plants grew in the cracks, and working with the fungi and bacteria, produced the rich volcanic soil supporting ever more wonderful creatures.

Creeping, or flying on wings spread by the gentle ocean breeze, life covered the verdant land, each species propogating to survive and seek dominion. The rain washed the soil and nutrients into the sea, feeding an endless cycle of life in the shallow waters, and spawning the fish that feed the monstrous creatures brooding in the great deep.

And so the great forces that built the paradise, now tear it down. Almost all our achievements, particularly our creative works, immediately decay from the moment they're made. After the paint dries, the roof is thatched, or fabric is prepared, then the paint peels, the roof rots, and clothing fades, withers, and rends. While the warm air, intense humidity, and fertile soil, support bountiful growth, they also attack everything with relentless, pitiless vigour. They corrode and crumble our works, wear them away, and finally wash the remnants back into the sea; it's a constant reminder of our transient mortality.

So, while Samoa is a paradise gained, it's also a paradise slowly and relentlessly being lost. Perhaps the paradox is most clearly seen by the fencing wire passing through rows of Samoan tree trunks. New fence posts usually sprout roots and branches, so fence owners routinely prune back the posts to prevent the fence from becoming a vegetation jungle.

The last arrival was mankind, made in the image of the Creator, who with his words, called the world into being. *"He has made everything beautiful in its time. Also, he has put eternity into man's heart,"* writes The Teacher. Mankind has a deep, heartfelt longing for the eternal, and an insatiable thirst to create and build - in structure, story, song, dance, and art. Cast out of the first paradise because we took from the Tree of the Knowledge of Good and Evil, we seek to restore our paradise lost, to preserve what we've made, and we hunger for significance. Ultimately, we want to find the Tree of Life and live forever. If we can't do that, we at least hope to be remembered.

During our pre-departure training, wise heads impressed on us the need to reduce the expectation we will achieve anything of lasting value in Samoa. At best, they said, aspire to be a 'happy memory' in the minds of a few people. They warned that because our Australian culture values achievement, we'll find it culturally difficult being unable to achieve tangible outcomes. And they warned darkly that many volunteers, due to their scandalous behaviour, were not even a happy memory.

While we found the advice understandable, it was emotionally hard to swallow. Aren't we here to help improve people's lives, and inch a part of the world a little closer to Eden? Surely, we're more than just entertainment value?

We've already emerged from an onslaught of great forces - a cyclone of wind, a deluge of rain, and battering of waves. Now we're going to do our bit, if not to restore paradise, then at least to catch up on lost classroom lessons.

According to Tavita, cleaning up the school, and cutting the grass, are the next steps in battling the elements of tyrannical decay. Sure, the herd of wandering cattle and the odd donkey do their bit to keep the grass in check. But they also leave piles of steaming manure in classrooms, and apart from being quiet by nature, appear devoid of other civil behaviours.

There's no routine maintenance, school cleaners, or grounds people, and cleaning is a student responsibility. On Friday, half the students return to work and assemble in the hall in mufti. Tavita assigns the girls to clean classrooms, while the boys do the heavy work of cutting grass and removing cyclone debris (tree branches, roofing iron, and building fragments).

"*Malo lava* (hello) Mr Reilly," says Avele, smiling as she walks into my classroom with a troop of girls.

Like most, she's dressed in a tee-shirt, with a faded yellow *ie solosolo* wrapped around her, and wearing *se'e vae* on her feet. While some wipe desks clean, Avele vigorously sweeps the classroom, making the dust fly off her Samoan broom. Unlike most classrooms, mine has a lockable door that has so far prevented cattle wandering in and dumping excreta on the floor. Other girls clean the remaining unbroken louvre windows and blackboard. It's obvious they don't need any help or instruction from me; they've cleaned their house, church, school, and yard since they could walk. I abandon my girls to their work, and venture outside to watch the boys cut grass.

Swinging bush knives in their hands, twenty to thirty boys stand in a large circle, while another drums a piece of roofing iron with sticks to keep time. At first, they all swing their knives together through the air - perhaps getting into the 'swing of things'. When a boy calls out *tas (one)*, they all sweep their knives down into the grass, their broad shoulders and powerful arms rippling muscle and glistening sweat. Swarths of grass fall or fly off their flashing blades, and with a backhand stroke, they sweep away the cut grass. After taking a step forward, they cut again in time to the beating drum - grass flying into the air once more. A group of girls follow behind the boys, sweeping the cut grass into heaps using Samoan brooms.

John wanders over and says, "Want to try cutting grass Samoan style?"

"Not a chance John." I've already tried cutting grass with a machete; it's almost impossible.

"They won't let you anyway," says John. "You're a teacher - you're not supposed to do manual work."

A group of excited boys suddenly appear. Says one of the boys, "We work at your house."

I'm puzzled. "What work?" I ask.

"Clean up," he says eagerly.

"Great," says John, speaking Samoan to better understand what they've been assigned to do.

"Tavita says they're to clean up your house. You must have something that needs doing. Now is your chance!"

I know Heather won't be comfortable having a group of unknown students inside our house, but they could remove coconuts and whatever else attracts the pigs. After the cyclone, scuffling pigs soon re-appeared, waking us every night.

Walking to our house, John instructs some students to clear away coconuts and fallen branches and sends others to clean his house.

"Feels a bit like slave labour," I say.

"Welcome to Samoa," says John, laughing. "Actually, to these kids, it's an opportunity. In Samoan culture, they say leadership is learned by service, so it's also a privilege to serve."

Looking back towards the school, we spy Tavita talking with a young palagi woman.

"Who's that?" I ask, intrigued.

"Dunno," says John. "Never seen her before."

"A yank?"

"Probably."

Though we can barely see her, somehow John and I have a strong sense she's American. Anyway, we're about to find out because she turns and walks in our direction.

"Hi guys," she says with an American accent, reaching out to shake hands. "I'm Olivia Ganino. Most of the kids call me Ganino or Nino for short. It's easier for them and sounds almost Samoan."

"It does," agrees John. "Are you teaching here?"

"Yeah - Tavita asked me to teach general science and biology. I did my Peace Corps training with Tammy and Helen."

Via the grapevine, Helen heard Olivia was available and introduced her to Tavita. Over lunch we hear she lives with Mama Sefina and her eight children at Fagamili-tai, a large village close to the airport. My student Valu is one of the eight children.

"What's it like living in a village?" I ask.

"Well, it can be pretty noisy and intense, cos there's always something going on - even at night."

"Where do you sleep?"

"We're all on the *fale* floor lined up like sausages - Mama, me and the kids. It can be hard sleeping some nights, but it's great experience, and my language skills are improving no end."

I try to imagine Heather and myself sleeping on the hard floor, hearing the neighbour's voices, lights shining, and radios blaring. We're looking forward to a village experience, but I'm not sure we're quite ready for it yet.

After Olivia leaves Helen says, "I dunno how she's gonna do it."

"What do you mean?"

"Just living in a village can be difficult for a palagi, but to do a full-time teaching load on top of that - that's tough."

"She seems pretty disciplined," says Tammy.

"She's gonna need to be," says Helen emphatically.

The students may be allocated to classes, but a constant stream of pastors and parents still make their way to Tavita's house pleading for their children to be enrolled.

Sometimes the student shows promise, and Tavita accepts them. More typically, the student can barely understand English, has repeatedly failed lower forms, but wants to enrol in Upper Five (year eleven) or Form Six (year twelve). Sometimes he knows they were expelled from another school for bad behaviour.

"Why do pastors come with the parents?" I ask him one day.

He groans and shakes his head. "Oh, you don't understand Samoan culture yet. The pastor comes and begs because they know it's very difficult for someone in my position to refuse a pastor."

"We'd tell them the classes are already full," I say.

"But you're palagi," he says, shaking his head and smiling kindly. "You don't understand what we Samoans have to go through. Sometimes I wish I was a palagi so I could just say no. I'm sorry about the large classes - I know many of these kids shouldn't be here, but we're a Congregational Church school and I can't refuse these pastors."

When I share Tavita's comments with Tammy and Helen, they shrug their shoulders because there's nothing we can do.

"If the students can't do Upper Five or Form Six, why are they so desperate to be here?" I ask Helen.

"It might be prestige, something they and the family can be proud of. But think about it - if you're a sixteen-year-old girl in a village, you can spend your time looking after your older sister's children, doing the laundry, preparing food, and God knows what else. Or, you can catch the bus to school, wear a nice uniform, sit in a shady classroom, then *tafao* (wander around) the streets of Apia talking with your friends. What would you rather do?"

"You make it sound like babysitting."

"It can seem a bit like that, but there's some great kids here who want to learn, and some are pretty bright. Anyway, if your classes are too big, you can always expel some."

"Expel?"

"When they misbehave, which they're bound to do, send them to Tavita. He'll either beat them or expel them - it's an easy way to whittle your class numbers down."

I'm taken aback by Helen's 'take no prisoners' approach. With secondary education such an important development goal, it seems counterproductive to expel students, ungenerous at best, and at worst, brutally heartless. But I'm unsettled by the nagging thought Helen's view might be culturally sound. Samoans seem to expect swift and (in our eyes) brutal judgement, not consistent with the peaceful, Pacific Island paradise of ill-informed Australian imaginations.

"And why are there so few boys?"

"You mean why so many girls? I don't know, but the girls are more responsible - all the boys seem to do is clown around and chase girls."

I thought girls were being left behind by the education systems of the world. Maybe they are, but not at our school, and not apparently, in Samoa. When I recall the leading Samoan people in government and the public service (those Mick had engaged to speak to us in our first week), they were women except for our language trainers. And at least half the teachers at our school are women.

Until we have water at the school, Tavita runs three classes a day instead of the full five. Each day starts with a staff meeting at 7:50am sharp; punctuality maintained by threat to shame latecomers.

While the staff meet, each class conducts their own *lotu* - a morning service led by a student. The sound of beautiful singing wafts from the classrooms as they sing hymns in parts. After a tense staff meeting, the music can be inspiring and uplifting, like a sweet perfume to the soul. It's a solemn, peaceful start to the day; a little order before chaos descends on us like a cloud, and things start to unravel.

We first mark the roll of our form classes, then teach three lessons, finishing with a final form class before dismissing the students at 11:40am.

A full-time teaching load is four subjects, but Heather and I take on five to make up for being short staffed. I teach Form Six and Upper Five Physics (two classes), Upper Five Maths, and General Science to my form class.

While I have no teacher training or experience (apart from my own high school years), I have the advantage of few preconceived expectations.

Seeking to plan out the year's lessons, I ask Arjun for the Upper Five Physics curriculum. Unfortunately, the school has none, so Tavita gets a copy from a friend at Samoa College (the best government school in Apia). I'm familiar with each major topic described on the single page curriculum. Since there's nothing to indicate a target proficiency level, I aim for Form Five level in Australia.

Much like Australia and New Zealand, the final year of high school in Samoa is an intense, stressful, marathon effort of study, culminating in assessment by a single, external exam, set by the New Zealand Education Department. While it can be difficult for students, it's also daunting for the teachers. They must nurture a class for a year through to the final exam, and then spend nervous weeks awaiting results. Fortunately, there's a detailed Form Six physics curriculum and some sample exams.

Tavita appoints Heather to the role of Head of the English Department, where she has a greater load, but an opportunity for greater influence. Besides teaching Form Six and Upper Five, she takes a Form Three class so she can understand the education standard of the youngest students entering the school. There are forty-seven students in her form three English class, but only eight desks, so thirty-nine students sit cross-legged on the floor.

Tavita sets the carpenters at Malua to work making desks, and since I have no desks at all in my physics room, I get the first batch. They're rough cut and nailed together, but still appreciated by teachers and students. Since the cut timber hasn't been sanded, the desks are often de-splintered by the soft flesh of unwary students.

The school issues stationery (workbooks, pens, and rulers) to students. Most families can't afford such luxuries, and if we rely on students to buy their own, the resulting mishmash in the classroom makes teaching even more difficult.

We do have blackboards and white chalk, but the chalk skates across many blackboards because they're in poor condition. I ask Tavita for some blackboard paint, but he's never heard of it, so I hunt in the hardware store in Apia and find a small tin. After washing my board clean, I cover it with two coats of paint. Suddenly, my classroom has the best blackboard in the school. I give the tin to Tavita, who gives it to the school carpenters, and I never see it again. No one paints any blackboards.

We have high hopes we might find some resources in the school library - the locked door and windows covered with wire mesh suggest it contains something of value. Perhaps there's a dusty class set of physics textbooks, or some works of great literature; something that might spark a fire in the heart of a future Samoan author or poet?

When we hear the library is open, we eagerly walk through the open door. There are several large working tables curiously covered with *fala* (pandanus mats Samoans typically sleep on) surrounded by bookcases.

I peruse a bookshelf but can't discern any order or theme. Classic literature (Dickens and Hardy) mixes with modern paperback thrillers, old mathematics textbooks, French language texts, history books, and university engineering textbooks. The disordered bookcases look like they were frozen in time while trying to organise themselves; some are back-to-back in a line, while others stick out at random angles.

Opening a book, I see 'Westlake Girls High School' stamped on the inside cover. Every book has a similar stamp, showing they're all castoffs from a school, university, or town library in New Zealand or Australia.

There's no card index system, and we soon realise Helen was right; there are no class sets of textbooks available for teacher or student use.

I'm surprised how well the books have survived after sitting for three days and nights in rain blowing horizontally through the open louvre windows. But I detect a mouldy book odour emanating from the shelves. Dust, decay, and cobwebs, hang darkly in the silent shadows, more threatened by ambivalence than ignorance as though all corporate knowledge lies dormant in a dark corner. And perhaps because it has no value here, or if it does, no one has the energy to do anything with it.

Patuina, Iosefa's wife and librarian, sits at her desk brooding like a mother hen.

"How do students borrow books?" asks Heather.

"Students cannot borrow books," says Patuina firmly. "They don't bring them back, and then there would be no library."

While disappointing, it also seems reasonable. Except that we think if the books were in a village, at least someone might read them.

"And how do teachers borrow books?" asks Heather.

"Bring the book to me, and I record it here," she says, pointing to an open student's exercise book with columns ruled in red ink.

Disappointed, we walk away, concluding the library is a mishmash of generously donated, but obsolete books. Instead of breeding knowledge in the minds of our students, the books breed insects, while the pages are digested, not by avid readers, but by fungus and microbes.

"Who uses the library?" I ask Tammy over lunch.

"Well, Patuina spends a lot of time there," she says with a wry smile.

"But what does she do if she doesn't organise the books or lend them to students?"

"She sleeps," calls Helen from the kitchen. "Apart from that, no one knows what she does."

"She makes sure no one steals any books," says Tammy generously.

"Don't you mean borrow?"

"Borrowing or stealing, it's sometimes hard to tell the difference in Samoa. Actually, Form Six students sometimes use it to study in their free periods, and teachers can use it for lesson preparation."

"And do they?"

"Are you kidding?" says Helen, walking into the room. "They sleep there - I hear them snoring."

"Maybe it'll be different this year under Tavita," I suggest hopefully.

"Maybe," says Tammy, but Helen sits down and rolls her eyes, as though pigs might also one day fly over hell's frozen lakes.

"I work in the library sometimes," adds Tammy. "The staff room can be noisy."

"It's like a library exists on paper, but it's unusable."

"Yeah, you see that a lot here," says John. "At Tuisivi there's a fully equipped science classroom, but the teachers can't use it because the principal wants to keep it pristine for showing visitors."

Asking students to buy textbooks is completely out of the question. A single textbook costs more than a term's school fees and must be paid for upfront before being ordered from New Zealand.

One afternoon we go to Wesley Bookshop in Apia with Tammy in search of textbooks. She recommends a Form Five General Science book.

"I worked through that last year and found it helpful. It covers the year's curriculum, and each chapter is a single lesson."

Great. Same for the Maths textbook.

Standing at the counter, I have the distinct feeling I'm buying the last copy available in Samoa.

Arjun tells me I can make the dedicated physics room my own. There's shelving down one side and a back room filled with devices in various states of corrosion and decay. Initially hoping I've found something useful, it's soon obvious most are beyond redemption.

To me, it's unthinkable to teach physics without engaging in the scientific method of experimental measurement and observation, which requires working equipment. But in Samoa, any device containing moving parts, or electrical switches, dies within a few months unless it's maintained by constant use. Without the heat generated by electrical components, insects soon move into the dark recesses of appliances, and engage in carnal orgies of reproduction to multiply their kind. The insects eat paper and wire coatings, build nests, and drop their excrement without regard to the health and wellbeing of vital electrical components.

Dust settles on surfaces and provides a safe harbour for fungal spores. They are carried on the wind, then nurtured by the damp air, and fed by nutrients from insect excrement, and dead carcasses not already carried away by the omnipresent ants.

Electrical contacts become covered with a resistant oxide layer, rust, or corrode away entirely, ceasing to conduct electricity. The same oxide layers grow on mechanically moving parts, which eventually seize up. Switches become permanently on or off, dials cease to turn, and the wheels of motion stop spinning. Even an empty glass beaker, left unattended on a laboratory shelf, gradually turns green with fungal growth.

However, there's a box of simple ticker-timers whose only moving part is a vibrating copper leaf spring. For decades, ticker-timers have been used the world over to teach the motion of bodies and lay a foundation for teaching Newton's Laws. A ticker timer vibrates a leaf spring, which imprints a dot through carbon paper onto travelling ticker tape. Attach the tape to a falling weight and the ticker-timer records the distance travelled for each 'tick' of the leaf spring. I can power them using AA batteries I can buy in Apia. Unbelievably, there's a box of ticker tape rolls in a cupboard, unconsumed by insects or moisture.

Carrying the ticker-timer remnants home, I cannibalise parts, disassemble and reassemble, sand brass and copper contacts with emery paper (brought from Australia because it's handy), and bend the important leaf springs into working order with plyers. I resuscitate enough ticker-timers to share amongst groups of three or four students.

There are Bunsen burners but no gas. It remains a mystery how they built a school with gas ports in the science classrooms, but without a gas reticulation system. But some wick-burning glasses filled with methylated spirits produce a cool, weak flame, sufficient to demonstrate some basic ideas; burning magnesium, heating compounds in a test tube, or making steam. After I fix the blackboard, repair equipment, and prepare lessons, I realise that I'm doing almost everything from scratch.

Since I'm starting with no teacher training whatsoever, I do what everyone else does. I copy my own teachers, including probably repeating their mistakes.

In years four and five, I was fortunate to come under the tutelage of an older teacher on the verge of retirement. Mr Stevenson was authoritative, strict, and stern, but also very kind and benevolent. He made all his own teacher aids and materials, long before similar manufactured aids appeared in schools. Besides a regimen of reading, maths, and academic learning, Mr Stevenson taught us a variety of arts and crafts, including woodworking, bookbinding, and how to marble our book bound pages. When the school softball bat broke, he taught the older boys to make a new one using his wood lathe and had us varnish it to bring out the wood grain. A rare and outstanding teacher, our parents were very sorry to see him retire.

When he did retire, the wheel of fortune reversed its forward motion, and for my last two years of primary school, a very different teacher was assigned to us by the Education Department's lofty and faceless decision makers. An alcoholic by habit, and slothful by nature, Mr Mallinder was often in the local pub during classroom time. When he arrived at school with a hangover, instead of learning English and mathematics, we played cricket, often for the whole day.

Learning languished under Mr Mallinder like a famine-stricken child. Our starvation was so severe, we arrived at High School as intellectually stunted specimens of humanity. I had no knowledge of a decimal point, and lacking other basic skills, I struggled in remedial maths classes.

But the real impact was far worse because I formed an opinion that I was somehow intellectually deficient in mathematics, as though afflicted by some sort of congenital defect. Considering I eventually studied advanced engineering mathematics, there's no doubt Mr Mallinder's fondness for the bottle had knock on effects that held many back. By making high school more difficult, the career train of some got diverted onto a dead-end track, limiting their opportunities for the rest of their lives.

However, through bitter experience, Mr Mallinder taught us all an important, timeless truth. Time is unforgiving, and a teacher can have a profoundly negative impact on a child, endowing them with a chronic sense of failure, that can imprison them for the term of their natural life. Or a teacher like Mr Stevenson can impart learning and skills to open up bountiful opportunities, provide a child with a sense of wonder at the world, and a capacity to always accumulate new skills and knowledge.

For childhood knowledge endures with us through all the turbulent years of our lives. More than a happy memory, knowledge not only keeps us alive, it also enables us to break free from the prison of ignorance, and soar on eagle's wings. Investing knowledge in a child is not only noble, it also leaves an enduring legacy - something unaffected by the great forces of wind and rain, heat and humidity, bacteria and bugs; something the salty sea cannot corrode, corrupt or consume.

Knowledge endures because it's eternal, as God is eternal, infinite, and personal. John writes how "*In the beginning was the Word, and the Word was with God, and the Word was God.*" When God said at creation, "*Let there be light ...*" he called everything into being by the Word, or Logos (in Greek). The apostle John is using the Greek concept of Logos to show that knowledge and truth are not only attributes of God, but they were made human in the person of Jesus Christ.

Our universe did not begin with atomic particles, or a quantum field, but with Logos in loving relationship within a triune God of three persons. Because God is truth, and love, and a person, knowledge is an attribute of a personal God we can know. A God who desires relationship with us.

It's fashionable today to believe there is no truth - that everyone has their own truth - but it's impossible to live according to that dictum. At a minimum we need to know truth about our world to survive, like how to grow food, find fresh water, or count money. But more deeply, we hunger for truth to fill the emptiness in our souls, a vacuum that can only be filled by knowledge and relationship with God, who is truth eternal. We all crave what is transcendent - something to believe in, a cause to give purpose to our otherwise meaningless lives. And while some people might claim there is no truth, they seem to believe in the truth of the righteous causes they use to satisfy their hunger for purpose.

We can live, not only with the confidence that truth is out there to be discovered, but also with the confidence that we can find and know that truth because we're made in the image of God. For we are created to know and learn truth about God and His world, and to grow in relationship with Him.

True, we are finite, fragile, and fallen human beings whose knowledge is imperfect and incomplete. But just as we don't need to know someone completely, or perfectly, to have a meaningful relationship with them, so our knowledge of truth, about the world and the God who created it, can be imperfect and incomplete, but still meaningful. However, it does mean we should expect our knowledge on any subject to grow, much like a relationship, always open to change and enrichment at a deeper level. And though weather, plants and bugs may well outlast, outwit and outplay our goals and aspirations, truth and knowledge are God's eternal truth, and we can be confident it will endure, long after we are gone.

The Word brings not only the created world and knowledge, but also meaning, purpose, significance, hope, and beauty. And our need for relationship with God gives us our deep longing to love and be loved, like the love of parent and child. These attributes of God are the intangible things we most treasure in our tangibly fleeting lives. And if to hold a child in our arms is to touch the eternity in our hearts, then to pass on knowledge to a child is to build something more significant and enduring than a happy memory. They might seem like lofty thoughts and heavenly aspirations, but without reaching for the stars, we have no chance of even finding the ceiling.

However, living beneath the ceiling, we must accomplish our noble goals through mundane tasks. Seeking to achieve more than chalk and talk, without textbooks we need to produce worksheets for our students, from scratch, of course. But as we're about to find, producing anything in Samoa is like walking through quicksand.

14
QUICKSAND AND CHAOS

"And which of you being anxious can add
a single hour to his span of life?"
Matthew 6:27

To get anything done in today's world, we depend almost exclusively on microprocessors embedded in computers, smartphones, and toasters.

But I started work when the peace and prosperity of mankind rested on the ability to communicate using a typewriter. With a typewriter, one could carve hitherto illegible handwriting into black type. Documents despatched to distant lands were now read with ice cold clarity by the recipient, even if they couldn't understand their import. With the typewriter's unmistakable clackity-clack sound, there poured out from every office worldwide, mountains of memos, missives, and communiques.

One had to be taught to type; it was a valuable skill.

Curiously, the ability to type was mysteriously designated as a female trait. Males need not apply, unless they're authors or journalists. Companies and governments set up vast pools of all female typists, who turned handwritten drafts, shorthand notes, or direct dictation, into legible documents. Stenographers (as they were called) who could convert dictation to error free documents with great speed, like my mother, were highly valued and sought after.

My mother commenced her career as a junior typist in one such typing pool, deep in the bowels of some Melbourne corporate entity. The best typists, or those displaying administrative talent, were promoted out of the typing pools to become secretaries to the great and powerful. Being one such fair maiden and fast typist, my mother soon scaled the lofty heights of an office atop one of the first skyscrapers in Collins Street, where she was secretary to a director of the mining company, Conzinc Rio Tinto.

My mother inhabited a world of thin white paper, black carbon sheets, and a firm belief that imperfection was definitely a mortal sin, if not a crime against humanity. Though errors might be verboten, it had to be acknowledged that by employing unusual cunning, combined with a brief lapse in concentration, an error could wheedle its way onto a page. On discovery, collective guilt applied to all hitherto typed words, with the entire page being untimely ripped from its typewriter carriage, executed without trial, and condemned to burn in the eternal fires of the municipal incinerator. When the souls of the deceased words promised to be error free, they were reincarnated afresh onto a virgin sheet of white paper, layered with multiple carbon copies.

When I started my engineering career in 1985, the curtain was about to fall on my mother's world, but the actors were still on stage, and the lights were shining.

The Australian Army employed me, and although it had a more tolerant approach to the odd typing error, it put a high value on following regulation and rigid processes. It was unthinkable for typing to be done other than by an all-female typing pool, in a dark dungeon, guarded by a fierce, female, fire-breathing dragon.

To have a letter or report typed, one first boldly approached the half door dungeon entrance, bowed to the dragon, and passed a handwritten draft into her scaly claw. Through her horned rimmed spectacles, the monster looked down doubtfully on both the draft document and her prospective prey. Meanwhile, we bowed submissively, and uttered what we hoped were the correct incantations. Withdrawing backwards, as in the presence of royalty, we then turned and fled to avoid having our heads bitten off.

The following day, if we were lucky, a typewritten draft magically appeared on our desk.

If we found a mistake, we amended the typewritten draft using the prescribed dragon code, and then cautiously approached the monster a second time. Fortunately, since my mother had taught me some limited dragon language, I had a better-than-average chance of getting work typed without being blasted by the dragon or losing any essential body parts. However, many colleagues were not so fortunate, being deficient in dragon arts, and their deprived upbringing having failed to teach them any dragon tongue.

The dragon guarding the army's typing pool may have been an archaic disciplinarian, but she at least had the latest equipment. The women typed on electric golf ball typewriters that also recorded every stroke on a tape or floppy disc. If a document needed a minor amendment, the change could be made to the floppy disk recording, and the document automatically re-typed by the typewriter, thus saving labour. But by the time I left for Samoa in 1990, word processors had replaced the typewriter, the curtain had come down on that world, and the typing pools were fast evaporating.

Newly liberated from constant threat of torture and oppression by the ruling typists and their dragon mistresses, a techno-egalitarian regime arose.

Now any unskilled bumpkin could effortlessly type and print as many copies as they wished. Much to the dismay of bourgeois dragons forced into early retirement at the sharp end of a few secretarial keystrokes, any peasant could now use the ubiquitous photocopier to produce countless copies without any training whatsoever.

However, at Leulumoega Fou, the typing regime is still in power, the stage lights are on, and there's no thought that the curtain might come down anytime soon. In contrast to the army's electric typewriters, Leulumoega Fou has a few, old style, purely mechanical devices. However, the old machines are very reliable, virtually indestructible in Samoa's climate, and completely unaffected by lack of electric power.

But typewriters do not multiply copies. At Leulumoega Fou, the Gestetner (Mimeograph) machine is the only method for producing worksheets. We need worksheets, because the library, textbooks, films or slide presentations used by teachers in Australia or New Zealand, do not exist. Instead, writing notes on the blackboard for students to copy into their workbooks occupies much classroom time. According to Helen, some Samoan teachers think this was the sole job of the teacher. The previous year, some teachers simply instructed a student to copy notes onto the board while the teacher went and smoked with friends or slept in the library.

When I describe the wonders of the Gestetner to my adult children, I could be talking about something the ancient Sumerians used before inventing the wheel. But, for the hundred years before the availability of low-cost photocopying, the Gestetner reigned supreme over the short run printing world.

In the staff meeting one morning, Tavita informs us that Alani, the school secretary, provides the teachers with the secretarial service to produce worksheets. Alani will type our handwritten draft onto stencils, print them on the Gestetner, then collate, staple, and deliver them ready for classroom use.

So Tavita instructed us.

Helen dismisses Tavita's direction, being already deeply scarred by her attempts to produce worksheets the previous year.

"Alani takes forever to do anything," says Helen. "And by the time you get your worksheet, it's full of mistakes."

Both she and Tammy laboriously type up their own stencils, and sometimes get Alani to run off copies on the Gestetner.

But "Alani's sloppy and sometimes tears the stencil," says Helen. They prefer to bypass the Alani bottleneck and print, collate, and staple worksheets themselves.

Heather and I want to do things the right way and think we should follow the principal's directive. Aren't we here to immerse ourselves in Samoan culture by doing things the Samoan way? We know that means taking some lows along with the highs. While it's easy to intellectually sip such ideals seated in the comfortable cultural armchairs of our palagi thinking, reality can be harsh.

If Alani had been as fast, diligent, and focused, as either my mother, or the army's dragon dominated typists, this process might have worked. To Alani however, stories of error free work by fair maidens in tall towers, or buried in dungeons guarded by scaly green dragons, were all wild fantasies. Bedtime fairy stories told to children, whose imaginations could effortlessly think three impossible things before breakfast.

As I approach the school office one morning, I hear shrieks of laughter from Mele, standing in the doorway, as Alani sits at her desk chewing gum. Her face animated with excitement, Alani breathlessly tells Mele a story, then tosses her head back and laughs loud and long. I stand in the doorway, politely waiting for Alani to stop. But she goes on and on, in vigorous Samoan, chewing gum, and leaning forward in her chair, getting more excited. Then Mele puts her hand to her mouth, and shrieks with laughter.

I understand almost nothing, and hope they'll eventually recognise my existence. After all, I'm hoping to discuss something work related - something needed for the school and teaching.

Finally, wiping tears of laughter from her face, Alani raises her eyebrows at me.

"*Malo* Alani."

"*Malo* Ian," says Alani, smiling beautifully and greeting me like a long-lost cousin. "*O a mai?*" (how are you?)

"*Manuia, fa'afetai*" (very good, thank you).

Not wanting to prolong pleasantries for fear she'll launch into another hilarious story before we can get down to business, I ask, "Do you have the worksheet typed for me?"

"Worksheet?" asks Alani, looking puzzled.

"The one I gave you Friday. Remember? We talked about it yesterday."

Her face is blank. Then she frowns like she's never heard of any worksheet, let alone the one I gave her.

"You said you'd have it ready to run off today?" I suggest.

She looks down at the confusion of papers on her desk and picks one up tentatively.

"What class?" she asks, looking up again while masticating gum.

"Upper five physics. You remember?" I ask desperately. "I've done all the diagrams, so you just need to type the rest and then run off copies."

"Maybe it's here somewhere," she says without conviction.

She sifts through several piles of papers and shows me one. "Is this it?"

"No, that's Tammy's worksheet."

Sneering in disgust at the offending paper, she tosses it onto a different pile and pulls out another.

"Maybe this one?" she asks, raising one eyebrow.

"Yes, that's it."

Alanis eyes light up and she smiles with satisfaction.

I briefly feel elated, knowing my stencil hasn't disappeared into a filing system black hole. However, to be fair, the successful progression of any piece of work through the school office owed more to the vagaries of climate and mathematics of probability, than laws of interstellar physics.

At least once a day, the sea breeze gusts through the windows, blowing the already random piles of paper in a whirlwind around the office and often out the door. After Alani and any nearby students run around retrieving wind-blown papers, recognising some may have escaped entirely, they're randomly reassembled into completely new piles - resulting in work being re-prioritised. That urgent and important job, sitting atop the work pile, might suddenly find itself at the bottom of a different pile, or disappear entirely into the nearby plantation, forever lost to humanity and the unfortunate teacher.

My heart sinks. Alani has made no progress at all, and I wonder if the office whirlwind has already reassigned my worksheet's priority several times.

"Can you type it today?" I ask desperately. If Alani types it without mistakes, then maybe she can print the worksheets ready for my class tomorrow?

But her face clouds - she looks crestfallen. "Today?" she says, looking at the draft as though pondering a radical new idea. "Maybe?"

She looks at me with sympathetic eyes, but I've learned that for Alani, and most Samoans, "maybe" is a face saving "no". On the other hand, she doesn't want to disappoint me.

"I really need it for my classes tomorrow, Alani. Could you do it today for me?" I plead, pressing my case home on her bleeding heart, as though I'm somehow special.

Then, with deep conviction, she suddenly sits upright and says, "I'll have it done for you tomorrow." Smiling, her eyes light up and she attacks the gum with renewed vigour.

"Don't worry Ian," she adds with a beaming smile, tossing the draft onto yet another paper pile. "Tomorrow!"

She turns back to Mele to finish her story, and I hear another shriek of laughter as I walk to my classroom. I'm unsure whether "tomorrow" means before my class or after it, but all I can do is leave the fate of my worksheet in Alani's uncertain but sympathetic hands.

The idea that while they are at work, they should be diligently working, or at least focussing their attention on work-related matters, did not seem to concern either Alani or Mele. I mean, to my way of thinking, Alani's priority should be to get my stencil typed, and then socialise after school, or during the morning tea break. And as the Head Mistress of the school, shouldn't Mele be setting an example for other teachers and students?

Isn't the purpose of the school to teach?

I get the distinct feeling that for many, the school's function isn't to teach students, but to socialise with friends. Teaching is just an annoying interruption to that primary purpose.

After dismissing my form class at the end of the day, I go straight to the office - ever hopeful Alani might have at least typed the stencil. Then maybe I could print the worksheets myself.

But Alani has already left for the day.

Perhaps I should type the stencil myself? After all, my mother taught me to type. "It's a good skill to have," said Mum. But I already have a lot on my plate, preparing lessons for subjects I've never taught, and trying to resurrect classroom equipment from a state of corrosion and decay. Besides, I think it's important to do things the Samoan way. I want to live the experience of being, if not a Samoan teacher, then at least a teacher in Samoa.

When I poke my head through the office door the next morning, Alani sits at her desk, beautifully dressed as usual, with a frangipani flower stuck in her hair, and chewing the omnipresent gum.

"Today, Ian!" she says triumphantly, as though the stencil was already typed and printed, instead of languishing for days in the office. At least, the fact she immediately remembers my need indicates my worksheet has transitioned to being a priority in her mind, no longer subject to ducking and weaving its way through the whirlwind office workflow.

Again, I make the end of day, dash to the office to find Alani gone, and the door locked.

Still no worksheets.

But when I look in the office the next morning, Alani smiles and graciously hands me a stack of printed worksheets, hot off the Gestetner.

I'm delighted.

Excellent.

Finally.

"Fa'afetai tele lava Alani"* (thank you very much).

"E le afaina" (you're welcome).

Maybe it really is possible to use the proper channels?

But when I sit down in the staff room and scan the top sheet, I see several mistakes.

Then I see more.

I groan, realising the worksheets are unusable without making hand corrections to every sheet. Perhaps I should ask Alani to correct the stencil mistakes, and run off another seventy-five copies?

That'll take another three days.

If I'm lucky.

"What's up Ian?" asks John, taking out his tobacco pouch.

"Alani's finally run off my worksheet, but it's full of mistakes."

"Why don't you get the students to make the corrections after you hand them out?"

"I s'pose I could do that."

Thinking about it, I remember my teachers doing that sometimes - for maybe one minor change. But Alani's made a lot of errors. Will that work? I don't know, but I guess I can try.

Later, I distribute the worksheets to the first of my two physics classes. I spend the first fifteen minutes writing the corrections on the blackboard and instructing the students to amend their worksheets. But later when I check their work, I see many students have also made correction mistakes, compounding the errors.

Then when I distribute the worksheets to the next class, I find I'm ten worksheets short. Alani's printed sixty-five copies, but I need seventy-five.

I tell some students to share their worksheets in class and promise to get some more printed.

This time I skip my form class and catch Alani before she escapes.

"Hey Alani, I didn't have enough of those worksheets. Can you run off some more? I need seventy-five copies."

"Oh, sorry, the stencil tear. It's no good," she says with great sadness, as though confiding the death of a loved one.

Foolishly, I thought Alani was the skilled operator, whose job it is to make sure a stencil doesn't tear. But in Alani's view, such calamities were more like acts of God, along with cyclones, earthquakes, and tsunamis. Her Samoan philosophy says we just accept calamities over which we have no control and get on with life as best we can.

"You want me to type another one?" she asks mildly, without enthusiasm.

"Maybe," I say, realising I've now become the face-saving Samoan because she knows I really mean "no".

I just can't summon the superhuman effort necessary to produce a simple worksheet. Feeling like I've just used my last ounce of strength to reach what I think is the mountain peak, only to discover the real summit is high above me.

I give up; the students who don't have a worksheet will just have to share.

Unsurprisingly, Helen is right again. Helen can be SO annoying.

Over lunch that day, I tell John what happened and how I feel.

"*Fiafia - aua le popole*" (don't worry, be happy), says John, laughing.

"Don't worry, be happy" is a slogan we see emblazoned on tee shirts in English and Samoan, and frequently verbalised. At first, we laugh - we think it's just tee-shirt humour.

But maybe they're serious? What if it's an actual way of life?

Because Alani is the living embodiment of the "don't worry, be happy" philosophy. While she does her job, she's not bothered by the odd, or even frequent mistake, or the timeliness of any task.

Samoans suggest that if we don't worry, we too can be happy.

But we are worried.

We're worried because we have a curriculum to teach, in a limited number of classes before the end of the year, and want to give our students the best education we can under the circumstances.

We're worried because, working back from those lofty goals, we need this worksheet available for class tomorrow, otherwise we'll have to teach it next week and we've already lost weeks because of the cyclone so it MUST be ready tomorrow. Why can't Alani just type it instead of telling stories to Mele and anyone else who peeks in the office door...?

We're worried because we may not achieve what we think is possible, and the goal we have set for ourselves. Ultimately, we're worried because we have set goals, even if we've set them unconsciously. Perhaps because we've invested meaning and purpose in achieving something that seems tantalisingly close, but ultimately unachievable.

And so, we are unhappy.

One solution to our problem is to avoid setting goals, or set goals that are easily achieved. But we feel that's like admitting defeat. Perhaps we aren't really unhappy, but just dissatisfied. For we need to be dissatisfied with our lot to summon the effort, and perhaps courage, to improve it. We need a vision for what might be, to be inspired to turn that vision into reality. Life may be a journey and not a destination, but without a destination, we don't embark on the journey. We are pilgrims, and though our road may be long and hard, without seeing the celestial city, we dawdle in the doldrums of mediocrity, or the slough of despond; we perish, thirsty for want of what might have been.

Perhaps God has placed us in Samoa so we learn to do what we can, and accept what we can't, without being anxious. Learning to start, without fretting for failing to finish in the way we planned. We produce worksheets because in our hearts we want to give our students the learning opportunities we had, or millions of other teenagers have in the world's advanced economies. But that may not be what God has in mind, or what's best for these students' futures.

Tammy advises us there's no point getting upset with Alani. She'll no longer be cheerful towards us. Work will arrive no sooner, possibly later, and contain at least the same number of mistakes - probably more.

"And don't forget, Alani handles your mail," says John.

True. We find our mail from Australia often arrives at the church office in Apia, where it rests from its long journey for an indeterminate time, before being given to someone going to the school. That person hopefully delivers the mail to Alani, or sometimes Tavita, in whose company it might further rest and recuperate, possibly sipping pina coladas on a beach somewhere before it's finally delivered into our hands. We find being on the right side of Alani is critical for our mental, if not physical welfare. Since our work will be untyped and full of mistakes, whether we have a cheerful, friendly Alani, or a grumpy Alani, we choose the cheerful, friendly option.

After a while, we appreciate the reality that no matter what happens, Alani is always happy to see us, welcoming us with a beaming smile, regardless of circumstance. Alani doesn't let any dark cloud of imperfection detract from her *joie de vivre*, or irrepressible happiness.

We meet people like Alani everywhere - in shops, offices, hotels, and government. They do their work without being highly competent, diligent, or timely, but they're always cheerful, friendly, and happy. Expat palagis often complain such Samoans are lazy, preferring to sleep, or sit around smoking, than lift a finger to help themselves or their students. We see plenty of evidence of laziness measured against our palagi values, but there are also plenty of examples of diligent and hardworking Samoan teachers. And looking back on my educational experience, I recall plenty of lazy teachers in Australia. And we've already learned the hard way that it's wise to sleep in the afternoon heat rather than persist working.

Some Samoan teachers know nothing else - they have no alternative vision to aspire to, or career path beyond their current station. They're local Samoans, not young, starry-eyed volunteers out to change the world - like we and many Peace Corps Volunteers. Their Samoan culture recognises status and relationships, not achievement. And achievement of anything permanent was extremely difficult in Samoa - whether because of the corrosive climate, the uncertainty and unpredictability of events, or the unreliability of people. Because everything might vanish in a puff of wind - another cyclone - or be eaten by insects, fungus and washed into the sea.

Perhaps Alani's attitude is more than understandable. Maybe it's a sensible survival strategy? Perhaps the whirlwinds blowing through the office, the fragility of stencils, the limitations of Alani's skill and ability, and our limited capacity for acts of superhuman effort, are all beyond our control? If they're really acts of God, then it's wiser to focus on preserving the peaceful status quo, than push ourselves to the brink of sanity trying to make changes.

On the flip side, when we fail in some way, Alani and the teachers are always disarmingly sympathetic and unfailingly kind. They might tell their friends, family, and everyone in the village, they think we're insane (we probably are). But while they might laugh privately, with face-saving comfort they publicly tell us, "Never mind, it was good you tried."

Of course, we could avoid any extra effort, make no worksheets, do the bare minimum, and settle for not teaching our students as well as we hoped. We have the uncomfortable thought that this is exactly what many teachers do, Samoan and palagi alike, to survive mentally and physically. For we don't want to make the palagi mistake of measuring our self-worth, by our ability to achieve standards or goals set by our culture. For neither the army's dragon lady, nor the Rio Tinto secretaries, could have survived in Samoa. Within a few months, the dragon would have self-immolated in a ball of fire, and the secretaries would have either fled, or leapt out of the skyscraper windows.

Nevertheless, these cultural insights do not solve our problem of how to produce error free worksheets in a timely manner. We know Tavita is not the 'do the bare minimum' kind of principal. He's committed to giving our students the best education the school can offer, and pushes for real, positive change.

And we can't stand by and do the minimum.

We're palagi.

We want to do the best we can.

It's obvious the only proper solution is to follow Tammy and Helen's example and do the stencil typing and printing ourselves. And since Heather and I foolishly agreed to take that extra class (to do our bit), we have no spare time during school hours. We do all the work at home. Since there's only one spare typewriter, we share it with the other palagi teachers, lugging it from house to house, or relocating ourselves to whatever house has it. We type in the afternoon heat, when our hands are so sweaty our fingers slip on the keys, or by candlelight in the evenings.

We correct stencil typing mistakes using a special pink correction fluid. It has the added benefit that the fluid vapours also facilitate a drug induced halo of peace and wonder, positively advancing our mental health and wellbeing, along with our stencil. Alani keeps the school's only small bottle of correction fluid under lock and key, but everyone knows nail polish remover also works. We borrow Heather, Tammy, and Helen's little bottles of nail polish remover, and sometimes even manage to return them.

Of course, from Alani's view point this arrangement is a win-win solution. It takes the pressure off her to type stencils, and once the Gestetner is set up, it takes less than five minutes to print enough copies for a class. Sometimes we also do the printing, collating, and stapling.

To be fair, if I compare it to Wangaratta High School, where I attended, Leulumoega Fou has over eight hundred students to my high school's six hundred. But my school had four secretarial staff running the office, three librarians, and at least one laboratory assistant, who prepared equipment for class experiments, and ordered in any new equipment or chemicals that might be required. All of which arrived promptly. Then there were maintenance and cleaning staff maintaining the buildings and grounds.

Tavita has Alani.

Meanwhile, to advance my mental and physical wellbeing, I join Ramon and John, who are keen to maintain their fitness with an early morning run. Up around six, we run along the road toward Saleimoa, when the early morning twilight is calm, soft, and beautiful. We're often up in time to see the sun peep over the sea's horizon, sending shafts of light breaking through the distant grey clouds. The bare and broken trees have all browned off, but we see green shoots budding on skeletal branches - perhaps heralding a coming spring of renewal after the winter of Ofa's desolation.

Villagers stare at us like they've never seen anyone run before. Some distance past the Saleimoa store, we turn around and head back to the Malua pool. We may run in the coolest part of the day, but it still feels like a sauna. Bathed in sweat, we jump in the pool to cool down and wash.

Tammy and Heather sometimes join us at the pool. Heather is still being coached by Tammy in the art of bathing wrapped in an *ie*. When some teenagers approach walking along the road, she freaks out, hiding in case they're her students. When the teenagers are out of earshot, we give her the 'all clear', and she emerges from behind a rock. Returning to a pancake breakfast prepared by Helen, we dress for school, and walk to the morning staff meeting.

It's not long before Ramon and John's desire to sleep overtakes their determination to run, and I run on my own.

One morning, a furiously barking dog runs across the road to sink its teeth into my ankle. Jumping away and slinging the dog off my leg, a man steps from his *fale* and hurls a stone at the dog, hitting it squarely on its hindquarters. It runs off yelping with its tail between its legs. As the man steps back into his *fale*, I'm suddenly left limping and bleeding. The man is unconcerned, like this happens every day because, in Samoa, dogs frequently attack people walking innocently along the road.

Limping home, I wash the wound and apply antiseptic hoping it's enough to stave off any infection. Heather shudders, thinking of the nasty bacteria inhabiting the mouth of a half-starved and neglected Samoan dog. John is sympathetic as I relate the story over breakfast.

"Dogs are nasty - y'gotta learn to do what the Samoans do - bend down to pick up a rock so the dogs run away. They know what's coming."

"That bloke was an amazing shot," I say. "He hit a running dog exactly where he wanted to."

"Yeah, they learn to throw early in life. The girls are amazing. They're not allowed to climb coconut trees, so they knock the coconuts off by throwing rocks."

"Why can't girls climb coconut trees?"

"Oh, don't you know," says Helen, rolling her eyes. "It makes them infertile."

"How is that?"

"Old wives fable," laughs John. "I dunno if anyone believes it, but I've never seen a girl climb a coconut tree."

"I reckon the boys are more likely to become infertile, if they slip and slide down the tree."

John laughs. "We wouldn't even make it up the tree. There's no danger to our fertility."

To avoid further mishap, I avoid the road and run around the track on the school rugby pitch. We also take John's advice, and whenever threatened by a dog, mimic reaching to the ground for a stone. Magically, the dogs always run away.

But attack by dogs remains a serious hazard. There are many stray, unkept, and uncared for dogs lurking everywhere. One evening in Apia, a dog attacks Doug, causing a serious wound that has to be stitched up at the hospital at Motootua. And a few weeks before she eventually leaves Samoa, Tammy will be savagely attacked in a village by a pack of three dogs. With torn clothing and several serious wounds, she'll leave Samoa stitched and bandaged.

Mentally, we know being a volunteer teacher can be hard. But physically and emotionally, we're now realising the vast difference between knowing about something, and the real, lived experience; how its wear and tear, fatigue, and tyrannical decay, threatens to overwhelm or undermine everything we attempt. Whatever we do, whether it's producing worksheets, washing our clothes, or going for a morning run, it's always a lot harder than we think, and often means doing everything from scratch. It's like being a carpenter making a chair but having to first make the nails on a blacksmith's forge.

Giving our students a better education with few resources has the combined effect of burning our physical and emotional candles at both ends. The candle hasn't burned out yet - we haven't reached the limit of our capacity, or willingness, to endure and work hard. But we're consciously and unconsciously adopting Samoan cultural survival skills, like picking up a rock to avoid dog attacks, and learning to worry less, be happy more, and enjoy the journey.

It's not only our hearts and minds that are adapting, because one morning I hear a piercing shriek from the bathroom.

"My hair's falling out," calls Heather, showing me a brush clumped with a wad of dark hair. "What's happening?"

I too notice a lot more hair on my comb.

"Oh yeah," says Helen when we mention it over breakfast. "Y' hair falls out here - you're moulting in the heat apparently, like a dog in spring."

"Don't worry," adds Tammy positively, "apparently it grows back."

"I hope so," says Heather, taken aback to be compared to a dog in springtime, and fearful she might have contracted some foul disease leaving her bald in her twenties.

"I thought only animals moulted," I say.

"Well, so do we," says Tammy. "Anyways, it's cooler with less hair."

While that might be the silver lining to the looming prospect of being prematurely bald, it also means we are now literally tearing our hair out.

And will we tear our hair out trying to renew our visas that will soon expire? Because if they're not promptly renewed, our immigration status will be in jeopardy, and we could find ourselves on a plane flying home.

15

FISHBOWL AND ROLLERCOASTER

*"Judge not, that you be not judged. For with the
judgment you pronounce you will be judged, and with
the measure you use it will be measured to you."*
Matthew 7:1-2

efore we left Australia, the OSB was emphatic, saying, "You must
not overstay. Make sure your immigration status is in order or
you could find yourselves on a plane home." The holiday visa the
Immigration Department granted on arrival is about to expire. Without
extending that to a work visa, we'll be overstaying, and technically, illegal
immigrants. But after Doug and Jill tell us their visa renewal story, we
wonder if the public servants also operate using the 'don't worry, be happy'
philosophy?

"They lost our passports," says Doug. "We travelled from Savai'i, so we
could personally take our visa application to the Immigration Office. After
a few weeks, they told us they need more time, but when we checked a
month later, they'd lost them."

"We were six months without a visa or passport," says Jill. "When they turned up at Samoa College and were sent to Vaipo'uli, our visa had already expired. We had to go through the whole process again."

"Lucky, we didn't need to return home in an emergency," says Doug.

"Didn't the High Commission help?" asks Emma.

"They said to wait for Immigration to find our passports. In an emergency, they'd give us something to get back to Australia."

But Doug and Jill's story fills us with fear and dread, because extending visas is a highly uncertain process over which we have no control.

One afternoon, armed with passports and a letter from Feilo confirming our employment, we follow directions to the Immigration Office behind the German-built Lands and Titles Court. Feeling like forlorn figures making supplication to a looming monolith of faceless bureaucracy, we climb an ancient wooden staircase and find ourselves in a bare, windowless room. Dimly lit by a naked bulb hanging from the high ceiling, we see ancient tongue-in-groove walls, peeling green paint, and an old wooden bench in the centre of the room. It looks more like a New York crack house, or place of ill repute, than a government department.

The floor is dark with muddy footprints, and the walls are dirty. On our left is a brightly lit hole in the wall, with a wall behind - possibly to screen nefarious activities from our view. But the bell on the countertop suggests it's more likely a place of official function, than a den of iniquity.

With hope, and the eternal optimism essential to accomplish anything in Samoa, we ring the bell. We're immediately relieved to see a young Samoan man appear wearing a dark *ie faitaga*, and a white short-sleeved shirt. Since he looks more like a civil servant than a cocaine vendor, we must be in the right place.

Tentatively explaining our need for a visa extension, the civil servant fills out a form retrieved from under the counter. He asks for Feilo's letter and our passports, then gives us a carbon copy of the completed form.

"How long will it take?" I ask.

"A week maybe," he shrugs.

Knowing "maybe" can mean almost anything, we're immediately anxious.

"Don't worry," he says, sensing our concern. Smiling, he waves our passports at us and disappears behind the bare wall.

His unconvincing words are unsettling. We like to imagine that behind the wall works a bustling office full of diligent public servants. But if they're like Alani and many others we meet, we have a nagging feeling they're spending their time smoking and gossiping about what happened in their village last night.

Contrary to what the OSB said, it seems we're the only people worried about our visa status; everyone else is blasé and unbothered, including the Immigration Department. After the debacle that separated us from our passports leaving Australia, we feel naked and vulnerable.

"What'll we do if we have to go home in an emergency?" asks Heather.

"I s'pose we go to the High Commission."

If we're learning anything here in Samoa, it's patience and trust in God.

However, there are advantages to living in a small country. The degrees of separation are smaller than in Australia, so we draw some comfort from the fact that people at the Australian High Commission know who we are. Our friends Mick and Hannah, whose houses we treat like our own, even have personal relationships with Basil, the High Commissioner.

Frequently lubricated by alcohol at Otto's Reef, these relationships extend via Basil all the way to Australia, and particularly Queensland. A few weeks after the cyclone, the Queensland Rugby Team arrives to play a friendly game with the Samoan national team. To celebrate this sensational event, the Australian High Commission organises a cocktail party for expat Aussies to meet the team at the world famous, and pristine, Aggie Grey's Hotel.

In the town they have water - sometimes. And electricity - mostly. But Aggie Grey's has its own water tanks and generators, so tourists continue to live in luxury, during and long after a cyclone devastates the rest of the country.

Invitees to this exciting event are selected and vetted by a thorough and exhausting process. At Otto's Reef one evening, the High Commission staff give Mick a stack of blank invitations so he can invite any Aussie he wants.

Coming from Melbourne (heartland of Australian Rules Football), we know little about rugby, and nothing about the players. But when our diet typically consists of large servings of boiled rice and tinned herring, free food and drinks at the best hotel in the country sounds wonderful.

Being our first formal event after arriving in Samoa, we're keen to arrive clean and spruced up. After catching a bus to Apia, we head to Hannah's house at Motootua for a proper shower. Neither Hannah nor her housemate are home, but that doesn't stop us breaking-in to use their shower. It's what Hannah would expect.

But after turning the bathroom taps, we see no water. Disappointed, we fruitlessly wait ten minutes, hoping the water returns. No water, no shower.

We might not feel clean, but we can always dress well. Sure, it's an Australian cultural event, but because it's a formal event in Samoa, I wear my newly purchased *ie faitaga*. Given the state of the country after the cyclone, we guess we're not the only people arriving a little dusty.

Concerned we might be late if we catch a bus and walk, we flag down a passing taxi. Chatting to the taxi-driver, we discover he's Tavita's cousin; demonstrating the web of interconnected Samoan relationships extends deep into every district and village. Feeling thankful we've said nothing negative so far, we say Tavita is a good Principal.

"*Poko tele, ah*" (he's very clever), he says.

By catching the taxi, we not only arrive at Aggies early, we're also the first guests to turn up. At the front desk, a very elegant receptionist leads us into an open area, with a few chairs and tables under ceiling fans. She serves us cold drinks from the bar, while we sip them under cool fans, waiting for other guests to arrive.

Soon, an older Samoan man enters. He's well dressed and wears black leather shoes - the lace-up kind - not the thongs (flip-flops) Samoans call 'shoes'.

Wandering over to us, drink in hand, he starts a conversation, asking where we're from and what we're doing in Samoa. He doesn't introduce himself (we know that's poor manners in polite Samoan society), but we tell him we're Australian volunteers teaching at Leulumoega Fou.

He's familiar with the Australian Volunteer Program and pleased to hear we're teaching at his old school. He asks how we like being greeted by a cyclone, and how the school is recovering. He talks about his recent visit to Tasmania, how he had stayed with friends in Melbourne, and how much he enjoyed his time there. His English skills are faultless, and he's obviously very well-travelled.

Thinking he might be an influential businessperson, I ask him, "What sort of work do you do?"

"Prime Minister," he says.

"Oh," I say, feeling embarrassed and suddenly lost for words, but desperately wanting to continue the conversation. I wonder how one speaks to a Samoan Prime Minister and ponder raising the current controversial topic of universal suffrage. We heard that currently only *matais* can vote for members of parliament, but unscrupulous families are creating new *matai* titles to rig votes in their favour. Proponents of universal suffrage argue change is necessary to preserve the traditional *matai* system, but I can't recall whether the Prime Minister supports the change.

Fortunately, when the American Consul walks into the room, the Prime Minister kindly introduces us, first to the Consul, and then to other entering dignitaries.

As the room fills up, the Prime Minister graciously moves on to meet and greet others. Finally able to relax, we join our friends, and even meet some members of the Queensland Rugby Team. While we make no friends in the international sporting elite, from now on, we tell people that Tofilau Eti Alesana, Prime Minister of Samoa, is our mate.

Discovering the taxi driver is Tavita's cousin, followed by our surprise Prime Ministerial encounter, drives a growing realisation we live in a fishbowl. Fishbowl life extends from the humble family *fale*, where neighbours watch over every activity, to the country's highest decision makers. We never know who we might meet, who their relatives are, and what influence they might have. But we do know they talk about us.

Anonymity is not possible in Samoa, but it might even be unthinkable. Cultural practices appear structured to ensure everyone knows about everyone else, not least to pay the proper level of honour or respect, and to save face. When everyone in the fishbowl knows everyone else, including who's honest, and who isn't, who's reliable, and who isn't, there is peace and security. The fishbowl maintains order because everyone knows their place or station relative to everyone else.

But while face-saving ensures people maintain a polite public face, privacy only exists within the confines of their thoughts. All this makes it difficult to know what people truly think, including our students. Fortunately, we get a glimpse into their world when Heather has them write a short essay about themselves.

While they are universally proud of their Samoan culture and heritage, it is with their *aiga* (extended family) they identify with most strongly. Actions and behaviours that are noble and good are those that contribute, or bring honour, to their *aiga*, their village, or their school. Obedience to elders and to God, and service to their *matai*, are pathways to honour and respect. Similarly, a high class ranking, a good job, or being awarded an overseas scholarship, are not just individual achievements, but also family achievements. At the school coalface, it might mean the family, or the *matai*, chooses the subjects a student studies. The worst behaviours are those that bring shame on their *aiga*, village or school. Poor behaviour at school brings shame on everyone in the family - siblings, parents, and grandparents.

Because their identity and aspirations are so coupled with their family, they don't see themselves as individual and autonomous people in the same way palagi teenagers do. Samoan culture actively discourages such thinking because it fosters unwarranted independence, pride, and selfishness. They use the derogatory word '*fiapalagi*' (wants to be palagi) to describe reluctance to share, or other selfish behaviours.

However, at school we actively encourage our students to think independently and pursue subjects they're good at or enjoy. By doing so, we create tension between traditional Samoan culture, and the external palagi world.

One morning Tavita announces, "This year the school celebrates its centenary." When he asks the staff for ideas to beautify the buildings and grounds for this significant event, Heather suggests a class garden competition. We're surprised when teachers enthusiastically embrace this idea, not realising that both teachers and students are fiercely competitive. Staff appoint Heather, Mele and Leua to be competition judges. We invite students to build a garden in front of their classrooms on Saturday mornings and after school. Tavita announces the garden competition at the next school assembly.

One Saturday morning half the girls in my class turn up to make a class garden. They bring some tools - bush knives and a small spade - but digging in soil generously impregnated with basalt rocks proves difficult. Within a short time, many girls sit in the shade watching others work, without the competitive enthusiasm and killer instinct of other classes.

However, Valu, Avele and Pelopia all work hard clearing the *vaofefe* and grass. When Valu slips and the spade hits her hand, I'm shocked when she says "*kefe*" (f*ck).

"Valu!" I say, frowning.

She grins sheepishly - obviously surprised I understand.

Then, on her way home later, Pelopia insists on giving me one tala "for your bus fare", which seems strange, but I assume is a cultural thing.

Despite an uneasy feeling that these nice Samoan teenagers might be more worldly than we think, I enjoy my form class. While they're often a noisy rabble of teenage girls, they sometimes exude the quiet maturity of young women. They listen attentively when I teach General Science, diligently copying notes into their workbooks. Getting a response to questions can be a challenge, and they're so quiet Helen calls my class 'the morgue', but sometimes Avele or Pelopia venture a suitable response.

After a few weeks of teaching, I give them a test to check progress. Using the Alani production process this occurs a week later than planned, and when I assess the results, I'm disappointed when only two pass - Avele with 54%, and Pelopia miles ahead with 75%. Since many only achieve single figure results, it's clear most of my class have learned little or nothing. I experience firsthand the problems Tammy, Helen, and John talk about, which I optimistically hoped wouldn't occur in my class.

However, what my students most care about is their class ranking - how they compare to others. Thirty-nine percent may signal failure in palagi eyes, but if that's top of the class, they're ecstatic. Class ranking appears meaningless to us, but while we try to push against it, we may as well hold back an avalanche with a placard.

Instead, we work on causes.

Since they may not understand what we say, we talk more slowly, speak more clearly, and use simple English wherever possible.

"Avoid idiom," says John. Being Australian, avoiding idiom is difficult, but we work on purging Australian expressions from our language.

Meanwhile, everyday student interaction helps grow our Samoan language skills. We find using our limited Samoan far more effective than English when giving directions. I use *"soia!"* for "stop", and *"aua le pisa!"* for "be quiet". While it helps a class run more smoothly, we know it's window dressing on an unavoidable reality. Students lack the earlier education and learning necessary to perform at the academic standard demanded by forms Upper Five and Six.

There's a school assembly every Monday morning in the school hall. Although it only takes twenty minutes, by the time it finishes, and all the students reach their classrooms, most of the first period is a lost lesson, much to our chagrin. Teachers sit on the stage on chairs during assembly, while students all sit cross-legged on the floor in rows. Led by a student or the music teacher, their strong, harmonious voices sing the school song and a hymn. Tavita always has a series of announcements to make, and there is a short devotional talk.

Upon learning we're members of a Presbyterian Church in Melbourne, similar to the Congregational Church, Tavita asks me if I would deliver the devotional talk sometimes.

John thinks it's a great idea. "From what I've seen, most of these devotions end up as threatening calls to obedience. Maybe you could give 'em something more positive?"

The following week I give the devotion. I read a Bible passage, and talk about it for a few minutes, speaking slowly and carefully, as loud as possible - there's no microphone or sound system.

One Monday morning I see Tavita frown at Helen when her dog Pe'a enters the hall. As Helen drags Pe'a away I whisper to Tammy, "What was all that about?"

"Ask Helen later," she says mysteriously.

Helen shares the story over lunch.

"Well, last year Pe'a sat under my chair during assembly - no one minded, and she didn't bother anyone. But she was on heat during Tavita's first assembly as the new principal... and another dog ... shall we say... demonstrated his affection for Pe'a in a very physical way on the stage behind Tavita while he was talking."

"Hammer and tongs, I heard," says John grinning.

"Anyway, the whole school thought it was hysterical, but Tavita was really embarrassed."

"I can imagine," I say.

"It was hilarious," says Helen, unrepentant, but adds sadly, "Now poor Pe'a is banned from assembly."

"And pregnant with puppies," adds John.

One Sunday morning Helen bursts through our back door.

"Sione tried to commit suicide!" she says, breathless.

Sione is a form six student living with Aputi and other teachers in the large old house near the swamp.

We're speechless with shock.

"Keola saw him and knocked the glass out of his hand," says Helen.

"Glass?" I ask.

"Weed killer, Paraquat. It was in his mouth, but we don't know if he drank much."

Drinking Paraquat is the suicide method of choice in Samoa, especially among girls. Boys might reach for a gun and blow their brains out or hang themselves from a tree branch. But girls often reach for the highly toxic weedkiller.

"Keola made him eat soil and then tossed him in the Landrover. He's taken him to the hospital."

"Why eat soil?" I ask.

"They say it absorbs weedkiller, but I dunno if it helps much."

We're shocked to hear about Samoa's high teenage suicide rate. Why, when people seem so happy and smiling in their Pacific Island paradise? And why weedkiller, which causes such a slow, lingering death?

We're told the story behind Sione's suicide attempt is unrequited love; an old story, and as far as stories provide explanation, unrequited love will do. But we all know that's the public face of a much deeper cause.

I grew up in a small rural community hearing stories about friends and family living in small outback Queensland communities. While a close community can nurture and support, it can also destroy those who don't fit in. In the fishbowl community, everyone sees and judges everyone else, remembers every miss-step, and while they sometimes laugh with us, they often laugh at us, pulling us down if we rise too high. When we frequently judge others, we then judge ourselves by the same measure, and find ourselves wanting.

More vulnerable than most, teenagers are sufficiently fragile and sensitive to feel the pain of every mocking dart, but adult enough to know its meaning. Feeling frequently judged, battered by fault correction, admonition, and punishment, they easily feel starved of love and affection. When we're young, the next year seems like eternity, and hope is easily lost. Perhaps every suicide happens when we peer into the darkness of a hopeless future.

Paraquat guarantees a slow, lingering, and painful death, over many days, during which the person is, for the final moments of their life, the centre of attention. As they lay dying, they hear and see the anguished voices and tearful eyes of their weeping family, hear the gratifying voices of regret for all the inflicted pain, and the satisfying knowledge that for one tragic moment, they know they're deeply loved.

A glass of weedkiller in exchange for feeling briefly loved may be a hellish bargain, but it's a bargain some Samoan teenagers make. Like a spectre lurking in the shadows of every Samoan family, teenage suicide is common and inescapable. Parents fear finding their child dead or dying like so many others. And not just in Samoa - it's a method of choice worldwide. Some countries have since banned the weed killer to reduce the suicide rate.

Keola returns a few hours later telling us they're testing Sione.

"If he drank any, we don't think it was much," says Keola. "Hopefully he'll be okay, but they'll keep him under observation for a week at least."

A few days later we catch a bus to Apia with Tammy and Helen and visit Sione at the hospital.

The hospital at Motootua is like no other hospital I've seen before or since. While it has wards full of beds like any hospital, there are also wards with no walls, much like a *fale*.

We find Sione in one such *fale* ward, where we greet him cheerfully, and pass him a gift of cream biscuits. He seems a little ashamed his palagi teachers have come to visit him, but also deeply moved. He sits on his bed and thanks us with an eloquent and teary speech. We all feel very emotional, wiping tears from our eyes.

A week later, Sione is back at school, apparently physically unaffected by his brush with death. While we hope he feels emotionally restored, it's impossible to tell.

Over the next few years more students attempt suicide, and some succeed. It's always a surprise, and we always feel we could have done more to prevent it, if we had known.

Thinking we were going somewhere easy going, peaceful and pleasant, Samoan life reality is proving to be a physical and emotional rollercoaster. As we lurch from hilarious comedy to deadly tragedy, we learn life lessons daily from every frequent life-changing event.

And the next anticipated life-changing event, is the coming of electric power, and with it, running water.

16

POWER AND WATER

"Blessed are the meek, for they shall inherit the earth."
Matthew 5:5

"Great news guys," Helen calls out one afternoon, walking through our back door. "The phone line's up again, and that means we can take calls from home - woo hoo!"

Wow.

A phone at our school. No more travelling to Apia and waiting for hours at the post office to call home. Now our family can call us. A simple, ubiquitous device in Australia has become an exotic luxury.

"Won't they have to call during school hours?"

"No, there's a phone on the same number at Tavita's house. We can take calls there if he's home."

Even better - a phone fifty metres away.

But the next day, Helen's back with bad news.

"Turns out the Church hasn't paid last year's bill. We're disconnected 'till the bill's paid."

"When will that be?"

"Oh, God knows," says Helen, shrugging her shoulders. "Sometime between next week and next year if you ask me."

Walking through Malua a few days later, we see technicians replace and repair damaged power poles.

"Maybe we're getting power?" suggests Heather.

"Hope so - or at least water in our tank."

Then, walking home after school a few days later, Tammy calls out, "We've got water guys!"

A small fountain pours from their water tank overflow. Finally powered, the Malua water pump is filling tanks.

I turn the tap on our tank and hear the satisfying sound of water pouring inside.

"Great," says Heather, her eyes lighting up with anticipation. No more bucket showers or tramping six hundred metres to the communal bathing pool.

Cold running water. A creature comfort of modernity.

Knowledge of its presence feels wonderful.

Almost decadent.

Since the school also has water, Tavita announces we'll now move to a full teaching day, while Arjun makes up a new timetable. Now we teach three, hour-long classes before morning tea break, followed by another two hours of classes, and finish the day around one-thirty.

I've never taught high school before, and while I know the subject matter, I struggle to teach science using only a blackboard and chalk.

As an experienced teacher, Heather tries to teach like she would in Australia, but finds it difficult working with large class sizes and poor education standards. Asking students to write an essay, results in up to fifty essays per class - more than doubling the class workload of an Australian teacher. Since the typical student has only a rudimentary grasp of English grammar, she must decipher their intent before she can meaningfully comment on their work. She sometimes works by flickering candlelight into the early morning, straining her eyes.

When we barely cope teaching three classes a day, the prospect of preparing and delivering another ten lessons each week is daunting. Sure, running water saves a little time, but constant afternoon heat, high humidity, and candlelight vigils, are more exhausting than we ever expected.

Fortunately, at breakfast the next morning John says he, "flicked a switch this morning, and the lights came on."

Helen's jaw drops momentarily, before declaring, "We're cooking dinner at your place tonight."

"The fridge is running again," says John. "We can break open the champagne."

"Champagne or not, we're gonna celebrate that's for sure," says Helen, always keen to party. "I'm going to Apia this afternoon for food."

While we hope Helen finds something luxurious in Apia, we creatively contribute food from our sparse cupboards, excited by the prospect of NOT having a candlelit dinner.

I plan to bake a rice custard in John's oven, because we have rice, eggs, sugar, and powdered milk. Carrying the prepared dish to his house that evening (and hoping his oven will bake), I find Helen busy unpacking.

"Look what I got," she says, brandishing a large block of Anchor Cheddar; real cheese we can store in John's fridge. While it's hardly Camembert, and about as plain a cheese as ever blessed God's earth, it's luxurious.

"I'm making spaghetti bolognaise," she adds, "with cheese on top."

"Real spaghetti? That'll be a treat."

"Yeah, the real thing, not like that canned stuff they sell here," she adds, with a derisive look in John's direction.

"You don't like our tinned spaghetti?"

"Is that an Aussie thing too? My God, I couldn't believe my eyes; who puts spaghetti in a can?"

"It's nice hot on toast," says John laughing.

"Well, the first time I saw it, my Samoan mother put it on my plate straight from the can - ugh!"

As we cram around John's kitchen table, he puts a jug of ice-cold water on the table. "Helen couldn't find champagne, but we've got *vai aisa*."

What could be more decadent than *vai aisa* in our own home?

Candlelit dinners no longer hold any romantic appeal. Not only do we revel in the splendour and brightness of a single incandescent globe, we also see what we're eating.

After dinner we crowd around John's table to work, or sit on his wooden deck chairs.

"I finally got my revenge yesterday," says Helen suddenly.

"Revenge?" asks John.

"You haven't heard about the soldier at the Tusi? He made unflattering remarks about my body shape last week."

"Body shape?" asks John.

"My posterior if you must know. Anyways, it turns out he's scared of bats, so I paid Vailuaga (a student in her class) ten *tala* to get me a flying fox. Yesterday I snuck into the soldier's hotel room and put it in his bed."

Like an Australian fruit bat, a Samoan *pe'a* (flying fox) is cat size with a wingspan close to one metre.

"Was it alive?"

"You bet it was," laughs Helen. "When he went to bed last night, he freaked out big time. The others said he nearly shat himself!"

"Oh Helen, that's terrible," says Heather.

"Isn't it just," laughs Helen, grinning and wiping tears from her eyes. "But I might have to go to confession this Sunday," she adds, affecting a saintly and penitential air.

"What happened to the bat?" asks John.

"The hotel staff took it away; I heard the Tusi's chef wants to barbeque it."

"Poor thing," says Tammy sadly.

"Will he really eat it?" I ask incredulously.

"Oh yeah," says John. "Samoans love eating flying fox. If you hear gunshots around dusk, it's often people hunting them."

"I can't imagine it tastes good."

"Me either," says John, "but I wouldn't mind trying it one day just to find out."

"You can have it," says Helen, screwing up her nose in distaste.

"The way they eat flying foxes, they'll be extinct soon," says John. "Like they ate all the birds."

"What do you mean?"

"There used to be a lot more birds in Samoa. They've excavated huge stone mounds on Savai'i that I heard were for catching pigeons. The Samoans ate'em all, and now there are no pigeons."

True, compared to Australia, we hear few birds. On any evening on my childhood farm, a chorus of raucous magpies, cockatoos, galahs, kookaburras, and other birds screeched and called from trees across the grassy plain. But we hear no morning or evening bird chorus in Samoa. Silence fills the vacant sound space left by birds that apparently filled the vacant stomachs of long dead Samoans, leaving only legendary stories of pigeon hunts and feasts.

"I thought indigenous people lived in harmony with nature?"

"Yeah, maybe, except if you're hungry and it tastes good. The Maori ate the moa to extinction, and God knows what else."

We're not the only bodies partying in a glorious light filled room. Tired of flying in darkness, the vast insect population swarms into the light, from tiny creatures we can barely see, to large flying beetles an inch long. They circle around the light bulb then kamikaze dive onto our work, into the typewriter, and into our hair.

Tammy is unfazed about pulling the odd beetle from her hair, but Heather and Helen are not happy. Occasional shrieks punctuate the night, before the offending insects are apprehended and flung back into the outer darkness.

Later, I hear scratching noises in the ceiling space. When I catch John's eye, he leans back in his chair, and smiles. "The rats are back everyone," he announces, sounding like a television news anchor.

Having had a food free kitchen for weeks, John's house has also been rat free. But the moment his cupboards and fridge are bountifully stocked with nutritious food, the news travels like lightning down the rodent gossip grapevine to every nearby famished rat. They're probably engaging in initial sniff reconnaissance before getting down to the business of 'sharing' John's larder.

"You seem to have a bigger rat problem than us John," I comment.

"Too many holes in my wire screens," he says, pointing to his broken kitchen window.

"Maybe Samoa has rats because there's no snakes here?"

"I'm not sure about that," says Tammy. "I heard there's a small snake about six inches long up in the mountains."

"Hardly going to prune back the rat population."

"'Fraid not," says John doubtfully. "Actually, there're no snakes in New Zealand either."

"Really? We've got heaps of snakes in Australia. "Y'can have some of ours if y'like?"

"No thanks - you can keep 'em."

"It's a wonder some Aussie hasn't let a few tiger snakes loose over there for fun."

"Knowing a few Aussies I've met, I bet they've tried."

"Seems like every animal in your country wants to kill you," says Helen to me.

"No, what about koalas!"

"Okay - I gotta admit, they look pretty cute."

"I heard koalas pee on you," says John, "and they're drugged up on eucalyptus leaves."

"I think being high on eucalyptus leaves is an urban myth," I say, "but it's true they can pee on you if you hold them."

With the ominous sound of rat reconnaissance, and John's admission of rat size gaps in his defences, Heather and Helen call it a night and head home. Tammy and I finish a little later, leaving John developing strategies for defence against the coming rodent blitzkrieg.

We live in John's house like we do in Tammy and Helen's, and they do in ours. Olivia sometimes stays overnight and joins us. Living in Fagamilitai village leaves little time for lesson preparation, particularly when power hasn't reached the village yet. I admire her discipline and diligence, but she's often so focused she speaks in monosyllables without looking up from her work, and we feel ignored.

Unlike Olivia, we're often distracted when working together, as spaghetti chatter has us following the soap opera lives of neighbours and friends, endlessly fuelled by the latest stories travelling down the volunteer gossip grapevine.

But through sharing we learn how others live and work.

Being the only Upper Five commerce teacher, Helen prepares one lesson and teaches it four times, sometimes in the same day. She admits by the third or fourth time it's "pretty boring", but it allows her to put more effort into preparation for each lesson and give more frequent tests. I adopt her strategy and give multiple-choice tests because "the kids like multiple-choice", and correction is quick and easy.

Teaching chemistry, John works hard to relate topics to materials familiar to students in their village. I'd like to follow his example, but unfortunately lack John's intimate experience of village life. I feel determined to get that experience somehow - when we have more time. Literally rubbing shoulders together, our relationships deepen, and as our sharp edges wear off, we learn to value our friends at a much deeper level. We form bonds as interdependent and vulnerable people - bonds so deep our surface frictions, necessary to round off edges, become trivial. Trivial though our differences may seem compared with the tumult around us, they're still there, and at close quarters the friction between Tammy and Helen becomes more apparent.

They're both professing Christians, and their faith, with its emphasis on sacrifice in the service to the needy, was a strong motivator for joining the Peace Corps. Helen is a committed Catholic while Tammy grew up in a Protestant evangelical country church. They're both adventurous and unfazed by hardship, and their strongly held Midwestern values of hard work, hospitality, friendship, kindness, and shouldering responsibility, also influences how they live and work. The bureaucrat who placed them together must have thought them an ideal match. But when people live together, it's the differences that matter.

Quietly spoken and reserved, Tammy appears meek (perhaps pointing to low self-esteem), avoids confrontation and any direct challenge to someone's dignity. Helen is opinionated, outspoken, and intolerant of hypocrisy and behaviour that hurts those she cares about. She passionately advocates for any person, or cause, she believes in, but too often speaks blunt truth to people's faces. While we know Tammy sometimes finds Helen domineering and overbearing, she rarely responds negatively, preferring to be patiently positive. Helen thinks Tammy should stand up for herself more. We wish Helen would stand up for herself less.

They both care deeply about their students, but express that in different ways. Learning from mistakes of the previous year, Helen has a 'take no prisoners' approach to class discipline, resulting in less class stress. She values self-care and often spends sanity restoring time with like-minded friends in Apia. Tammy struggles to control her classes, frequently works herself into the ground, and often wipes tears from her eyes. But while many Samoan teachers respect Helen, they like Tammy; identifying with another vulnerable person, who like them, struggles in the whirlwind chaos of Samoan life. How do the meek inherit the earth? I'm not sure, but I know Tammy received enduring love and affection in a way Helen did not. A happy memory that persisted long after she had gone, and a living lesson to us how God uses the most unlikely people - choosing the weak, instead of the strong, to achieve his goals.

One day we see workers climbing the poles near our house and stringing wires. We stand around salivating like kids at an ice-cream truck in summer. Seeing the work done fuels anticipation and justifies hope; and hope is rewarded one evening when we see our bedroom light shining in all its glory. In our excitement we go to turn on other lights, but we've forgotten the location of the switches.

Power is back and so is music. Next door, Tuala, and his family broadcast 2AP through our open windows from dawn until ten at night (when the station finally stops broadcasting). If we go to bed before ten (which isn't often), we turn on our noisy fan, creating enough white noise to drown out the radio and constant nattering next door.

I turn on our digital clock and set the alarm for six, for an early run before breakfast. The alarm also wakes Helen next door because there are no closed windows in Samoa.

When students ask for Saturday classes, we foolishly agree to teach them because we want to make up time lost by the cyclone. Although electric lights give us a few extra hours each day, the additional preparation and classes consume more time and leave us exhausted.

At eleven o'clock one evening, Heather sighs and says she still has two lessons to prepare for tomorrow. After working until after midnight, she accidently sleeps in. Feeling embarrassed when teachers smile and smirk as she arrives late to the staff meeting, she apologises to Tavita. Helen feels indignant and angered by the smirking teachers, but John sees it differently.

"Don't worry about it, everyone laughs at everyone else in Samoa," he says. "Samoans are quick to turn anything into a joke."

John's words bring little comfort, suggesting Helen's laughed at more than she realises, which is both true for all of us, and humbling. We also know now that Samoans laugh for many different reasons, including just happiness. The children calling out, "Palagi, palagi" are often simply curious and happy to see us. Their parents might laugh because they're embarrassed by their children. Whatever the reason, they usually mean no harm, however disconcerting it might be for visiting palagis.

Fortunately, a new teacher named Ape (short for Apevai) arrives to teach after finishing a postgraduate degree in New Zealand. Her father being the Principal of Malua Theological College, Ape is well connected, qualified, and helps ease the teaching load on Heather.

Since we now have working lights, stoves and refrigerators, there's no need for communal meals. While we miss working together around John's kitchen table, we're more productive as the volume and pace of work increases.

Curiously, we're thankful now for the period without power because it gave us time to learn the ropes of teaching in Samoa at a pace where we could cope. We learned to love and care for neighbours, bear their faults, celebrate their strengths, and befriend people that rub us the wrong way. We discovered that shared struggle through the storms of life, strengthened the bonds we formed in the cauldron of shared suffering. We learned skills necessary for living in community with others, including the reality that living harmoniously means living with tension, disagreements, and getting on each other's nerves. Living more like Samoans helped us establish a bridgehead in understanding Samoan culture through lived experience. Experience that planted our feet firmly on the ground of our new culture and country and taught us the reality that "*each day has enough troubles of its own*", and that we only need to trust God for each day as it comes.

One day I ask Helen if they'd like me to roll away the tank I provided to collect rainwater after the cyclone.

"Yeah," says Helen. "It's only breeding mosquitoes now."

"I'll let the water out then and roll it somewhere."

"You know, it really meant something to me when you put that tank there."

"Well, we needed water, and it was hard work carrying water from Malua."

"Sure, but that's not what I meant. You gave us a tank before you set up yours. I know we don't always agree, but you were giving and caring, and that really meant a lot to me."

It's humbling to realise that little action had such a significant, positive impact on Helen. It makes me reflect on the much larger positive influence she's had on our lives since we first met at Otto's Reef. We were wary of her then afraid she was a stereotypically loud American.

Curiously, while most of our fears were realised in some way, Helen is also generous, hospitable, diligent, reliable, and endlessly kind. She cares deeply for her students, and she cares about us. She has boundless energy for injecting fun into life, and she's a wonderful friend. Never one to shrink from pushing a new boundary (like putting a live fruit bat in a soldier's hotel bed), she often flouts rules and propriety, without breaking laws. Helen also sizes up a situation shrewdly, and I'm learning the wisdom of seriously considering her unsolicited and brutally delivered advice, even if I don't always take it.

Everyone is more complex than their labels, and our initial response to Helen exposed our own prejudices about Americans, and the attitudes we interpreted through the lens of cultural imperialism, fuelled by American popular culture flooding the English-speaking world as we grew up. For Helen, speaking up is driven less by American culture, and more because she's the youngest of six kids. She says she had to speak up, or her brothers and sisters would trample all over her.

While we still groan when Helen speaks up in staff meetings, when we think she should be silent, she has grown from someone we're wary of, to someone we love and want alongside us, and someone we often need. One day she'll push a boundary too far, but not yet.

But Ramon does.

One evening he collapses in Leua's kitchen with an asthma attack, or something worse, we're not sure. Latu runs to Ape's house and calls the only ambulance in the country, which miraculously arrives rapidly from Apia.

Paramedics bundle Ramon into the ambulance with an oxygen mask on his face, and Leua goes to help translate at the hospital.

A few days later Ramon is back, a little shaken and taking things more slowly. We wonder whether his vegan diet is a good idea in Samoa, but realise our own diet is more vegetarian than it was in Australia. We rarely eat red meat because it's expensive and typically as tough as old boots. We eat a lot of tinned fish because it's cheap and doesn't need refrigeration.

Buying food in Apia after working a full teaching day is proving physically demanding. Since I can carry a much heavier pack than Heather, I often do the shopping alone, leaving immediately after school.

I stand waiting for a bus by the road along with hundreds of students. Since the bus is always crowded, I typically travel with a student sitting on my knee - usually one of my girls. Sometimes Fuli or Avele, hopefully Mutini who's much lighter, or someone getting off a few villages down the road, rather than going all the way to Apia. As much as I might want to avoid it, I'm expected to nurse students on my knee so more people can fit into the bus, enabling students to get home at a reasonable hour. To refuse would be considered very selfish in Samoan eyes, like we're not contributing to the community, or acting as though we're above our station in the social hierarchy.

It's important to make a toilet break before travelling, to avoid being tortured by the recurring impact of an eighty-kilogram teenager sitting on a full bladder, for thirty minutes, over every bump in the road. I'm also careful to avoid being hit by the elbow in my face or gash my unguarded knee on the bolt protruding from the seat in front.

By the time I finish shopping, I catch a bus back before nightfall and have dinner around six.

In contrast to Helen's pessimistic expectations, the Church pays their phone bill, and the phone is reconnected within a few days. We notify our parents in the next air-letter home and two weeks later, we're called to Tavita's house to take a telephone call. Heather lifts the receiver and breaks into a radiant smile when she hears her mother's voice.

Tavita's roof hasn't been repaired yet, so we stand talking under his remaining roof as rain pours down, forming pools on the linoleum floor.

Finding few students have dictionaries, Heather asked our parents to scour charity shops for books to ship to the school. She also requested comic book stories because pictures better communicate context. Heather's mother has questions about the books, but the line crackles and then cuts off.

Our first call from the school is comforting, making us feel a little closer to family back home, but it reinforces the reality that Helen and Tammy are our family now. We've grown to love them. Heather and I have only brothers in our families, so they've become the sisters we never had. Helen is the irritating sister who thinks she knows what's good for you but will stick by you no matter what. Tammy is the sister who's always there to offer a sympathetic ear and a kind word.

We thank God for his mercy and goodness in providing us with Tammy and Helen. Together with John, they're the people we need in our lives right now. Imperfect, and on their own journeys, but sharing this part of their life journey with us.

I'd always thought of culture forming through the lens of ideas, not by brutal necessity of working together to survive harsh realities. Samoa might be paradise compared to other places, but life is still hard, and culture is moulded by the need to share common tools and resources. Because we need each other, it's essential to trade privacy and independence, not only for human help, but what comes with it - community, a sense of belonging, being cared for, and caring for others.

Living in a modern city like Melbourne, with its abundant prosperity and everything anyone might want or need, it's easy to drift apart from friends and neighbours, simply because we no longer need each other.

In contrast, Samoa constantly reminds us of the fragility of our lives. Like a balancing tightrope walker, we're only one misstep, or severed strand, away from disaster. And now we know one strand of the economic tightrope is affordable and reliable energy. While most Samoans are subsistence farmers, oil and falling rain (hydroelectricity) provide the power that frees up time, and transports the goods and people that create family wealth, and prosperity.

It's the job of each elected *matai* to ensure every member of their *aiga* (extended family) has land to grow food. People typically grow at least enough coconuts, taro, bananas, and other important foodstuffs to feed their families, and contribute to celebrations and other community obligations. But they need cash to buy other household essentials, like a machete, cooking pot, lamp, or cotton cloth to make clothes. Acquiring these basic items not only improves their quality of life, but also helps build resilience to hard times, like the aftermath of a cyclone. People therefore produce more than they need, transport it to the market by bus or pickup, and sell it for much needed cash.

They also need cash to pay school fees. A high school education is recognised worldwide as one of the critical enablers of economic development. It can lead to a well-paid job, or a better operated family business, and provide regular cash income. But for a child to complete their education, and get that well-paid job, they need to do homework. They do homework in the evenings when it's dark, so they need a bright light, made possible by affordable and reliable power.

To a poor subsistence farming family, access to that energy source results in improved education, increased resilience in hard times, better health, and wellbeing, and sometimes a roof over their heads. Without accessible, reliable, and affordable energy, prosperity runs out of steam, and economic development is not possible.

With power, water, and a telephone nearby, life appears to be returning to some sort of 'normal'. One afternoon I return to the Immigration Department and pick up our passports with their three-month visa extensions. Delighted to have our immigration status in order, and with things finally falling into place, we look forward to settling into some sort of routine, and maybe even achieve something.

Or are we being naïve yet again?

17

RATS

"... and forgive us our sins, for we ourselves
forgive everyone who is indebted to us."
Luke 11:4

One Sunday morning, while walking to the morning Malua church service, we drop in on John.

Walking through his open door, we see blood dripping down a wall and a dead body on the floor. It lies twisted in its death throes and smeared with congealed blood. An overturned chair and a saucepan on the floor suggest a lethal struggle, and nearby lies the obvious murder weapon - a blood spattered broomstick.

The dead body doesn't belong to John; he sits on a chair finishing a cigarette.

"I got one Ian," he confesses, with a satisfied smile. "It was a hard-fought battle, but good triumphed over evil."

Heather looks with horror at the bloody carnage, and dismay at the dead rat on the floor.

"Sorry, haven't been able to clean up yet," says John, waving his hand over the field of battle. "Still celebrating. The others got away, but they'll be back; there's always next time," he adds, tapping his smoke into a can.

Instead of fighting the Battle of Britain, John battles a persistent guerrilla campaign waged by infiltrating rodents. Like the Vietnam War, there are more nightly raids and skirmishes than pitched battles.

John has located the rodent Ho Chi Minh Trail to a hole in his flywire screen, and like the Americans in Vietnam, he's hoping technology will turn the tide of battle. Instead of closing the hole, he sets the two exposed wires from a modified electric toaster cord across the opening, plugs it into the 240V wall socket, and waits.

A few lizards, obviously deficient in the art of war, are fried to blackened crisps, but rats are not called 'cunning' for nothing. They studiously avoid the exposed electric wires, and deviously make new trails into John's kitchen.

Undeterred, John places a traditional mechanical rat trap on his kitchen bench. However, shrewd Samoan rats wised up long ago to the danger of traps, sharing their wisdom and lore with colleagues and offspring. The trap remains untouched.

One evening, some boarders knock on John's door with homework questions. While they talk, Lomitusi fiddles with the unset rat trap on the table.

"Careful Lomitusi," cautions John.

"Don't worry," says Lomitusi, "I know about traps."

John is unconvinced by Lomitusi's confidence but doesn't want to dampen his curiosity when he pulls back the spring arm, and carefully sets the trap. Then, Lomitusi slowly extends his index finger to touch the bait tab.

WHACK - the trap slams down. He winces, jerking his hand back with the trap dangling from his finger. John stares speechless and horrified.

Carefully extracting his unbroken finger, Lomitusi puts the trap back saying, "I don't like that trap."

Since high-tech and traditional methods fail to deter vermin ingress, John resorts to what works best, the nightly ambush with a broomstick. Few things are more satisfying to a noble knight defending his home, than visibly vanquishing an enemy by spilling blood and bashing brains on the battlefield. Waking to rat noises in the night, he grabs the broomstick, creeps slowly and carefully into the darkened hallway, flicks on a light and swings valiantly at the first rodent in reach.

Having pet mice as a child, and gone searching for field mice with friends, I have some affection for small rodents. Centuries of undeserved false accusations, rarely proved in a court of law, have severely damaged the rat's reputation. More like poverty-stricken parents petty thieving to feed their starving children, they're innocent victims of mainstream media bias, not least being blamed for the Black Death. Science now says the fleas spread the disease, exploiting the innocent rodents who were unwitting bystanders to the tragedy. Since then, media hysteria portrays the species as mass murdering, disease carrying harbingers of the end of civilisation.

Far from being a threat to humanity, wherever people have bravely explored the far reaches of the globe, rats have been there alongside their human partners, sharing the dangers, the hardship, the unbearable heat, and bitter cold. They also shared humanity's provisions, which from the rat's perspective, was only fair. And by taking early leave of any unseaworthy ship, rats have frequently performed a valuable early warning service to sailors, who were otherwise unaware the buoyancy of their vessels was under threat. All the rats expect in return for this valuable partnership is a little food.

Heather is not convinced of the historic benefit of the human-rodent partnership. She shows ambivalence towards their innocence with respect to crimes against humanity, and feels very differently about sharing her home with any rodent like creatures, small, large or otherwise. And while rats have rights too, and I'm sure they have a vital role to play in our ecosystem, it doesn't mean we have to share our home with them uninvited, or our food. So far, while we see rats scurrying from house to house on the power lines, and hear them in our roof each night, they haven't infiltrated our home.

Not yet.

As an experienced teacher himself, Tavita knows the value of being able to provide student worksheets. Realising their production consumes much of our valuable time, Tavita successfully lobbies the church authorities to purchase a photocopier.

It's the smallest photocopier I've ever seen, and when it's delivered from New Zealand, I wonder how it will survive Samoa's salty air and lack of maintenance. We soon have it chugging away, but the rate at which it consumes expensive paper and toner alarms Tavita. He rations it's use, so it's only for urgent copying, or what the Gestetner can't do.

"I thought they might have a spirit duplicator," I say to Helen one afternoon.

"What's that?" she asks, as she types a stencil.

"A little machine that wets the paper and uses a coloured stencil."

"Like a Roneo?"

"Yeah - a Roneo."

"I think there's one in a staffroom cupboard, but no one knows how to use it." She types a few more letters before saying, "Anyway, it's probably broken."

Roneos used a simple ink stencil fitted to a rotating drum, and an organic solvent that smells wonderful. As a student, I fondly remember teachers arriving in class with newly Roneoed worksheets that were literally intoxicating. Holding damp worksheets to our faces, we inhaled hallucinogenic vapours that transported us to our very own happy place, and probably also dissolved a few brain cells.

In a staff room cupboard, I find the machine in pieces alongside a box of blank stencils. Re-assembling it at home, and using methylated spirits for fluid, I soon have it working.

Newly liberated from the tyranny of the Gestetner machine, and the frugally rationed photocopier, I use the spirit duplicator for all worksheets except end of term exams. While it's true successful operation requires some tradecraft peculiar to the machine, it's easier to operate than the Gestetner. Surprisingly, other teachers show little interest in it, and it becomes our personal printing device.

When I ask Tavita to pay for more bottles of methylated spirits, he seems disturbed at how much I'm using. In Samoa, metho is expensive too, and it's sad to think improved education depends on something as simple as a bottle of methylated spirits.

Now that we've broken some physical barriers to giving students homework, we're frustrated to find many don't do it. While initially that's no surprise, we're surprised when the primary complaint is that they have to do their housework before homework, and then it's dark.

"What housework?"

"Sweep da *fale*, wash da clothes, make da food, scrape da taro."

While thinking that's just a typical student excuse (some tried the same excuse at my Australian school), John confirms the problem is serious for Upper Five and Form Six students.

"Culturally, they're supposed to work and serve their elders. Many parents think kids learn at school and don't understand the need to study at home. They think the kids are just shirking housework."

We're sympathetic now we have experience working without power and running water. I imagine Avele working till dark before trying to study sitting cross-legged on the *fale* floor by a flickering lamp. It's clear that for students to do homework instead of housework, then change - behavioural or cultural - is necessary.

After three hours of teaching each morning, we look forward to morning tea in the staff room. Rostered on prefects serve 'tea' and something to eat.

At first, our ingrained Australian culture suggested being served by students was like slave labour. But now we accept the rightness of our adopted culture. And from our student's point of view, it's a privilege to serve, and it's culturally right - the younger should serve the older. Since everything revolves around relationships in Samoa, it's also an opportunity for them to build relationships with their teachers, including the new palagis.

One day when Sydney and A'a are on duty, A'a offers me a cup to hold, while Sydney pours out 'tea' from a large kettle.

Sydney has her hair set in a beautiful French plait. She would have laboured long doing her hair early in the morning. They might live in simple circumstances, and wash in the village pool, or shower under a standpipe, but they always come to school immaculately groomed; their blouses spotlessly white, and the pleats of their skirts carefully ironed.

Taking a sip of the lukewarm liquid, today's beverage lottery has delivered the taste of tea with a hint of coffee. Depending on the diligence of yesterday's kettle rinsing, and the prefect's preference, we drink tea, coffee, or tea flavoured coffee, or coffee flavoured tea, with or without sugar, all poured from the same kettle. If there is sugar, it's sure to be laid on thick.

"Mostly tea today," I tell Heather.

"Oh good," she says, eagerly taking a cup.

A tray of *pani popo* (sweet buns covered in sugary coconut sauce) beckons from the nearby table. Every day a bakery in Apia delivers something - like pork buns, German buns or sweet dumplings. After three hours teaching in the heat, I'm always hungry by morning tea and need the sugar hit to finish the day. Whether overcooked and burned, or undercooked and doughy, they're always welcome. Sometimes they arrive too late for morning tea, and we feel famished teaching the last two periods.

But biting into the pastry and savouring the sweet taste, I look down to see dead insects in the pastry - like currents in a current bun. About five millimetres long, and dark brown, I clearly see their heads and little legs protruding from their torsos.

"There are weevils in the *pani popo,*" I say.

John looks over and raises his eyebrows. Heather hasn't started on her bun, so she tears it in half and sees weevils too. She frowns and is not happy.

Meanwhile, Olivia takes a bite from her bun. "It tastes good," she says. "Don't worry about the weevils. They're baked so they should be sterile. Think of them as a protein supplement."

Since Olivia, John, and I, are hungry, we eat our buns with relish, receiving a necessary energy burst to teach the day's last two classes. Heather declines her weevil protein supplement, preferring fasting to eating insects.

One day, when I return to my classroom after the tea break, I find it completely empty of students. Then I notice the entire school seems strangely quiet - there are no students anywhere in sight.

Or teachers.

They've suddenly vanished.

Tammy walks by with all her books in her arms, looking like she's going home.

"Hey Tammy, where are the students?"

She stops, rolling her eyes at me. "School's dismissed. I dunno why, but I guess there's no water again."

"Why didn't someone tell me?"

"Who knows, I just found out myself. Anyways, time to go home," she adds, like it's something that happens every day.

I like to have a plan, and I've planned out the year's curriculum. I feel that when I have a plan, I can be confident, knowing each small step, each class lesson, is a step on the journey to achieving my goal. Above all, an achievable plan gives hope, and to work without a plan seems defeatist and irresponsible. But now my lesson plans are totally screwed up, and I feel deflated and annoyed. Now I'll have to make a new plan.

John joins us as we walk home, while in the distance a few straggling teachers and students walk to the road.

"This happens a lot," says Tammy.

"Happened at Tuisivi too," says John, "for one reason or another."

"Why didn't Tavita announce it at our morning tea break?" I ask in frustration.

"Tavita's gone to Apia," says Tammy. "He probably told Iosefa, who told a few Samoan teachers and thought everyone else knew."

Somehow, the students, and everyone else, always seem to know what's going on, while we're completely in the dark, the last to know anything.

Tavita tells us later that officially he had to send the students home because the school has no water. Unofficially, he went to Apia to chase the carpenters who are supposed to be building desks. They didn't turn up for work until nine, and then inexplicably disappeared into Apia for the rest of the day.

We thought the restoration of power and water might bring some stability and routine. Instead, it feels like the uncertainty, chaos, and confusion, just stepped up a gear. We live on a bed of shifting sand, making lesson plans so we can teach the curriculum, only to have classes shift, mysteriously vanish, or slip away like soap in a bath.

Then, one morning Tavita is quietly angry.

The previous morning, he attended an important meeting in Apia, leaving Iosefa to run the staff meeting. Seeing Tavita's absence, some Samoan teachers abandoned their classes and went home. He has to chastise these teachers and discourage that sort of behaviour. But while Tavita has some authority as the church appointed principal, and some cultural clout as a *matai*, he's younger than some teachers, and more important *matais* outrank him.

He begins by raising a different matter.

"If students are absent, they must bring a note from their parents. If not, send them home until they bring a proper note."

While he addresses all staff, everyone knows he's talking to the palagi teachers, who have a deserved reputation for being a soft touch - easily manipulated by the superior cunning of Samoan teenagers.

We know this, but we and our students find ourselves between a rock and a hard place.

Most of the parents don't speak or write English, and our limited Samoan can't detect student forgeries. If the parent can't read or write Samoan, they must ask the student's aunt, uncle, or even pastor to write the note. Alternatively, they might have the student write the note in English, which we understand, but then it looks like a forgery.

We accept these notes because it's the best a student can do and think it's better for a student to be in class than wandering the streets of Apia.

Tavita recommends a Samoan teacher review the provenance of each note. But without knowing the student well enough to judge a forgery, the Samoan teachers often just shrug their shoulders, and by the time we do all that, the day is over.

Of course, we know Tavita's notes reminder is really a face-saving prelude to his real message.

He first apologises to the palagi teachers because he needs to speak in Samoan. Partly because he's ashamed of his own people and wants to speak only to them, but also because English lacks the utility, weight, and emotional leverage of Samoan.

A skilful *matai* needs to be a great orator, and we know Tavita carefully chooses his words for maximum effect. He talks quietly and gently, and although we don't understand his words, we feel the tension in the air. Without yelling, table thumping, or visible display of anger, he leverages shame to induce improved future behaviour. We're not supposed to know what's happening, even though we do, so we deliberately act bored by the whole procedure, to save face for our fellow teachers.

Meanwhile, we think the behaviour of these teachers is unforgivable. While we work hard, sacrificing our time and risking our health, they take it easy. It appears to us that poor teaching in lower grades makes our work that much harder. Such behaviour makes Tavita ashamed of his own people.

But our problem is that we work too hard, tempted to meet every need in the stream of urgent needs constantly flowing by, fearful we'll end up collapsing like Ramon. But seeing a need isn't the same as hearing God's call. Just because something can be done, doesn't mean we should do it.

To discourage laziness, our hardworking parents and palagi culture had admonished us "don't put off till tomorrow what you can do today". The idea we might work ourselves into the ground, fighting battles we can't win, wasn't on their horizon. While it's countercultural to put things off till tomorrow, for us, it's become a necessary survival skill.

While we frequently wish Samoans wouldn't put things off till tomorrow, we're beginning to appreciate the value they place on prioritising time and effort towards wellbeing and survival, instead of achievement. But it's going to take us a lot more time fighting fruitless battles before we change our approach. Perhaps hard times are always necessary to learn hard lessons, and maybe we can't truly find boundaries without crossing them first.

Meanwhile, the palagi teachers argue and discuss what to teach and how to teach it. John thinks chemistry is useful to anyone in a Samoan village, but he'd like to focus on practical knowledge and less on passing the exam.

Most students are going to fail anyway, so why not?

Because we all know there are one or two bright students in each class who might pass and even get to university. Should we diminish the opportunities of the two academically strong students for the sake of the others?

It's not a new problem in teaching, but Heather is the only trained and experienced teacher, so it's new to the rest of us. In my case, the subject matter is also new.

"I think I'll need help with General Science Biology," I say to Olivia one afternoon. I avoided biology at school (too much memorisation) in favour of the simple mathematical elegance of physics. Now my youthful disdain for biology might return to haunt me. "Form Four was the last time I did any biology."

"What level is that here?"

"Maybe Lower Five?"

"Well, we don't start biology till third term, so you've got plenty of time. Tammy and I can bring you up to speed."

"There's nothing to it Ian," adds John, with the supreme confidence of someone who doesn't teach biology.

"I remember dissecting a frog in Form Four," I say.

"Well, y'not gonna dissect any frogs here," says Olivia, refocussing back on her work. "There are no frogs in Samoa."

"Really?"

"Zilch - it's a problem with the textbooks here, because the kids don't even know what frogs are, and they hear tadpoles become frogs and get really confused. You'll have to dissect something else."

"Don't worry Ian," says John, "there's plenty of rats!"

Now that physical barriers raised by the cyclone devastation are disappearing, it becomes clear the most pressing problem isn't lack of time or resources, but people's behaviour - whether absent teachers, runaway carpenters, or misunderstanding parents. People can choose to be better, but frequently choose otherwise. While God teaches us patience, we find it easier to be patient with the weather, the lack of power, water, food, and even the rats, than with people. We accept we have no control over the weather but think people ought to do what we think is right; as though giving us some measure of control. But we don't control people. Instead, God asks us to pray for the patience, forbearance, and willingness to forgive the debtors who wrong us.

Although we hold everyone responsible for their choices, we know culture influences behaviour, and there are cultural pressures we know nothing about. We hope there's more reason for teachers absconding other than being lazy or selfish. For it seems to us, no teacher would abscond unless their behaviour was at least partially culturally acceptable to their village community or family. To understand the motivation for such behaviour, we need to better understand Samoan village culture - the beating heart of the *fa'asamoa*.

But how do we spend time in villages and engage with village culture, when we're so mired in schoolwork? We feel frustrated, having been in the country nine weeks, we're yet to set foot in a real Samoan *fale* in a real village.

18

ELISAPETA

"For where two or three are gathered in my
name, there am I among them."
Matthew 18:20

Some might argue we experience the *fa'asamoa* working at a Samoan school. But the school operates more like a palagi organisation, where we work alongside both palagis and Samoans. The school is a community, but not a Samoan village. We also walk through Utuali'i and Saleimoa, buying food at little *faleoloas* (stores), watching children play, and observing village life. But like visiting an aquarium, we see the fish, and they see us, but we don't swim with the fish. Until we experience a fish's life, we don't understand what being a fish really means. If we're not immersed into the life experience of our students, how can we truly understand them?

We've learned from Tammy, Helen, and John, who have all acquired (been adopted by) Samoan families and spent weeks at a time immersed in village culture. But we haven't yet grounded that learned cultural knowledge into our own lived experience.

"Ask a student if you can visit their family," suggests John.

"It's a good way to start," says Tammy.

We consider visiting Elisapeta, a very friendly, chatty girl (never lost for words) we both teach, living in nearby Le'auva'a village.

"She's well-mannered and from a good family," says Helen. "They should look after you properly."

One day, I ask Elisapeta to stay back after class. Initially looking worried, as if she's in trouble, her eyes light up when I ask if we can visit her family, like she just won the lottery.

"You come *to'ona'i?*" (Sunday lunch) she asks.

"*Ioe* (yes), if that's okay with your parents?" I add, not wanting to invite ourselves to lunch.

"You come church," she says, almost instructing me.

"We'd love to come to church," I respond, "But maybe ask your mother first?"

"*Popole fua,*" (don't worry) says Elisapeta dismissively, and smiling with obvious pleasure, says "*Fa'afetai tele lava,*" (thank you very much) before running off to join her friends.

While Heather is concerned we might have rudely invited ourselves to lunch, Leua says not to worry.

"They'll expect you to come for a meal, it's an important part of Samoan hospitality. You should bring a gift though, something they'll appreciate, like a tin of *pisupo*" (tinned corned beef).

"How big?"

"Oh, say a kilogram tin. I wouldn't worry too much, just make sure you bring a gift."

On Friday Elisapeta hovers behind after the final form class. "I come Sunday morning," she says, "catch bus to Le'auva'a."

"We can meet you at Le'auva'a," I say.

"*E leai*" (no), I come here, she says firmly, as I sense our roles suddenly reverse. Elisapeta has become my teacher.

"Okay, what time?"

A confused look crosses her face, before she declares, "I come eight o'clock."

At eight o'clock Sunday morning, filled with excitement and apprehension in equal measure, we're dressed and ready. While we know better than to expect Elisapeta to arrive promptly at eight, we wait patiently, hoping to see her approach our house.

Nine o'clock, and there's still no sign of Elisapeta. Not knowing when their church service starts, we worry we'll be late.

Nine-thirty, and no Elisapeta.

"Maybe she thinks we're coming next Sunday?" suggests Heather.

"She might be sick."

"May she's forgotten?"

"Hard to imagine. She looked excited."

A little later, a girl in a white dress steps from a bus and walks down the laneway. She carries a blue umbrella, wears a white hat, and makes a beeline for our house.

"Elisapeta's here," I announce.

Appearing at our back door, effervescent with excitement, and sweating with exertion, she seems in a hurry.

"*Malo* Elisapeta," says Heather.

"*Malo*. You come now?" she asks expectantly.

"We're ready; we've been waiting since eight o'clock."

She looks confused. Obviously, the "meet at eight o'clock" idea was something she said to help the palagi, who for some obscure purpose, needed a meeting time.

"We go now," she says earnestly.

Feeling like a chastened student, I pick up my daypack containing the tin of *pisupo*.

"The bus come!" she adds more urgently, like we're dragging our feet and making her late.

Walking to the road, Elisapeta sets a cracking pace - no leisurely Samoan saunter today. It's becoming a familiar experience. We spend hours patiently waiting, surrounded by relaxed, indolent Samoans, who then frantically rush about in panic-stricken haste, suggesting we're holding them up!

Hot and sweaty, we stop and wait for a bus. Although the sea breeze blows, it's oppressively hot standing in the sun, with no shade from the bare, cyclone-stripped trees. Elisapeta opens her umbrella to shade herself and Heather but ignores me.

Wearing a simple white dress with red trimmings matching her red school thongs, it's obvious she's wearing her best outfit. A few strips of expensive, hand sewn lace, decorate the wide brim of her white hat. The dress was probably hand made by someone in her village - perhaps her mother, aunt, or neighbour. All precious, it's probably handed down by an older sister or cousin.

Elisapeta soon flags down a bus, and we're on our way. Le'auva'a is a village founded by people who relocated from Savai'i after the Mount Matavanu volcano erupted eighty years earlier. As the slow-moving lava approached the villages of Mauga and Samalae'ulu, they moved to land gifted by people on Upolu, creating new villages.

There are no signs showing where each village starts or ends (one merges into another), but Elisapeta painfully jabs my ribs to signal "time to get off".

"How much is the fare?" I naively ask.

"No pay," says Elisapeta dismissively, as she gets up.

Putting coins into a tin near the driver, she pays our fares. Being wealthier than Elisapeta's parents, I feel a little embarrassed, but such generosity is an important part of Samoan hospitality. In response, we have a tin of *pisupo* in my daypack, and we're told further exchanges of generosity will accompany our developing relationship.

We join a scattered throng of well-dressed people converging on the village church. Even children wear simple but obviously formal clothes. Many girls wear white dresses, while the boys and men wear *ie faitaga*. Women wear hats and *puletasi* in a variety of colours, but white and cream dominate. Since no men wear hats, I wonder if the hat wearing is a religious observance, or just fashion. While their dress looks quaint to palagi eyes, like stepping back to our grandparent's time, white clothing and a wide-brimmed hat is both beautiful and sensible in Samoa's climate.

The Le'auva'a Congregational Church is one of the large, white, concrete buildings, that so impressed us on our first day in Samoa. We walk up steps to a semi-circle patio in front of a large entrance doorway. Two men sit behind a table with a large ledger book, and an offering plate filled with notes and coins. As a middle-aged Samoan woman puts money in the offering plate, a man writes in the book.

As we enter the building and walk down the aisle together, many heads turn to scrutinise us. Elisapeta appears pleased; her visiting palagi teachers are on display, sitting in the wooden pew beside her.

Peering over the pew in front, two pairs of children's eyes stare shamelessly at us like we're exotic animals; having probably never been close to palagis before. When I smile at them, they duck down, and giggle. The woman sitting next to them, perhaps their mother, looks with scorn as she swats their heads down with her fan.

Is the woman sitting near us, wearing the colourful green *puletasi*, Elisapeta's mother? Or the older woman on the other side in the white dress with the frilly hat? Since no one is going to introduce us, we feel bad. Being ignorant and unskilled palagis, we forgot to do our homework and ask Elisapeta about her family - the names of parents, siblings, who's married, and who isn't.

We sweat in sweltering heat, because unlike a *fale*, the church is a palagi style building with walls blocking the cool sea breeze. Many people fan their faces with *ili* (fans). Seeing we have no fan, the woman in the white dress gives an *ili* to a young boy, who runs to Heather, putting it in her lap.

As Heather says *"fa'afetai,"* (thank you) the boy runs back to the woman, who scowls at him. The boy delivered the fan, so why did she scowl? We're confused, unsure what to make of it. Did we get the boy into trouble?

There's no music before the service, just a buzz of voices, and the occasional 'whack', signalling realignment of some child's behaviour to their parent's preference.

Hearing a clang, clang noise, I realise someone is ringing the church bell by hitting a gas cylinder hanging from a nearby tree. Sensing church is about to start, I retrieve our Samoan Bible and hymn book from my pack. When the pastor announces the first hymn, we miss the rapidly spoken Samoan, but Elisapeta finds it for us.

Expecting to stand, like in a church service at home, we're surprised when everyone sings while seated. But their loud, thunderous voices blend in harmonious, perfect pitch, without any musical instruments, filling the building, and the village, with heavenly music, uplifting and stirring the depths of our souls.

Almost no one uses a hymnbook - they all sing from memory. Fortunately, we recognise the tune and sing along reading the Samoan words in the hymnbook, without understanding their meaning. While we can't speak the language, and our cultures are very different, we find ourselves singing in worship together in a unity that transcends culture, language, and time.

We experience the tangible reality of the apostle Paul's words *"Here there is neither Greek nor Jew ... barbarian, Scythian, slave or free, but Christ is all and is in all"*. It's no surprise music plays such an important role in Christian life and worship. For music is a universal language, awakening beauty in the hardest heart, and hope in the most downcast spirit.

Fascinated to learn Samoans sing in harmonies they call 'voices', without reading music, we wonder how they know what note to sing? It could be because they're surrounded by music and dance from birth, but I'm open to the idea it's in their DNA - God's special gift to Polynesian people.

Like a rippling brook, Samoan vowels, long, short, and joined together, bubble and modulate their way over the rocks and pebbles of teeth and tongue, swirling in rhythmic eddies of accentuation, intonation, and inflection. It's a language of singing spirit, sound, and song.

After various words from the pastor, followed by another hymn, someone reads a passage from the Bible. Again, we fail to understand, and can't find it in our Samoan Bible. But no one else looks at a Bible; they sit listening and fanning themselves in the heat.

The pastor then preaches his sermon. We catch a few words here and there but understand little. Feeling bored, my eyes wander around the concrete church walls, and my mind follows.

The church interior is plain. There are pale green painted walls without decoration, except for patches of ubiquitous mould - probably inflamed by the recent cyclone. The church obviously survived Cyclone Ofa, perhaps due to its high peaked roof and reinforced concrete structure. I expect many villagers found refuge here; people whose *fales*, even if they survived, offered no protection from the wind, rain, and flying debris. Churches have long been a refuge in time of trouble - from rampaging enemies, for body and soul, a quiet place to pray, a shelter from the storms of life, and all that threatens our peace of mind.

When a young child in front makes a noise, an elderly woman sitting behind leans over and whacks him over the head with her hand. The child doesn't cry but settles back into his seat. His grandmother perhaps? A neighbour?

I see moulded gothic arches - a medieval architectural invention enabling cathedral builders to create large, light filled spaces. Although the reinforced concrete here doesn't need a gothic arch for strength, it's here, on a tropical island, eight hundred years and half a world away from the first arches of medieval Europe.

After what seems like an eternity to us, the pastor finishes, and we sing another hymn in thunderous voices.

Then the two men we saw at the entrance doors walk to the front. Holding the ledger book, they read out names followed by:

"... *sefulu tala*, ... *lima tala, lua sefulu tala* ... " (quantities of money).

When a man walks to the front, they stop reading while he gives them money. They make an entry in the book before continuing: "...*tolu sefulu tala...*"

"What's happening Elisapeta?" whispers Heather.

"Peoples give money," says Elisapeta.

We gathered that much, but it appears they're publicly announcing how much each person gave. Surely not?

Another woman gives more money: "... *fa sefulu tala* ... "

Perhaps they're fund raising for a building program? That would make more sense. Maybe we should ask Leua?

The men finish and as they walk away, the pastor prays, before everyone stands up to leave.

We expect people to congregate and chat, perhaps welcome us, or even meet the pastor, like we would at home. After all, the church is a community, isn't it? But everyone ignores us, and Elisapeta makes no effort to greet anyone. Swept out with the stream of people passing through the doors, we're soon walking down the front steps. Elisapeta opens her umbrella to shade herself and Heather.

Walking down the road, we're delighted to see Patisepa, a student in my class, wave from the opposite side, dressed in an *ie solosolo* and obviously working.

"Patisepa doesn't look like she's been to church," I say.

"Patisepa seven day," says Elisapeta.

"Seventh day Adventist?"

"Ioe" (yes).

"She went to church yesterday?"

"Ioe, aso to'ona'i" (yes, Saturday).

Says Heather, "I have relatives who are Seventh Day Adventist."

"We say, *fitu aso, leai se ka'ele,*" says Elisapeta, which she translates as "seven days, no bath!" - laughing hilariously at her own joke.

We both smile because friendly rivalries and jokes between churches is culturally something we understand.

"Why doesn't Patisepa go to the Seventh Day Adventist school?" I ask.

"Her father say, 'Seven day school no good.' Bad!'" she emphasises by shaking her head.

I know enough now to realise "bad" could mean anything, but one thing it probably didn't mean, is poor academic standards. It turns out Patisepa's father's family had some sort of conflict with the principal, or the principal's family. Like most relationship conflicts in Samoa, the causes might be a little hazy, but they're universally the fault of the other party.

Turning into a narrow rocky road heading inland, we walk between brightly coloured *fales*. Fire smoke mingles with the distinctive odour of baked taro, *palusami*, and other *umu* baked foods, as families cook rice, heat kettles, and prepare *to'ona'i*, the most important meal of the week.

Parents sit in *fale*s directing children, who run hither and thither carrying bowls, dishes, kettles, and food.

Elisapeta soon turns off the road, heading towards a palagi style *fale* - rectangular, with a concrete floor, and a shallow, blue corrugated iron roof. Traditional Samoan *fales* have semi-circle shaped ends, and a high domed roof of coconut thatch. Instead of the traditional blinds of woven coconut branches, Elisapeta's *fale* has blue plastic tarpaulins on wooden rollers tied up under the roof eaves. The roof looks like it's been hammered into shape and nailed back onto the frame, suggesting Cyclone Ofa blew it off.

Stopping at the *fale* edge, Elisapeta slips off her *se'e vae*, and knowing one doesn't wear shoes in a *fale*, we remove ours too. When she directs us to a *fala* (mat), we carefully sit down cross-legged. She stays behind us out of sight, as an older couple enters the *fale* and sits opposite. Elisapeta doesn't make any introductions, and when I glance behind, she's gone, leaving us with two people we assume are her parents. Although she's changed clothes, I recognise Elisapeta's mother as the woman in the white dress in church.

After initial greetings of, "*Talofa lava*," and "*O a mai oulua*" (how are you both?) followed by, "*Manuia fa'afetai*" (assurances that we are well), it becomes apparent that Elisapeta's mother and father speak almost zero English. Coupled with our limited Samoan, the conversation quickly grinds to a halt.

I take the tin of *pisupo* from my pack and put it on the floor, saying it's a, "*Mea alofa*" (gift). Elisapeta's mother smiles saying, "*Fa'afetai lava*" (thank you very much) and calls out loudly to nearby children. A young teenage boy, perhaps Elisapeta's brother, takes the *pisupo* away.

We sit in silence again, trying to scrape together a few Samoan words to say something - anything to break the silence.

When Elisapeta's mother calls out loudly, a young boy appears thrusting a heart-shaped *ili* at Heather. Heather gratefully takes the fan saying, "*fa'afetai lava*" (thank you very much) to the boy. He shows no recognition or acknowledgement and immediately runs off. Perhaps he didn't understand?

Elisapeta's mother calls out loudly again, and another young boy presents Heather with a *niu* (green drinking coconut), pre-cut and ready to drink. A moment later a young girl, around seven years old, gives me a *niu,* and then runs away, as if she's scared, or embarrassed, it's hard to know.

Are they the children we saw in church? It's difficult to know because they've all changed clothes. Elisapeta suddenly reappears wearing an old tee shirt and *ie solosolo,* while other children are similarly dressed in faded, and slightly ragged clothing - a total contrast to their church attire. Since there are no bedrooms, or any other rooms, how did they change so quickly with no one noticing?

We're thirsty and *niu* are always refreshing. But drinking from the cut coconut, juice dribbles down our chins onto our clothes. Unlike orange juice, *niu* juice isn't sweet and sticky, so it probably doesn't matter, but our clumsiness embarrasses us.

Since we might be the first palagis Elisapeta's parents have hosted, they're probably uncomfortable too. While it's obvious we can't carry on a normal conversation in Samoan, it's also clear they're surprised and pleased whenever we try to use what we hope are appropriate Samoan words and phrases. They politely sit with us, probably also pondering what to say and do.

I wish Elisapeta would sit with us and translate. But while we see her come and go, directing the younger children, and getting some linen from a large chest, she otherwise ignores us. Is that because, compared to us and her parents, she's too far down the social hierarchy?

A shirtless young man with long, ragged hair, steps into the *fale*, and sits near Elisapeta's mother. Wearing a dirty, faded *ie solosolo*, it's clear he hasn't dressed up for the occasion, and has been roped in to translate.

"What is your age?" asks Elisapeta's mother via the young man.

"Lua sefulu valu (twenty-eight), and *lua sefulu fitu"* (twenty-seven).

"How long married?"

"Three years, nearly four," we say, thinking this is good because it suggests we have a level of maturity.

"How many children?"

"We have no children."

Elisapeta's mother's face falls, and she shakes her head.

"What's wrong?" I ask.

"She say, 'No children, and married four years.'"

"Talofa e" (what a pity), adds Elisapeta's mother sadly.

To be married at twenty-seven without children is a Samoan catastrophe. Most Samoan girls were married by twenty and have three or four children by our age. A family with eight or nine children is normal. We're obviously troubled by a severe health problem.

"We hope to have children one day," I say.

The young man translates, but then a long conversation with Elisapeta's mother follows, suggesting he's doing more than just translate. Her frown changes to a smile before she laughs heartily.

"I tell her palagis have good family planning," he says with a grin. "Now she understand."

We heard improving family planning has been a decades long government program, partly to limit a predicted population explosion. While parents are aware of family planning methods, we heard the concept is counter cultural and unpopular. Samoans love a large family of healthy, well-behaved children. Not only do the children contribute to the family (work), they're also a symbol of admiration and success, along with security for old age.

The government needn't have worried about a population explosion. Fast forward thirty years and the best export from Samoa has been its own people. While the population in Samoa today is similar to what it was in 1990, there are now three times that number living overseas, sending back money in US, Australian and NZ dollars. Emigration has made Samoa more prosperous, enabling communities and families to pay for the growing import of manufactured goods, including cheap ready-made clothes.

While the personal nature of these questions is a little confronting, we know Elisapeta's mother is simply raising subjects important to any married Samoan woman; having lots of children and bringing them up to marry one day and produce grandchildren. Our lack of children frequently emerges in conversation on family visits and referring to 'good family planning' always puts a smile on our hosts' faces.

I ask where they sheltered from the cyclone.

"You were here in cyclone?"

"*Ioe*" (yes).

Elisapeta's mother looks impressed, perhaps seeing us with newfound respect.

"Cyclone very bad," says the young man. "We go to school" (village primary school).

"What about your *fale* and plantation?"

Elisapeta's father waves at the roof as the young man translates, "*Fale* roof blow away, but we put the roof back."

"*E leaga tele*" (very bad), says Elisapeta's mother shaking her head sadly.

Children appear carrying dishes of food, and Elisapeta's mother directs where to place them on the floor. We identify *umu* baked food - *talo* (taro), *i'a* (fish) wrapped in foil, and *palusami*. Also, cold palagi food - *pisupo* (canned corned beef), *supageti* (spaghetti from a can) and *masi sao* (Arnotts Sao biscuits). There are spoons for us in case we don't eat with our hands.

"Eat!" says Elisapeta's father abruptly.

As we eat using our hands, like we learned at Moira Walker's *fiafia*, weeks earlier, we feel like we fit in. The *umu* baked Samoan food is delicious, but not the cold palagi food, which we suspect is there in case we don't like Samoan cuisine. To be polite, we eat a little of everything.

When I ask Elisapeta's father, "Did you catch the fish?" her mother laughs, looking at her husband with derision.

Her father smiles saying, *"E leai"* (no), and I hear *i'a* (fish) and *va'a* (boat).

The young man translates. "He have no boat, not know how to fish. He buy fish from man in village who has boat - *o le paopao"* (dugout canoe).

I tell him I would like to buy a *paopao* and go fishing.

Elisapeta's father raises his eyes and smiles.

"He say *paopao* cost many *tala,"* translates the young man.

"Does he know where I can buy a *paopao?"*

"E leai" (no), says Elisapeta's father, shaking his head.

While they talk with us, Elisapeta's parents look outside the *fale* to avoid eye contact. While we know they're being polite, we still feel unsettled, as though lacking their full attention. The habit of looking directly at someone while speaking is so embedded in our subconsciousness palagi mind, it seems impossible to change.

While they studiously avoid eye contact, we know they watch us carefully. They look pleased when we eat the taro and *palusami*, and Elisapeta's mother sometimes calls out to Elisapeta or another child, who then appears offering some implement, or another dish of food.

"Manaia tele le mea ai" (the meal is very nice), says Heather, taking the opportunity to practice some language.

"Manaia le i'a" (the fish is nice), I add.

Samoans don't put value on served food being hot, so everything is lukewarm or cold. To ensure food is eaten hot, the family needs to align serving the meal with building the *umu*, the church service, and their guests' arrival; an almost impossible feat when few people have clocks or watches.

In a society that doesn't use timepieces, timeliness is not only unimportant, but also meaningless. What matters is availability - being available when an event or task arises. Elisapeta expected us to be available when she arrived to travel to her village. Similarly, Elisapeta's parents expect the *umu* to be cooked, and food prepared, so that whenever church finishes, or whenever we arrive, the food is ready, whether hot, lukewarm, or cold.

While people laugh about 'Pacific time', meaning an event starts an hour or two late, unless everyone has access to time, it neither makes sense, nor is it possible to run on time, or be on schedule. Meanwhile, palagi cultures pile needless stress on themselves attempting to cram as many events as possible into their available days, using the omnipresent time, such as clocks in cars, at bus stops, on walls, watches, and now phones.

My foot and joints ache from sitting cross-legged. Although we sit on *fala*, it still feels as hard as concrete. I need to change positions but need to avoid pointing my feet at our hosts. Since I'm still adjusting to wearing a skirt, I also wonder how I can adjust my legs with appropriate discretion. Realising it's something I should have practised before we came, I decide to suffer in pain rather than risk offence. Seeing Heather squirm, a little, I guess she's feeling the same pain.

I also begin to wonder if the young man in front of us is a wayward relative, because I have the feeling he hasn't been to church, and there's something about his manner that's different to Elisapeta's parents. While I can't explain what's different, I wonder if we're able to pick up signals that transcend culture?

We feel bad being unable to finish all the food on offer. But when we conclude we've eaten enough, Heather turns to Elisapeta saying, *"Ua o ma'ona"* (we have eaten enough).

"Ma'ona" (finished)? asks Elisapeta, confirming she heard right.

"Ioe" (yes).

After Elisapeta's mother calls out instructions, a child whisks food, and plates away. A plastic bowl of water appears in front of us with a neatly folded tea towel. After washing our hands in the bowl, and drying them using the towel, another child takes them away.

A young girl places two cups before us and Elisapeta pours tea from a kettle - lukewarm, weak, and very sweet, a welcome injection of fluid and sugar.

Meanwhile, in the next *fale* a few metres from ours, the children start their meal. It's customary in Samoan culture for the oldest, or most important people, to eat first, attended and served by the younger. When the most important have finished, the younger eat what's left, with the youngest children eating last.

Shrieks of laughter emanate from the children's *fale*; the sound of raucous revelry suggests their meal is a livelier affair than our quiet and respectful conversation. We look wistfully across at the party and wish we could join the children; unfortunately, it's not possible when we're honoured guests.

However, perhaps we shouldn't feel bad about failing to eat all the food placed in front of us. Perhaps we weren't expected to eat it all, because we realise anything left over is being appreciated by the teenagers and young children.

Eventually Elisapeta's father says something we don't understand. Then they all get up, leaving us alone in the *fale*. Knowing I can't make any faux pas now, I finally adjust my sitting position to relieve the aching pain in my legs.

A little later Elisapeta rescues us, asking if we'd like to go for a walk around the village.

Unfolding our aching, stiff limbs from the floor, we slip on our thongs and sandals, as Elisapeta retrieves her umbrella. Sidling up to Heather, she holds her arm to keep her close under the umbrella's shade.

"Don't you like the sun?" I ask Elisapeta.

"*E leaga*" (bad), she says, wrinkling her nose.

"Why is it bad?"

"Make skin dark."

"Is dark skin bad?"

"Samoa girl - they wants white skin."

"White? Like mine."

"Like Eta," she says, looking at Heather in admiration.

"Is that beautiful?"

"*Ioe*" (yes), she says, "Samoa girls - they wants beautiful."

Elisapeta, like many Samoan girls, sees a pale complexion as desirable beauty. And Elisapeta is pretty - her friendly face, attractive smile, and dark, wavy hair, beautifully frame her olive complexion and dark eyes. Obviously, she carefully guards her lovely complexion from the sun, and naturally expects Heather to do the same.

"Many palagi want to make their skin dark," I tell her. "They lie in the sun to tan their skin brown."

Elisapeta looks puzzled, as though I'm telling her something that can't possibly be true.

"Sometimes they pay a lot of money to make their skin dark," adds Heather.

Elisapeta frowns, shakes her head, and looks affronted, as though we're deliberately lying or teasing her with a tall tale.

"It's true," I say earnestly.

"*Valea tele*" (very stupid), she spits contemptuously.

"What about me?" I ask, "don't I need pale skin too?"

"Ha," bursts out Elisapeta, covering her mouth with her hand. "You - man!" she says pointing at me, as though that says it all.

Walking back down the lane, we hear neighbours call out, "... *Elisapeta, o le a ... ai ... le palagi?*" Hearing the intonation of a question, we guess they're asking who we are.

"... *O'u faia'oga ... Leulumoega Fou...*" (my teachers, Leulumoega Fou) says Elisapeta, followed by a comment that makes the neighbour laugh.

Then the echo of another neighbour a little further away.

"Who's that with Elisapeta?"

"Her teachers from Leulumoega Fou," followed by more laughter.

Then another, "*E a?*" (what?)

More words follow about "palagi teachers from Leulumoega Fou", and so the news transmits from *fale* to *fale*, along with the joke, whatever it is they find amusing about us.

It crosses our mind that the whole village, possibly several thousand people, will soon know Elisapeta's palagi teachers visited her family today.

They attended church with Elisapeta?

Did they eat Samoan food?

Did they speak Samoan?

We expect they might read things into the event. It's also possible Elisapeta has read far more into our visit than is warranted. After all, out of all the students in our classes, we chose her to visit first, and that must mean something. It isn't every Sunday a palagi couple visit their church and join Elisapeta's family for *to'ona'i*.

So what does all this mean for Elisapeta and her family? As the story passes from person to person, growing with gossip through the village rumour mill, morphing through Chinese whispers, by the time it reaches the last person, it might be entirely different.

Finding ourselves back at Patisepa's *fale*, we chat with her briefly as she sweeps her house yard. Patisepa looks at us, partly curious, partly something else. Through the veil of teenage Samoan culture, I recognise the universal human emotion expressed on Patisepa's face - raw envy.

I wonder what impact this visit might have on our relationship with other students in our classes? Perhaps we should soon visit another student to avoid showing favouritism?

Then I realise what's happening; in Samoa, one thing happens on the surface, while another happens underneath. Ostensibly, Elisapeta is showing us her village, but actually she's showing us TO her village. We are the ones on parade, not the village.

Eventually finding ourselves back at Elisapeta's family *fale*, we take leave of her parents, saying "*Fa'afetai lava*" (thank you very much), and "*Tofa soifua*" (goodbye and good health). Then we walk with Elisapeta back to the roadside to wait for a bus.

It's Sunday afternoon, so there are few buses, and we wait for some time. Despite the gentle breeze blowing off the sea, it's oppressively hot, so we find a place under a shady tree sitting on a fence made of basalt rocks cemented together. Since my frame is pretty much devoid of any fat or muscle, the rock's uneven surface painfully digs into my flesh. To make a cushion, I put our Samoan Bible on the fence and sit on it.

Elisapeta's jaw drops, as she stares at me, horrified.

19

LOGOS

"In the beginning was the Word, and the Word
was with God, and the Word was God."
John 1:1

"**W**hat's the matter?" I ask.

"You sit on the *Tusi Pa'ia!*"

"The fence hurts," I say, jumping up as though sitting on hot coals. "Is it bad to sit on the Bible?"

"Samoan people not sit on *Tusi Pa'ia*. You are very bad."

Putting the Bible in my pack, I look around furtively, hoping no nearby Samoans saw my faux pas.

"We don't worry about that," says Heather. "It's what's inside the book that matters."

"Bad for Samoan," says Elisapeta, looking distressed. "We not put anything on the *Tusi Pa'ia* - not even cup."

"Really," says Heather, impressed by Samoan reverence for God's Word.

Then Elisapeta's face brightens. "But you are palagi," she says smiling. "You don't know. *Popole fua!*" (don't worry), she adds, pleased to find a ready excuse for my terrible behaviour. We're dumb, ignorant palagi; how would we know any better? Fortunately, Samoans are very tolerant and forgiving, with low expectations of palagis - low expectations I just amply justified.

Eventually, Elisapeta flags down a bus going past Leulumoega Fou. We climb up the steps, and as the bus takes off, wave goodbye through the window.

Practicing language and culture, even in a small way, confirms by lived experience, what has so far been second-hand knowledge. In a genuine village context, we've seen, heard, and lived many cultural experiences, and most importantly, we've begun to find our sense of place. For as palagi teachers, and as a married couple, Samoans have made a niche for us in their culture. We have our place, our station in the hierarchy, with its privileges and responsibilities. Whether we're comfortable with our privileges and responsibilities is irrelevant; they are thrust upon us.

We made a good choice visiting Elisapeta. Her effervescent personality made the day eventful, and her family were kind and hospitable. As the year progresses, Elisapeta continues to work on capturing our affections, and knowing her better, I also detect a hint of mercenary cunning that seems a little coquettish.

Being married provides some privileges that make integration into Samoan culture a little easier than if I were single. All the unmarried, male palagi teachers, are walking targets, fair game for any plucky female student intent on a life in New Zealand, Australia, or the United States. But although I'm married, and my wife is her English teacher, the barrier isn't high enough to stop Elisapeta trying to flirt with me. Or others apparently, because by the time we left at the end of the following year, I'm not surprised to hear Elisapeta is pregnant and married in that order. She had a little baby boy, and knowing Elisapeta, I expect she was very happy with all she accomplished.

When the bus stops by the Saleimoa store, we get off and buy a loaf of bread. Having been repaired since the cyclone, the store is even open for a few hours on Sunday, obviously for those like us, who lack essentials.

Walking along the road towards Leulumoega Fou, trees and *fales* silhouette the Saleimoa lagoon's bright blue water on our right. On our left a group of children carry buckets and saucepans, with strings of empty kettles hanging about their necks.

Seeing us, the children's eyes light up, and calling out "Palagi, palagi," they scamper across the road and mob us like paparazzi around movie stars.

Keen to try out his English, one boy looks at us sheepishly and says "Hello."

"Hello," we respond, smiling to encourage him, as the other children squeal into peals of laughter.

The speaking boy looks momentarily embarrassed, then thumps the boy next to him with his fist and a friendly skirmish breaks out. Hampered by the kettles hanging around their necks, they settle scores in an almighty racket.

"You like UB40?" asks another boy.

We care little for reggae, but we know Samoans can't get enough of it, and that UB40 is currently THE band of choice.

"*Ioe*" (yes), I say.

The boy suddenly launches off into singing, "*Cherry oh, cherry oh, baby,*" and the other children join in, effortlessly singing the English lyrics, or simulating the percussion instruments with their voices. They can't be more than twelve years old, but they're such excellent mimics they could be an a cappella cover band.

"Very good," says Heather, clapping when they finish.

"Can you do '*Red, red wine…*'?" I ask.

They launch into the song, each child singing a part or an instrument. Then they burst into laughter, and running across the road, call out, "*Kakou o*" (we go).

The sound of clanging kettles and saucepans fades as they disappear into a grove of trees.

Samoan children might play *volipolo* (volleyball), *lakapi* (rugby) and *kilikiti* (cricket), but they don't have toys like palagi kids. Instead, they work as soon as they're old enough to be useful, and effortlessly create their own entertainment. Mimicking older children and adults, they turn work into play, developing very early in life the skills necessary to survive and prosper in their community. And one way they turn work into entertainment, is to blend in song and dance.

In 1990, Samoan villages appear to largely function as oral societies, regardless of having had a written language for one hundred and sixty years. Typical of oral cultures, work, speech, song and dance, are threads woven into the fabric of life; a twisting pathway through a rich tapestry celebrating past tradition, and future hope, for every family and community.

Palagis use their writing skills to record notes in diaries, plan their future, or leave a permanent record of their past. But in oral cultures, people must use alternative, non-literate skills. When we can't read books, we get very good at reading people, and cultivate a reliable memory.

Not only is a good memory available to most people possessing a functioning mind, it's also conveniently always present, and costs nothing. While reading and writing provide more reliable and durable methods for palagis to record and plan, and may be essential for a more complex economy, palagi memory skills weaken and wither without exercise.

While other cultures rely on books and written records, in oral societies like Samoa's, it's non-literate, poetic art forms that transfer intergenerational history and complex skills necessary for survival. Rhyme, rhythm, and alliteration, are not just poetic devices, they're also aids to memory. They act as self-correcting mechanisms if an error wanders into the developing code of cultural DNA, enabling knowledge to be passed down accurately from generation to generation, without the need for writing.

Without theatre, film, musical instruments or literature, it's the human voice and movement that are the instruments, lyrics, and images that tell stories and move hearts. Poetry, song, and dance, not only beautifully express the full spectrum of human emotions, but also, they're activities in which almost everyone can participate - art forms needing nothing more than our voices and bodies. Music and song can also happen while we're doing other things - like carrying kettles, pots, and pans along a road. Young children, barely able to talk, can take part in the family *lotu* (service) - a peaceful moment of singing, prayer, and contemplation of God's gifts to us all.

Moreover, it's story, in prose, poetry, song or dance, that create the mind images that most stir our imaginations, enabling us to participate vicariously in the lives of people we'll never meet, places we'll never go, and live in past and future worlds. For a picture says a thousand words, whether conjured up by prose or poetic form, painted on a canvas, carved in wood, or danced in a story. Raw emotion, stirred by poetry and song, tugs our heartstrings, carving indelible images into our hearts and minds, to reach all that transcends our mundane existence. For it's through art, whether visual, poetic, or story, we open a window to the transcendent truth, beauty, and goodness of God.

For God is the Logos, the Word, and the knowing from which all our knowledge flows. God is the creator of all things, so all our art is a work of sub-creation using materials called into existence by the Logos. Made in the image of God, we create, weaving ideas, emotion, and narrative, into a structure of words, colour, and music, reaching deep into our hearts, wordlessly touching our deepest longing, and filling the God-shaped vacuum in our soul.

I'm not surprised God not only reveals himself through his creation, but also through an inspired body of written artwork; a collection of books filled with story, song, sublime poetry, and exquisite prose. Such art is perhaps the most effective way to reveal the transcendent reality of a transcendent God. For in story, we see transcendent truth in context, just as we're learning Samoan culture in the context of Elisapeta's family life. It's essential we learn transcendent truth, because elements like beauty, goodness, and love, form the bedrock on which we build our lives, and the axle about which our relationships turn; not only in our relationship with God, but also with each other.

Some complain the Bible isn't history, but it contains history, and without a knowledge of God, history has no purpose. Others complain the Bible isn't scientific, but it contains truth about our world, and without a knowledge of God, science can't say why we're here. Science can't help us find transcendent truth, because such truth speaks to our meaning and purpose, and we cannot detect, touch, or feel it. But we can reason the transcendent with our minds and know such truth in our hearts. Some complain the Bible doesn't condemn what we think is wrong, but without a knowledge of God, there is no good or evil, and as Dostoyevsky pointed out, *"everything is permissible"*. Without a transcendent God there is no goodness, beauty, or truth.

Great art is frequently misunderstood, and the Bible is no exception. Many misunderstand Bible stories, because the stories don't hold back from the grittiness of life. We read about a great hero who risks his life to save people, then murders a man to steal his wife. The story is not an example to follow, but a warning to us all, because while we're all made in God's image, we're all deeply flawed by the Fall. Good people do bad things; bad people can be very noble. Oskar Schindler was a greedy womaniser, war profiteer, and Nazi, but he risked his life to save more than a thousand people.

Since we seek to live our lives through the stories we tell ourselves, it's important to tell true stories. Stories we hear and tell, lay down the logos forming the bedrock of our lives, from which we draw a wellspring of emotion and ideas that stir those memories that so entwine us, they hold us together, and make us who we are. Sometimes I listen to UB40, not because I like reggae, but because in my stirred memories, I walk once again through Saleimoa in the company of happy, laughing children.

However, while Samoans are great lovers of music, they don't love all music.

"*E leaga*" (bad), says Vailuaga, hearing Mozart's Clarinet Concerto for the first time. He spits on the ground as though encountering a malevolent odour. As the clarinet's beautiful but haunting melody grows, he becomes visibly agitated and alarmed.

"*E leaga tele!*" (very bad), he says. Shaking his head in horror, he escapes, running away from the awful noise.

Typically confronted with Mozart, Beethoven or Tchaikovsky, Samoan students' faces crumple in visible distress, disgust, or horror.

"It's a great way to clear students away from your house," says John. "Play Puccini, it's like an air-raid warning - they run for cover!"

So whenever we want a relaxing, student free zone, we play classical music.

When Leua drops by that evening, I tell her, "A funny thing happened in church. Elisapeta's mother sent a boy to give Heather a fan, but when Heather thanked him, his mother seemed angry."

Leua smiles. "When you thanked the boy, his mother might worry he'll get a swelled head."

She explains that in Samoan culture, "You don't thank someone for doing their duty, because they're just doing what they should do."

"But what about encouraging him for obeying his mother?"

"Kids don't get much of that here. Not getting cuffed over the ear, or laughed at, is about all the encouragement they ever get."

"That's sad," says Heather.

"I know, it can seem hard on kids, but that's the way it is," says Leua, shrugging her shoulders. "It's what kids know and understand."

Although our students and teachers sometimes remind us not to thank people for doing their duty, we find it almost impossible to do. The sense of cultural rudeness is so ingrained into our palagi psyche from a young age.

"At the end of the service," says Heather, "they seemed to spell out how much money each person gave."

"Yeah, some churches do that," says Leua groaning.

"But why? Some people gave more money while they were reading it out."

"That'll be right. Someone's ashamed to hear their neighbour gave more than they did, so they give more."

Helen joins us after hearing Leua's voice from her house, keen to hear about our Elisapeta adventure.

"I've seen the same thing in Si'umu," says Helen, sitting down. "They pressure poor people into giving more money to the church - money they can't afford. I think it's disgusting."

"But you know giving is a really important part of Samoan culture," says Leua. "It's what we do, and the higher our status, the more we're expected to give."

"Sure," says Helen, "but isn't it about raising your status too? Aren't they saying, 'Look at me everyone, I gave more money than Sione over there.'"

"But," I say, "Jesus said we shouldn't let our left hand know what our right hand is doing, God loves a cheerful giver, and people shouldn't feel compelled to give."

"Well not here," says Helen. "Here they read it all out in public so they can shame poor people and scrape more money off of them."

"That's not right," says Leua. "Announcing people's gifts is what we do at every *fa'alavelave* (event) - like a village celebration, wedding, or funeral. Then it's all distributed publicly, so everyone knows who gave what and where it went."

"Like public accounting?" I suggest.

"Yeah, like accounting in an oral culture. It's all open, said in everyone's hearing, so everyone knows what happened."

I thought I was on Helen's side, but now I'm stunned by a new way of seeing, having given no thought to how public matters, accounting or otherwise, should be done in an oral culture. What would we do in Australia if most people couldn't read or write?

"Not all churches do it that way," says Leua, "and some pastors like my Dad discourage it in church. But his people insist on doing it because it's what they know and understand."

"Maybe," says Helen doubtfully, "I bet they also want to get more money and build a bigger church than the next village."

"But Leua," asks Heather, "how do they reconcile that with Jesus' teaching?"

"I think giving and distributing gifts this way is what people know and trust - we've probably been doing it like this for thousands of years. Even if many people want to change, it's still difficult."

The way Samoans come under pressure to support their *aiga* (family) or village, helps me understand why they insist on doing their public accounting 'in public'. While it might be open to unscrupulous people shaming others into giving more than they can afford, all systems are corruptible. We think our systems are better, but I now understand why Samoan villagers want a process they literally see and hear, to support their public confidence. A practice that's part of the fabric of their culture, is always going to gain people's trust more than an alien process they neither know nor understand.

"Isn't it a choice between Jesus' teaching and culture?" I ask.

"The *fa'asamoa* will always win that contest," says Helen.

"That's not true," says Leua.

What is true is that Jesus' claims have been a serious challenge to every culture from the moment he first preached the Sermon on the Mount two thousand years ago. "*Blessed are the meek,*" might seem sublime words today, but to the Greco-Romans the idea was morally wrong.

But while Jesus' teaching has influenced cultures throughout the world, cultures have also influenced Christian worship and practise since the earliest Christian church.

Romans celebrated the festival of Saturnalia on the winter solstice. To provide a Christian alternative, early Christians began celebrating the birth of Christ instead - now known as Christmas. Similarly, when Germanic cultures celebrated the birth of spring with Eostre's Feast, Christians in these cultures celebrated Christ's death and resurrection (Easter). They were similar concepts, the new life of Jesus' resurrection, and the new life of spring. At the time, many Christians worried these festival alternatives might infect Christian celebrations with pagan beliefs. They had good reason - chocolate Easter bunnies are a pagan hangover from Eostre's Feast.

Worshipping in a Samoan dominant culture increases our awareness of how modern Australian culture and values influence how we worship at home. As Presbyterians (originally Scottish), we have accumulated Celtic, Anglo-Saxon, Scandinavian, and Greco-Roman influences on our order of service, music, hymns, and even how we collect, check, and bank funds. How much of what we believe is right in church worship and practise, is simply self-justified cultural comfort?

On the other hand, shouldn't people express their worship of God in ways that are culturally resonant? After all, worship itself uses different forms of human expression and forms of art. Ways of singing, style of music, clothing, speaking, teaching, and prayer, are all influenced by our language, and language is the key that unlocks the door to any culture. While Jesus' words challenge every culture, each culture, time, and place, brings its own unique issues that need practical resolution. In Western cultures heavily influenced by Christianity, we take concepts like 'equality under the law' for granted, as though they're a universal truth. But what does equality mean in a culture as hierarchical as Samoa's?

It's universally true that we're all equally made in the image of God; something that sets us apart from animals and makes every human life equally precious to God. From the time Paul wrote, *"There is neither Jew nor Greek, …neither slave nor free, …no male and female,…"* his words have challenged and influenced philosophers, scientists, artists, monarchs, and lawmakers, resulting in, among other changes, the abolition of slavery and the United Nations Declaration of Human Rights.

But the application of that truth into cultural practice, and local laws, needs to work within the struggles, constraints, role expectations, and survival strategies of each culture. We need to have the humility and grace to recognise that each culture, in its time and place, may practically apply truth in ways difficult to understand when we look through our own cultural lens. It also requires change to ancient cultures that remain challenged by God's truth, including our own.

For are we any more ready for Jesus' challenge to our palagi culture? Are we eager to change? Samoans easily embrace Jesus when he says, "*Give to anyone who asks and whoever wishes to borrow from you, do not refuse him.*" But after two thousand years of Christian influence, palagi cultures still struggle with such generosity, while it's unthinkable for Samoans to do otherwise. It leaves me wondering if the partly literate culture of a Samoan village in 1990 might be closer to Jesus' time and place than modern palagi worlds. Hearing Jesus speak through Samoan village ears, might well provide new insight into Jesus' words; insight to which my modern palagi mind is still deaf.

We often attend the church service at the Malua Theological College with Tammy, and sometimes Leua, Latu and Anita join us. If the minister spots us in the congregation, they usually give a potted summary of the sermon in English just for us, before going on to preach in Samoan. It's a very kind gesture that we appreciate and makes us feel very welcome.

Ape invites us to *to'ona'i* with her family after church one Sunday. As Principal of the Malua Theological College, Ape's father shares his extensive knowledge of Samoan church history.

He says in the decades prior to John Williams' arrival in 1830, there was some contact with Wesleyan missionaries in Tonga, and some form of Christian presence. Samoan Christians brought Williams from Tahiti to Savai'i, where he met with the then current Samoan ruler, Maleitoa.

Ape's father says an ancient Samoan prophecy said, "People will come from over the sea and proclaim truth. Embracing the truth will stop fighting and bring about an era of great peace and prosperity."

Like many people groups, Samoans believed in one over-arching God called Atua. Understanding God described by the missionaries as Atua and believing their message of good news to be fulfillment of their prophecy, Maleitoa enthusiastically embraced the Christian message, spreading it throughout Samoa. The missionaries put the Samoan language into writing, created dictionaries and grammars, and began making permanent records of Samoan legends, history, and culture.

It's common to view missionaries coming to colonise, destroy traditional culture, and substitute a European way of life against the will of indigenous people. However, not only were missionaries welcomed into Samoa, but Samoans also wanted more. When the Congregational Church couldn't provide enough missionaries, some Samoan districts invited Wesleyan missionaries from Tonga, while others brought Catholic priests from Tahiti. Christian teaching influenced Samoan culture, but Samoans also incorporated their culture into their growing Christian thought and practise.

As for having a European way of life thrust upon them, for nearly two hundred years Samoans have been very adept at adopting what they find useful and ignoring everything else; much to the dismay of past European powers, current overseas aid organisations, and visiting palagis like us.

The view that colonising missionaries destroyed Samoan culture is both patronising and paternalistic - believing Samoans to be simple, powerless, and undiscerning people, easily hoodwinked by superior, crafty Europeans. But the Samoan people weren't hoodwinked by anyone, and their choices deserve our respect, and their discernment deserves our admiration.

After all, what culture isn't changing? Unless they're completely isolated from the world, all cultures change over time; influenced by neighbours, visitors or changing technology. Something as simple as a bus produces its own uniquely Samoan etiquette.

Prior to European arrival, Samoans engaged with Fiji and Tonga. Tongans even ruled Samoa for a long time (something unforgotten by Samoans). I'm as certain Tonga influenced Samoan culture, as I'm equally certain Samoans took what they wanted and 'Samoanised' it.

Samoans may have created the impression they're slow to change and touted by many as the cause of Samoa being one of the least developed countries in the South Pacific in 1990. But I think they're wisely cautious, and caution is an asset supporting a strong culture and a unique way of life that is seductive in its simplicity and beauty.

It's only been two months and we're irrevocably changed. Are we too being Samoanised?

20
TRAVEL

*"Blessed are you who are poor, for yours
is the kingdom of God."*
Luke 6:2

One afternoon in Apia, Heather bumps into Hannah, who says all the Australian volunteers are going to Vaipo'uli over Easter.

"Why not come with us?" suggests Hannah.

Vaipo'uli is a government school on the mysterious and legendary island of Savai'i, 'the Cradle of Polynesia'. We're keen to visit this important island, and the Easter break also promises to be a temporary retreat. A few days of immersion back in our own culture (not Samoan, or American), means we can talk without the constant cloud of potential miscommunication. And breaking from the confines of our school to the wider Samoan world, we hope to learn from Doug and Jill, and other Aussie teachers with Samoan teaching experience.

We think we'll catch an early bus to the wharf, buy tickets, and cross on the first ferry leaving at eight o'clock. Provided we catch the right bus at Salelologa, and get off at the right place, we should be with our friends for lunch. But there's only one ferry operating now from the damaged wharf at Mulifanua, and there'll be crowds at Easter. We want to be optimistic but feel daunted by the dark cloud of uncertainty that hangs over every plan.

Up at four-thirty, we eat a quick breakfast, sling packs on our shoulders, and carry string bags filled with food - gifts for our friends. Setting off for the main road, we thread our way through wet grass under shining stars. I feel tingling excitement and anticipation. The approaching sun brightens the dark horizon.

Standing in the dark by the roadside with our backs to the lagoon, we look hopefully for bus lights coming from Apia. Our shoes drip wet with dew, and our faces glisten with the first sweat of the day.

Where are Leua, Latu and Anita?

"Let's travel together," says Leua. "We can help you find the road to Vaipo'uli." They're spending Easter with their parents in a village near Vaipo'uli.

Hearing the growing sound of an approaching bus, lights appear around the bend, and we flag it down. Climbing the steps into the brightly lit cabin, I look hopefully behind us, but there's no sign of Leua in the darkness.

Perhaps she caught an earlier bus and they're already waiting at the wharf?

The bus travels briskly down the road, lurching around potholes and pigs. Goosebumps appear on our arms as the cool wind blows through the open windows. We pass dark *fales* full of sleeping families, occasionally stopping to pick up more people spending Easter with relatives on Savai'i. They carry bags of food, packs, and suitcases.

The sky is lighter at five-thirty when the crowded bus stops at the wharf. A good start. All is well.

We stand outside a crowd of people milling around a small wooden ticket office.

"Open six o'clock," says a woman standing next to us.

My heart sinks, knowing when the office opens, everyone will rush to buy tickets, and a melée will ensue. We've learned by now that queuing is cultural, and Samoans don't queue. At first, the absence of queues and frequent hustle was a curious novelty. Now I grit my teeth at the prospect of having to elbow my way through a crowd, like I do at the bank on Saturday mornings.

A growing line of cars, trucks, and pickups, wait to drive onto the ferry when the gates open. Fortunately, vehicles can't melée, so they queue. If only people here would do the same; life would be so much easier. At least for us. For everyone, as I see it.

We can't see any sign of the ferry.

"Come from Savai'i," says the same woman reading our thoughts.

We scan the crowd but can't see Leua anywhere.

Standing close as possible to the ticket office, Heather chats with an elegant young woman dressed in a beautiful sari standing beside us. Beside her stands her husband - a tall, thin man wearing a turban.

"We're teachers who got out of Burma," she says.

Another bus arrives, swelling the crowd around the ticket office.

Suddenly a ticket window opens and light streams out, revealing a man behind a counter. As expected, the crowd surges forward to the small window, forming a dense barrier of bodies. When our turbaned neighbour offers to buy our tickets too, we give him some money, grateful for his kindness.

When another bus arrives, we see Leua, Latu and Anita emerge carrying bags and packs.

"Sorry. We slept late," says Leua, holding a tray of eggs.

Latu smiles, while Anita looks anxiously at the crowd.

"No matter," says Heather, "the ticket office just opened."

"I better get our tickets," says Latu, who also disappears into the crowd.

"The eggs are for Mum and Dad," says Leua. "I'm holding them to make sure they don't break."

Fifteen minutes later we all have our tickets, and the sun has risen. Picking up packs and bags of food, we make our way towards a large, steel walled building with a concrete floor. Through windows and gaps in the steel sheeting, we should see the ferry when it arrives. A steel fence along the inside wall forces people into a queue forty metres long, leading to the ferry entrance gate. People and their belongings pack into the narrow space. There are coconut leaf baskets, plastic bags filled with food, boxes of tinned food, rolls of woven pandanus mats, and the occasional suitcase tied up with string.

Outside the queue, a loose crowd gathers - growing larger as more people arrive. Tired of standing, we sit cross-legged on the concrete floor like many others. We're learning that waiting, and doing nothing, is a very important Samoan life skill.

Around seven-thirty, we hear a distant chugging noise grow louder. People stand, watching the ferry approach the wharf, move slowly past the building, and then stop. With a clang and crash the front ramp lands on the concrete, and people stream off onto the road.

We stand up too, eager to finally get on the ferry. After all, we've already been travelling and waiting for nearly three hours.

"We have to wait for the vehicles to get off," says Leua.

Sure enough, when the last passengers walk off, vehicles drive down the ramp.

When we lift our packs Latu says, "Not yet. They load the vehicles on first."

Soon we see the long line of vehicles cautiously move up the ramp onto the open deck.

When the last vehicles drive on, everyone stands up ready to go. With a clang, the passenger gate opens, and in the distance, I see the queue move.

Around us, the crowd surges forward and we're swept along with it. Another crowd of bodies. No queue. Don't panic. Be patient. It's a large ferry and there should be plenty of room for everyone.

I'm shoulder to shoulder with a Samoan woman holding a small child in her arms. Heather is in front.

People pack closer together. We can't move forward.

"*Aua!*" (don't) calls someone.

"*Soia!*" (stop) says another.

A basket scrapes my legs.

An arm digs my ribs.

"Make space," says a man beside me as he pushes people away.

"Stop pushing," says another.

The crowd surges forward a step and then falls back.

A woman screams.

What's happening?

I'm pushed from behind and stumble forward into Heather. The small child grabs my shirt as her mother stumbles. A roar of voices behind us as the crowd surges back again.

I glance behind and see several middle-aged men, with both arms outstretched, push people forward.

When they push again, I stumble forward, and Leua crashes into the person in front - crushed egg spurting over her.

It's dangerous. A child might be crushed.

The men push again and the crowd surges once more.

I see terror in the young mother's eyes, as she fearfully holds her child.

Shrieks of terror. A child screams.

People yell, "Stop!"

I'm separated from Heather.

We slam together again.

Bags of food and belongings tear apart and feet trample spilled food into the concrete.

Leua loses Anita but Heather grabs Anita's hand.

Parents scream for lost children, as they're crushed with every surge.

Leua yells at the men behind in vigorous Samoan, as others swear violently.

"Stop doing this."

"You're going to kill someone."

Where is Latu?

Now everyone yells.

"Someone should do something."

"Where are the police?"

"Why doesn't someone stop this?"

Someone might die.

"O God," we pray, "save us from these foolish people."

Terrified, Anita cries for Leua as Heather holds her tight. She wants to comfort Anita, but she's jammed into the back of the person in front.

We forget the ferry.

We want to stay alive.

Someone throws a fist at the pushing men - striking a blow. Stunned, the struck man throws a punch back but misses. A scuffle follows, ending with men eying each other. It isn't much, but it's enough to make the pushing stop.

A man in uniform appears, not the police but a wharf employee.

The crowd eases away from each other.

Leua pushes through a gap and grabs Anita.

Children find parents again.

"Thank God," says Leua.

I can't see Latu.

People in front move again. We inch forward slowly. As we near the steel fence we breathe freely, relieved we're alive and unhurt.

Suddenly, like water bursting from a dam, we're swept into the queue moving to the gate. Slowly but steadily.

About fifty people ahead of us.

The line grows shorter as we inch along, seeing people disappear through the gate and onto the ferry. The bright light streaming through the gate beckons at the end of a dark tunnel.

Only ten people ahead now. I feel relieved. We are finally boarding the ferry.

Now only six people, as two more proffer their tickets.

Now only four - we'll be on the ferry in a moment and on our way to Savai'i!

But the gate swings shut with a loud clang.

We stop, staring through jail door bars in disbelief.

It can't be.

They're not leaving without us.

Are they?

The ticket attendant stands on the other side holding the gate shut.

"They might open again," says Leua hopefully.

The ticket attendant ignores us, looking expectantly towards the ferry.

We stand, holding our bags and packs in hopeful expectation.

A little later we hear the engine noise change tempo - rising a little.

We stare through the vertical steel bars and see the blue side of the ferry. Just twenty feet away.

So close.

We hear more clangs, and men calling to each other.

It hasn't left. Perhaps we can still get on?

The ticket attendant walks away. Not a good sign.

The ferry moves.

"It's leaving without us," I say.

"Damn," says Leua. She holds Anita's hand, looking out through the gate. Egg remnants stick to the front of her shirt.

I can't believe that what is happening, is actually happening.

We were so close.

Now I hate the jail door that cruelly crushed the life out of our hopes at the last moment. We hear the noise of the ferry engine increasing tempo again, but fading as it departs on its journey.

Without us.

Heather looks crestfallen. "What do we do now?" she asks.

"We'll have to wait for it to come back," says Leua despondently.

"How long will that take?"

"An hour and a half each way, plus another hour to load and unload. All going well."

"Four hours?"

"If we're lucky."

"What time is it now?" asks Heather.

"Eight-thirty," I say, glancing at my watch. We've been waiting here three hours already. Are we going to wait another four hours? I look at the long queue of people behind us, and the growing crowd in the terminal building.

"I'm not losing our place in the queue," I say. "Not after what we've just been through."

"We'll just have to sit and wait," says Leua.

"Four hours," says Heather in dismay, looking down at the hard concrete floor.

"Here's Latu," says Anita.

We turn around to see Latu grinning at us through the steel fence.

"Hey," he says, putting his hand affectionately on Anita's head. "I got separated back there and ended up out here."

"We have to wait for the ferry to come back," says Leua.

"Going to be a while."

"Yeah, but what else can we do?"

"I'm not even in the queue out here," says Latu. "I might not get on."

"Maybe you can hitch a ride on a vehicle?"

"Maybe," he says doubtfully. You want me to get something to eat and drink?"

"Good idea," says Leua.

I give Latu some cash, saying, "Whatever you can get."

"Back soon," he says, threading his way through people sitting on the concrete.

"We may as well make ourselves comfortable," says Leua sitting down.

My heart sinks at the prospect of sitting four hours on a concrete floor. Samoans are used to sitting cross-legged for long periods. They grow up with it. Not us. We're adjusting, but it's still painful. Concrete has one advantage though - it helps keep us cool. And we need cool, because there's no sea breeze inside the building, and we're already sweltering in the stifling heat.

By the time Latu returns with soft drink and German buns it's nearly nine o'clock.

Leua and Anita drink straight from a bottle. Heather and I share the other bottle, sitting on our day packs to be more comfortable. It's over four hours since breakfast, so the German buns feel good after the long wait and recent terror.

"Want to play cards?" I ask.

Anita's eyes light up.

Having learned that long waits are essential to Samoan life, we always carry a pack of cards, or a book to read. We play hearts and Latu joins in, passing cards between the steel bars.

Around us people sit, talk or sleep. I feel envious of Samoans who can sleep anywhere, even lying on bare concrete. Leua wipes the sweat from her face with her *ie*. As the heat rises, we all sweat.

I check my watch. After nine-thirty.

"Another three hours before the ferry arrives."

"Then half an hour to unload," says Leua. "And another half an hour to load on the cars and passengers."

"So, we won't leave 'til one-thirty, and the crossing's another hour and a half?"

"Yeah, then another half an hour to unload and hopefully get on a bus."

"It's about an hour-and-a-half on the bus to Vaipo'uli," adds Latu.

My heart sinks. We won't be at Vaipo'uli until at least five o'clock tonight. Maybe after dark sometime. If we're lucky. If the ferry's not delayed, and nothing else goes wrong. We've still got a long day ahead. Another eight hours travel through the hottest part of the day.

"Hey Latu," I say, "could you buy us something more to drink?"

He goes away with more money and returns sometime later with two bottles of Coke.

"Only drink they had left," he says.

The concrete is painful now. We change positions. Stand up. Sit down.

We've come to Samoa to be immersed in a different culture and way of life, to live with some of the world's poorest people - knowing it might be difficult and demand patience and perseverance. Perhaps we're learning what patience and perseverance really means.

When Latu leans on the steel bars, we notice they bend a little.

"Maybe you could slip through?" I suggest.

"Maybe," he says. "You push on that one and I'll pull on the other."

Counting "one, two, three", we push together, and Latu is suddenly on our side. We're reunited again.

We start another game of cards.

"What's the road like to Vaipo'uli?" I ask.

"Not bad," says Latu. "The cyclone damaged sections, but there's some bitumen."

"Some?"

"A lot of gravel," says Latu. "It's okay, but it gets dusty. They had to move the road because the cyclone washed some villages away."

Although it seems long ago, the cyclone came only nine weeks earlier, and the experience is still very raw. I imagine the anguish, fear, and sadness of terrified people. Their homes and belongings battered for days by wind and rain, then savagely destroyed by the waves of the rising sea, leaving only rocks and concrete.

"What happened to the people?"

Latu shrugs his shoulders. "They were okay, they're building new villages. Further inland this time."

Now it doesn't matter how I sit; every position is painful.

More patience.

A little longer.

Suffering is good for the soul.

Is it really? I doubt the person who said that was sitting on this concrete floor.

At the other end of the terminal, more people stand up.

"The ferry's coming," says Latu.

"Oh, at last," says Heather, reaching for her pack.

I glance at my watch, it's twelve-thirty. "It's on time," I say, jubilant at the simple pleasure of seeing something go right.

Thank you Lord, we've learned our lesson in patience and perseverance. No further lessons are necessary today.

The noise of the engine grows as the ferry approaches, and a few people cheer as the vessel slides back into view and stops. The front ramp crashes down on the concrete, and we see passengers from Savai'i pass by, walking down the road to waiting buses. Then we hear the noise of vehicles driving off, and through the gate I see vehicles drive onto the waiting ferry. Anticipating the passenger gate opening soon, we all stand up and gather our belongings.

The same stoic gate attendant appears on the other side to open the gate. Stepping through, the sunlight blinds us momentarily and we shade our eyes. We walk up the vehicle ramp onto the open deck. Ahead of us we see parked cars, trucks, pickups, and a few motorbikes. We follow Leua toward the passenger cabin at the back above the vehicle deck, but the stairway is blocked by a man in uniform.

"Cabin is full," he says.

Leua looks crestfallen as we stand beside a group of motorbikes. The stream of people flooding up the ramp behind us, gradually fills the vacant deck space.

I recognise Hannah's motorbike. Great, she must be here somewhere. Probably up in the cabin.

As more people crowd onto the open deck, a man in uniform uses a loudhailer to call out instructions.

"What's he saying?" I ask Leua.

"He says this is the last ferry today, but they're taking everyone who wants to go to Savai'i."

"Everyone? They can't take everyone. It'll be overcrowded and unsafe."

Leua shrugs her shoulders. "That's what he said. What can we do?"

We could get off again, I think. And not go to Savai'i. But we've already waited over eight hours. We've been crushed in a crowd, and just spent hours sitting painfully on a concrete floor. We're too invested to give up now. Plus, we really want to see our friends at Vaipo'uli.

So we stay on the ferry, standing in the tropical sun in the hottest part of the day. Sweat runs down my arm and drips off my fingers. If we felt hot sitting in the terminal, we're now being deep fried and parboiled in our own sweat.

As more people join the crowd on the open deck, we're pushed closer together. I'm jammed against Hannah's motorbike, with the brake lever in my ribs. Anita sits at one end of the seat, while another woman sits her young child at the other.

I can't sit down. It's literally standing room only.

People climb onto vehicle roofs, while others climb onto the ramp winding motors. Soon, a person occupies every foothold or place where anyone can sit or stand. People even climb up the radio mast on the cabin.

I'm an engineer. I know for certain they didn't design this ferry to carry so many people.

What if we sink?

Scanning for lifesaving equipment, I see an orange life raft attached to the cabin. It'll hold about thirty people. Not three hundred, and now there's easily over five hundred people on board, not counting the people in the cabin.

Heather and I can barely swim. If there's an accident, and the ferry sinks, we'll either drown or be eaten by sharks.

I recall seeing news reports in Australia about a disaster somewhere in the world, "...*hundreds of people drowned in the Philippines when an overcrowded ferry sank ...*".

That all seemed so distant. So unreal.

But this is our life, not some television news story.

Are we going to end our lives foolishly boarding an overcrowded vessel in a remote corner of the world? Is the sum of our lives going to be a footnote on the evening news?

Now I realise how easily these disasters happen, and why poor people put their lives at risk. Because when you're poor, you have little control over your life. Life itself is high risk, and often all available options are poor.

I've faced fear before, like during the cyclone. But if I'm honest, I always felt like we had a small measure of control. If the worst happened, we had contingency plans, and friends to help.

This time we have no control, we're completely dependent on people we don't know, who seem unreliable, and we find difficult to trust - like the ferry captain overloading his vessel, or the men who earlier caused a dangerous crush.

When Jesus told us to pray God will *"... deliver us from evil,"* he didn't just mean deliverance from our propensity to do wrong, but also deadly accidents, disasters, flood, fire, famine, pestilence, and war; events over which the poor and powerless have no control. Suddenly the Lord's Prayer seems very real - not something recited in Sunday School, or mindlessly parroted in church liturgy - but a living reality.

When we hear Jesus say, *"Blessed are you who are poor, for yours is the kingdom of God,"* we find it puzzling, while sceptics dismiss the statement as just fluffy words. How can we be blessed when a life of poverty is so hard? Perhaps the answer lies in the fact that the very nature of poor people's existence draws them closer to God in faith and dependence. When we have a safety net, we put our faith in it, rather than God.

Living in a wealthy country we easily feel like we have control over our lives. We rely on our insurance, our governments, police, doctors, regulations, and emergency services to keep us safe, or rescue us from calamity. But our sense of control is an illusion, for we have no more control over such events than people did in Jesus' day. Without insurance or emergency services, Samoans typically look to God to deliver them. There is nothing else.

After half an hour standing in the sun, I fear our lesson in patience and perseverance is only just beginning.

The ramp finally winds up, and the ferry heads out to open sea. The island of Upolu shrinks behind us. On our left I see Manono with Apolima in the distance. Further away, the dark shadow of Savai'i looms over the horizon.

The ferry pitches and rolls in the large ocean waves. Waves crash into the bow and spray cold, salty foam over lucky people near the front.

I wish spray would land on us, but we're too far back.

We drink more soft drink. Must keep our fluids up.

The sun beats down, as nearby Samoans spread an *ie* over themselves to create shade. Leua pulls one out of her bag and spreads it over herself, Anita, and Heather. The *ie* must be the most versatile and useful piece of clothing known to mankind.

Oh, for a shower of rain. Where are rain clouds when we really need them? When we arrived in Samoa two months earlier, it rained three times a day, every day, and overnight. But with the dry season beginning, a whole day passes with no rain at all. Almost unbelievable.

Hannah's brake lever skewers my back. By twisting and jiggling, I make room for Heather to sit on the footrest.

Be patient. After all, we're just learning how most people in the world travel. If we must wait for eight hours, then we wait. If we must stand on a steel deck in the tropical sun for a few hours, then we stand.

In less than two hours we'll be off this ferry and on a bus.

If we're lucky.

If we're unlucky, the overcrowded ferry will sink, we'll all drown, and our lifeless bodies will wash up on a beach somewhere or be eaten by sharks.

On the positive side, either way we'll be off this blasted ferry and out of this infernal sun frying us into human potato chips. I pray again God will keep us safe from accidental drowning, sunstroke, and the stupidity of mankind.

On the open sea, the wind picks up and we have a little cooling relief.

Around two we take out the few bananas we packed and share them with Leua, Anita and Latu. We didn't bring lunch because we expected to be at Vaipo'uli by midday. Leua has a little food too, but her eggs were all smashed in the crush. We sip the soft drink, wanting to ration it to make sure we don't run out.

Manono recedes behind as we pass the unmistakable volcano shape of Apolima.

A plumpish Samoan woman stands next to me wearing a blue tee-shirt and yellow *ie*. Fanning herself with an *ili* (fan), she chews gum as sweat runs down her face.

"*Vevela tele*" (very hot), she says.

"*Sa'o*" (true), I say.

Her beautiful, dark, wavy hair, so carefully set in a neat bun this morning, is falling apart in the sweat and heat.

After another hour of rolling and pitching in the sun, our hopes rise. We make out the green mountains of Savai'i, and the crashing white foam on the outlying reef.

All Polynesian cultures say their people came from a legendary place with a name sounding like Savai'i, and the oldest Polynesian archaeological sites in the Pacific are on this island. At least that's what the Samoans tell us. They also tell us the people on Savai'i consider themselves to be the true guardians of the *fa'asamoa*. Not surprisingly, people from Upolu seem to think the people on Savai'i are more like a bunch of backward hillbillies.

Finishing the last of our soft drink, we pass through a gap in the outer reef, and the pitching and rolling slows and stops. Amongst the coconut palms and the aqua blue lagoon around Savai'i, I make out the Salelologa wharf buildings. Approaching the ferry terminal, the captain reverses the engine and slowly noses in. Even if we feel like fried potato chips, we've made it to Savai'i without sinking, drowning, or suffering sunstroke.

After the ramp crashes down onto the concrete, people walk off the ferry.

"We need to find the Asau bus," says Leua, "or the Safotu bus."

"Asau or Safotu," I say, "right."

I wonder where Hannah is. Maybe we should try to find her?

Finally, as the people around us move away, we gather our belongings and walk off. With my legs and back stiff from standing so long, it feels good to move again.

Knowing we have a few more hours to travel, Leua and Heather go to buy something to drink.

Taking Heather's pack and food, I walk to the bus 'terminal' - a collection of buses parked in no discernible order in a gravelled area. I locate an empty bus marked 'Safotu', but the engine is off, and there's no driver. However, several people appear and climb in.

"Does this bus go to Safotu?"

"*Ioe* (yes), go to Safotu."

I climb on and stash our packs and food under a seat. As more people climb into the bus, a middle-aged man wearing a faded and stained *ie* climbs into the driver's seat. When he starts the engine I worry the bus is going to leave without the others. But soon Latu and Anita climb the steps, followed by Heather and Leua. Panting in the heat, they sit holding fresh bottles of Coke.

Heather can't open her bottle because her hands are two slippery with sweat. I hold the cap with my shirt and twist it off. She drinks gratefully, wipes her mouth with her hand, and passes the bottle back to me. Her face is red and dusty. Her dark hair is wet and matted from sweat running down her face and dripping off her chin.

I guess Hannah must be off the ferry by now. Probably riding happily down the road to Vaipo'uli.

The bus departs when it's full, and we soon pass through Salelologa, a small collection of stores and houses. Not even big enough to be a village.

As the bus picks up speed, the wind blows through the open windows and cools us down. We pass through villages filled with colourful *fales*, white stone churches, coconut palms and other vegetation growing back after the recent cyclone. Banana trees are recovering, but we see no breadfruit trees. Occasionally we pass near the sea and see the azure blue lagoon water.

Heather points to a sign amongst the trees that reads 'Tuisivi College', where Emma teaches. We haven't seen her since we left the Seaside Inn.

"I wonder how she's getting to Vaipo'uli?" says Heather.

"Bus, I suppose."

"It'll be good to see her again," says Heather, taking another swig from the bottle.

Yes, it will.

Suddenly the bitumen vanishes, as the road turns to gravel and dust. The driver slows to a sedate forty kilometres-per-hour or less, as the bus bumps and lurches around, hitting potholes and rocks. With each bump, our bones grind our flesh into the hard wooden seats.

Approaching a village, I notice the driver slows down further. Are we letting someone off? No, he increases speed again.

"He slows down, so dust doesn't blow through people's houses," says Latu.

That's thoughtful. But while no dust blows through people's houses, we're not so fortunate. Every time we stop or slow down, a dust cloud blows through the open windows, settling on our sweaty faces, arms, and legs.

After a while we turn further inland and the landscape changes to a vast expanse of jet black, volcanic rock. Scattered across the black plain are small green shrubs and a few ferns.

"The lava field," says Latu leaning forwards in his seat behind us.

As lava flowed from the eruption of Mount Matavanu eighty years ago, it created the vast rock plain we're now crossing. Occasionally I see a small tree gaining a foothold in the rock.

We stop at a village built on the lava field. A woman and three children get off the bus and we move on. Feeling the heat rise off the bare rock, I think it must be very hot and uncomfortable living here.

We soon leave the lava field behind as the road winds closer to the coast. My watch says it's four-thirty. Meanwhile, the wooden seats become harder with every bump in the road. We drink more Coke, and as the road goes ever on, we stop more frequently to let people off.

Around five o'clock Latu stands up and taps the bus driver on the shoulder. As the bus slows, Leua gathers her belongings, and they prepare to leave.

"I've told the driver to drop you off at the road to Vaipo'uli," says Latu. "It's not far."

Latu and Anita get off first, and as Leua pays their fares, she turns and calls out "*fa*" (bye). We feel very grateful for their friendship and help.

A few minutes later the bus stops again, and the driver calls out, "Vaipo'uli." We gather our packs and bags full of food, pay our fares, and climb down the steps.

As the bus moves away dragging its cloud of dust, we find ourselves alone on the road. Behind us is a narrow beach and lagoon. A little further down the road are some *fale*s, and a church rooftop - probably the village of Safune. On the opposite side is a narrow, red, dusty road winding up the hill - apparently the road to Vaipo'uli. The sun is low in the sky, but there's no let up from the heat.

We sling our packs on our shoulders, pick up our bags of food, and walk up the road. It starts out flat, but soon rises more steeply as it curves around to the right.

"How far is it up this road?" asks Heather.

"I can't remember what Doug said. Maybe a kilometre or two."

"Only one I hope."

Two kilometres uphill in this heat is more than half an hour's walk. But we're carrying stuff. We know now that trudging up a hill in the tropical heat and intense humidity of Samoa, is ten times harder than in a temperate climate. But we're exhausted, hungry, and thirsty. As we look up the dusty, winding road ahead of us, it feels more like ten kilometres, or a hundred.

"What we need right now is a lift," I say.

"Do you think someone will come and get us?" asks Heather.

"No," I say wearily. "They don't know we're here, and no one has a car. I was just hoping against hope."

But as we trudge wearily up the road, we hear the noise of an approaching vehicle. Turning around, we see a truck slow down on the main road, turn, and come towards us.

"Are they going to Vaipo'uli?"

We raise our hands to flag it down. As the truck goes past, we see Emma sitting on the tray with other people.

"They must be going to Vaipo'uli," I say, breathless with excitement.

We wave to Emma, and she waves back as the truck stops fifty metres ahead.

Wonderful. We can ride after all.

God is good.

We pick up our pace, walking to the truck, feeling relieved and happy. We don't have to walk up this horrible road after all.

But then someone gets out of the truck and walks off.

A creeping doubt. Have they stopped for us?

We start jogging, as packs and bags bang into our legs.

It's okay. The truck is only twenty meters in front.

We wave to Emma who waves back and smiles.

Suddenly the engine roars, and smoke pours out as the truck accelerates.

No! Don't go!

"Wait for us," we cry.

We wave and Emma waves back. She's calling out but we can't hear her. The truck picks up speed, roaring up the road in a swirling cloud of dust. We wave and cry out fruitlessly, as the truck disappears round a bend in the road hidden by trees.

We drop our bags and packs in the dust, staring in disbelief at the dust cloud drifting into the undergrowth.

Speechless. Too cruel for words. The driver must have seen us. We know Emma saw us! Why did they leave us here?

I see tears in Heather's eyes.

It's the last straw. A final crushing blow.

How could anyone do such a thing?

"Looks like we'll have to walk after all," I say, picking up my pack. Heather reluctantly reaches down for her daypack too.

"Let's go. It's only a little further up this hill," I say unconvincingly.

Picking up our bags of food from the dust, we start wearily trudging up the hill again. With the sun beating down, and sweat running in our eyes, we put one foot in front of another, plodding up the dusty road.

Unfortunately, Heather thought we'd take something special to our friends - a watermelon. She also brought some tinned fruit, and other vegetables - carrots - something difficult to buy on Savai'i, and a special treat for our friends.

I look down at the watermelon in the string bag which is now cutting into my hands.

"Why don't we ditch the watermelon?" I say.

"No, I got that specially for Doug and Jill."

"We could throw it under a bush and come back for it later?"

"No, we can't do that, the ants will get it."

I know that's true, but I think the ants are welcome to the rotten thing. Why did we have to bring such heavy things? Why not dried noodles?

We stop to wipe the sweat from our eyes. Heather's blue eyes are bright spots in a red, dusty face, framed by matted, dark hair.

We're desperately thirsty but there's nothing to drink. We finished the Coke long ago.

Stoically trudging further up the mountain road, we turn round each bend looking with hope for some evidence of our destination, but there's just more road, and another bend ahead.

"Maybe it's two miles," I say.

A little further, we come to a sharp bend with trees overshadowing a shady glen. We cross a small bridge over a mountain stream and look down on a rippling brook cascading into pools of cold, dark water. We leave the road to walk through the grass to the stream.

I know exactly what's happened. We've just died and gone to paradise. We say nothing, we both know exactly what we're going to do.

Heather drops her pack and bags on the ground and walks into a pool. I drop everything, the pack, the string bag with the blasted watermelon, the tinned fruit, and the carrots - I drop it all on the ground and step into a cold pool of dark water. Shoes, socks, and all.

I sit down, literally at rock bottom, feeling the delicious cold water embrace my weary body. Holding my breath and closing my eyes, I immerse myself into the mountain stream - a baptism in crystal clear water. I feel the water lift my muddy, matted hair from my head, hear a gurgling sound in my ears, and feel the lovely, cool, sensation of water washing and caressing my skin.

I want to stay here forever, but I eventually run out of air. Emerging slowly from the pool, I stop with the water just up to my neck.

I open my eyes and look across the water. Unbelievably, in front of my eyes, a can of Foster's Lager floats slowly past me in the mountain stream.

I reach out and grab it.

It's empty.

21
JUSTICE

"Or those eighteen on whom the tower in Siloam fell and killed them: do you think that they were worse offenders than all the others who lived in Jerusalem? No, I tell you; but unless you repent, you will all likewise perish."

Luke 13:4-5

The growing noise of an engine breaks the sound of bubbling water, and a red motorbike stops after crossing the bridge.

"God, you look like drowned rats!" says Hannah, taking off her helmet.

"Hi Hannah," says Heather. "We're having a break from walking up the road."

Hannah suggests she take Heather on her motorbike, and then return for me. As Heather climbs on behind Hannah, I give her a string bag of food to hold, and they roar off. A little later Doug appears on his motorbike and takes me to Vaipo'uli.

Like our school, Vaipo'uli occupies a large, open, grassy area, with a group of teacher's houses clustered away from the school buildings. Unlike our school, both the buildings and houses appear in good condition, but without a sea view.

Climbing off Doug's motorbike, I see Emma emerge from a house.

"Why didn't you pick us up?" I ask.

"Sorry, I dunno why the driver did that," she says with disgust. "I banged on the roof and yelled at him to stop, but he just drove on."

After showering in Doug and Jill's bathroom, and changing into clean clothes, we feel refreshed, relaxed, and hungry. Fortunately, preparations for a barbeque dinner are in full swing.

Doug cooks freshwater eels (caught in a home-made eel trap set in a mountain stream), and fish caught on the nearby beach. They already have an abundance of watermelon (much to my chagrin) but are grateful for the carrots, which they add to a salad.

Mick sits in a chair holding a beer, while Bruce talks to Chris, another Aussie teacher at Vaipo'uli, who suddenly laughs heartily.

"What's the joke?" asks Emma.

"I got robbed," says Bruce, smiling.

"Where?"

"At home. I wake up last Monday morning and see a man holding a knife to me. They took my cassette tapes."

"They didn't take money?"

"No - they stole my music!"

"What music?" asks Doug.

"UB40 of course."

"Mate, they was doin' you a favour," says Emma.

"Well anyway, I go straight to the Apia police station and report the theft. When I describe the bloke and his tattoos, the police say, 'Oh we know him. He's here in jail.'"

"Whaat?"

"They take me downstairs and there he is - listening to my music. It turns out he's serving a sentence, but they let him out on weekends to work his taro plantation. He was on his way back when he wanted music to pass the time in jail. I got my cassettes back."

"He didn't steal'em Bruce, he was just 'sharin'," says Emma.

"Yeah, right, that's why he needed a knife."

Mick told us about 'sharing', and Samoan's attitude to personal property, the first morning we arrived. Traditionally, property belongs to the *aiga* (family) or *nu'u* (village). Even land isn't 'owned' in the same sense as in European cultures, and they see sharing differently. In a Samoan village, people live in houses without walls, windows, or locked doors. Everything is open for everyone to see, demonstrating a level of trust and transparency that's unthinkable and perhaps impossible in a palagi world. If we want to live by the eighth commandment, "You shall not steal" in a culture with different concepts of property and property rights, then what constitutes theft takes on new meaning.

My large, strong, and preciously guarded umbrella vanished one day because a teacher 'shared' it. Because when everything belongs to everyone, and a teacher needs an umbrella, they simply 'share' any available umbrella. Fortunately, it re-appeared in the staff room several weeks later, so I 'shared' it back.

"They've definitely got different ideas about prison," says Mick.

"And justice," adds Doug.

"What do you mean?" I ask.

"The village council does traditional justice. Here, the police just deal with roads and ports."

"It's the same on Upolu," says Mick. "The police operate in Apia, but the villages operate traditional law, decided by the village council. It means if you have a problem in a village, don't go to the police; go to the village council - the *matais*'ll sort it all out."

"Last year," says Doug, "someone put sand in our petrol tank when we stayed in a village, so we complained to a *matai*. Within half-an-hour they rounded up some teenagers and gave them a beating. Everyone knew who did it. I gotta say, it might've been brutal, but it was swift and effective."

Palagis see justice, not only in terms of crime and punishment, but also maintaining equality and fair distribution of goods and services. But the Samoan concept of justice seems to be more concerned with maintaining the correct order of society, matching a person's behaviour with the position, obligations, and responsibilities of their status in the social hierarchy. Meanwhile, maintenance of adequate food, shelter, and care for all, happens through a culture communal obligation. This might mean a Samoan is obliged to give food to a neighbour in need, not because they think everyone should be the same, or for reasons of equity, but because it is the right behaviour for someone in their position.

Justice includes giving a person the honour and material stuff consistent with their status in the social hierarchy; so a *matai* should have a seat on the bus in preference to me. In some palagi societies, the concept of honour has become foreign, but in Samoa, honour is highly valued, so a high-ranking *matai* must be served and supplied according to their rank.

We're not surprised to find the idea of justice at school is influenced by village concepts of justice. But if it's confronting to hear stories of brutal but effective village justice, seeing and hearing students beaten in nearby classrooms is gut wrenching. It feels worse when we see Samoan teachers hit students for getting a wrong answer, in anger or frustration, or for being in the wrong place at the wrong time. They claim they're punishing laziness, failure to listen in class, or do homework, but it seems counterproductive, making our job teaching senior students harder. For by senior high school, students appear well-schooled in violence avoidance, but struggle to think independently.

What our students know and understand, is a world where punishment is painful, but over quickly, allowing the misbehaved to start afresh with a clean slate. However, punishment can sometimes be accidentally permanent. I teach a girl blind in one eye, because (I'm told) her mother threw a rock at her.

Meanwhile, Samoan teachers think we're naïve, ignorant of Samoan culture, and a soft touch. Sure, we're experienced teachers in Australia, have university degrees, and understand our subjects, but what good is all that in the face of Samoan teenage cunning? In their view we're hopelessly outclassed. And they're right. After all, our Samoan teachers were Samoan teenagers themselves not that long ago; they have inside knowledge and extensive experience.

Samoan teachers and students believe class quietness and control is the measure of teacher competence. We might think some healthy discussion is helpful to learning, but this is an alien concept in Samoan culture, where children are expected to sit down, be silent and obey. Palagi teachers are frequently judged by their classroom noise level, and by that measure, found wanting.

I'm sympathetic to their view. My Australian high school years were peppered with classes where I learned little, because my teachers had no control over students who ran riot. We knew some teachers suffered nervous breakdowns or left the profession due to stress.

We learned best in classes taught by strict teachers who had high expectations of us and enforced high standards; the sort of people you don't mess with. When our learning progressed, those teachers also gave us a sense of achievement - a sense we were going somewhere. Students who run riot, and the teachers who enable them, create lost learning opportunities, and steal from the future of students keen to learn.

Some order is essential for student learning, but maintaining order in a class of fifty students (common in Samoa) is far more difficult than in a class of twenty; particularly when there are no textbooks, equipment, or other teacher aids. And having heard about riotous classrooms in palagi countries, neither Samoan teachers, nor their students, want their school classrooms to sink to such alarming levels of palagi depravity.

In Samoa, parents hit their children to discipline them, because they love them, and need to teach them important life lessons. Strong discipline is evidence of deep love, because ensuring children learn critical skills and behaviours, gives them opportunities and potential for a sound future in their community. In Samoan culture, we take the place of parents at school; our students expect the same hard discipline, including hitting them so it really hurts.

"If you really love us, you'll hit us," they say.

While we might think avoiding corporal punishment is being kind and understanding, our students think we're not taking our role seriously, that we don't care about them - not like Samoan teachers do.

However, the expectation to use corporal punishment is really on me, perhaps because in Samoan culture, physicality is one measure of a man. Heather, Tammy, and Helen are expected to send poorly behaved students to Tavita, perhaps resulting in a beating with a rubber hose he keeps by his desk, or a few days of hard labour, or expulsion. But Tammy and Heather can't do that without feeling somehow complicit in any violent outcome.

It might seem obvious, but to effectively communicate with someone, we must speak a language they understand. Love languages are as cultural and practical as the words we speak. So disciplining students by methods imported from our Australian culture, risks sending wrong and confusing messages.

How are we going to bridge the cultural gap? How do we communicate in a way they understand, without resorting to physical violence? How do we discipline using methods that are culturally resonant, that send the right message in the right language, without compromising our own ethics?

And isn't it my own cultural baggage that makes me feel unethical? Baggage I picked up in Australia, like measles and mumps. Corporal punishment may be unpleasant, distasteful, and arguably unnecessary, but not ethically wrong by any principle that transcends time, place, and culture. While we can argue taking corporal punishment out of our schools was a positive step forward in our country, expecting another culture and country to do the same reeks of the very worst kind of cultural imperialism.

I decide to discuss the problem with Doug tomorrow. For tonight, the balmy night air is soft, peaceful, and pleasant. We feel relieved and at home; relaxed in the company of friends - people who we feel know and understand us. Because, for the first time in twelve weeks, we're immersed back in a little oasis of our own culture, even if it's a long way from home.

The next morning, we all trek up a rainforest path to a waterfall cascading into a large mountain pool. Surrounded by undergrowth and shaded by tall trees, the crystal-clear water is cold, and deep. It feels like a magical, faraway place, with the sound of falling water, and the flash of scintillating sunlight in dark shadows.

My reduced buoyancy in the cold, freshwater, alarms me at first. I've become used to floating high in the warm saltwater lagoon at our school. With my eyes open, I peer down into the water, where I'm even more alarmed to see black, snake-like forms, weaving their way over the rocks below.

"Don't worry, the eels only swim at the bottom," says Jill.

We walk back feeling refreshed in our sodden clothes. Doug and Chris check their fish and eel traps, anticipating more fresh food for dinner. Set in a narrow stream, the homemade traps are empty today.

"How do you catch fish on the beach?" I ask Doug.

"We spear'em," he says. "We made our own spears."

"Do the locals do that here?"

"Nah, they paddle out into the lagoon, or open sea, and fish with hook and line."

"Or dynamite," adds Chris laughing, as he leads us back through the undergrowth.

"Not anymore thank goodness," says Jill. "They banned dynamite fishing because it damages reef coral."

"And blows arms off," says Chris turning around.

"Really?"

"Yeah, there's a bloke in the next village who lost half his arm. He made a mistake dynamite fishing."

"It kills a lot more than fish and coral," says Jill, "like turtles."

"Don't worry, the Peace Corps'll bring them back," says Doug, and they all laugh mysteriously.

"What's the joke?" I ask.

"The locals catch live turtles to sell in the market. Some idealistic Peace Corps buy the turtles and let them go. The locals think it's great, because they catch'em again and sell them back to the same Peace Corps. It's like printing money."

"They think they're saving the environment," says Jill. "But they're really incentivising its destruction."

As we pass by the school buildings, we peer inside curiously. The classrooms are in better shape than ours, like there's been some maintenance, but they're dark and gloomy. Suddenly I appreciate the wisdom of whoever designed our school, with its two walls of windows on each side, open to the sea breeze all day.

We pass the school truck parked under a lean-to roof, with the school's name emblazoned on the side in large letters, and a broken windscreen.

"What happened?" I ask.

"The driver got stoned," says Chris.

"Stoned?"

"He drove through a village too fast, and people don't like it, 'cos it blows dust through their *fales*. They knew he was coming back, so they put a line of rocks across the road and waited for 'im. When he slowed down to go 'round the rocks, they pelted the truck with stones."

"He drove back covered in blood, with a broken windscreen and smashed driver's side window," says Doug.

"Village justice," adds Jill. "He'll drive slowly through that village from now on."

"People easily take things into their own hands here," says Chris. "We heard there was a bloke in a nearby village who went a little strange. He lived by himself up in the plantation between two villages. But when he used his rifle to take pot-shots at people, both villages got together, went up there and chopped him up with bush knives. That's what we heard anyway."

Being an experienced science teacher in Australia, and a one-year teaching veteran in Samoa, I'm keen to pick Doug's brains for practical teaching advice.

Knowing students are accustomed to learning by rote, he says he collects their workbooks every few weeks and checks each one. "It helps make them pay more attention in class, and they write and learn from better notes. At least they're learning something, even if it is by rote."

While I admire his commitment, the thought of adding another round of checking and correction, seems daunting when I already feel overloaded. When I explain I'm teaching five classes, Doug says that's too much.

"I know," I say. "I feel like I'm spread too thin."

When I ask if he's expected to hit misbehaving students, he says, "The kids just want to know you'll do it, so do it once at the start of the year, and you'll never have to do it again."

"It's a bit late for that - we're already eight weeks into the term."

Eventually we settle for Tammy and Helen's preferred deterrent punishment, which combines shame with self-inflicted pain. We send students out to weed *vaofefe* in the hot sun.

A feral, thorny weed, *vaofefe* (literally 'afraid plant') closes its leaves when touched. Using their bare hands, misbehaving students extract ten *vaofefe* plants by the roots. Working in the tropical sun is unpleasant enough, but *vaofefe* thorns compound their suffering by painfully tearing skin, leaving dirty and bleeding hands. Punishment is augmented by the shame of being on public display in the school grounds, and the high risk of being seen by Tavita. They know Tavita considers the palagi teachers too soft and might measure out additional punishment - beating, expulsion or hard labour; all more painful than thirty minutes weeding *vaofefe*.

Removing *vaofefe* is not only an effective means to curb misbehaviour, it also performs a valuable community service. And since it grows everywhere in profuse abundance, there'll always be *vaofefe* to be weeded.

When I describe our approach to class discipline on our return to Australia, we see disapproving frowns, harsh condemnation, and sneering self-righteousness, particularly on the faces of those who see themselves as enlightened but sanctimonious champions of social causes. And I might well have done the same, if my world had not been enlarged by harsh lessons learned trying to bridge a chasm between two cultures. If we're learning anything, it's how much cultural baggage we carry, baggage we cling to like a comfort blanket, but hinders our crossing cultural gaps, and prevents us making deeper connections.

We all want to shrink our complex world to a size and simplicity that makes us comfortable, or at least enables us to cope. But when we most think ourselves enlightened and open-minded, when we think we have God and the world all sewn up in a neat little package, it's in that moment we most risk becoming narrow, critical and judgemental. If we always leave the door of our minds ajar, just a little, we're always open to learning a little bit more about ourselves and others.

Our judges are people less able to open their minds to living in a different time and place; and closed to the idea that weeding *vaofefe*, with its accompanying pain and discomfort, could be necessary. That what they think is kindness, could, in reality, be harmful, or even cruel, in another culture, and a different time and place. In the same way buying turtles to set them free, could be harmful to a turtle population. Instead of doing our students harm, we demonstrate love in a way they understand.

Having been judged harshly, I find myself wary of making easy judgements on others, or claiming what I would, or would not do, in circumstances others find themselves. Who knows what I might do in another time and place, if I truly walked in someone else's shoes?

While we might think ourselves to be wonderfully tolerant and non-judgemental, when we encounter any new culture, we're compelled to make judgements, if only to keep ourselves safe. We need to separate truth tellers from liars, and ultimately discern good from evil. But without the crutches of our own culture, we're tempted to lean on the tantalising simplicity of our favoured ideology. Ideologies attract us because we want causes to believe in and causes offer purpose to our otherwise meaningless lives. And since we consider our causes absolutely worthy, they can become our absolute measure of good and evil.

But ideologies blinker us to view the world through a single, ideologically tinted lens. Marxists see world history through the single lens of class struggle. To free market capitalists, every problem can be solved through competition. Environmentalists judge actions by their perceived impact on the natural world; nature is benevolent and good, while human impact is evil.

Before leaving Australia, we were made aware of how ideologies give us false stories to interpret the confusing and unpredictable world around us. But interpreting reality through a single story narrows our perspective and limits our opportunities to find real solutions to real problems. In our hammer ideology, we see every person as some type of nail; while the real world is filled with screws, bolts and things that aren't even fasteners. When something doesn't fit into our ideological box, we're tempted to break it, to force it in.

Unfortunately, the world God created is too big, too complex, and too nuanced, for our simple ideologies to grasp, however desperately or passionately we believe them. If we want to really understand a culture, we must set aside our ideological glasses, and see the world with fresh eyes.

Myths and ideologies offer the simple but false idea that virtue or vice can be imputed to a people group, whether class, sex, race, culture, voting preference, or religion. If owners of capital are intrinsically evil, while the working poor are intrinsically good, we only have to determine a person's class, skin colour, sex, or identity, to know whether they're good or bad people, and judge them accordingly.

Today, in our public discourse, we've officially disowned the colonial myth that indigenous people are morally beneath us, that they're simple, their cultures inferior, and need benevolent care. However, we see it subconsciously practiced by aid delivering government bodies (western or not), and non-government aid organisations that vigorously profess otherwise. Similarly, neo-colonial, self-appointed progressive activists, and other moralising idealogues, who look down their nose at Samoan's Christian worship, corporal punishment, role of women in Samoan culture, and a host of other 'evils', now hope to enlighten Samoans to behave better.

But perhaps the more damaging myth is the belief in the noble savage - the idea that all indigenous societies are naturally good, and would live harmoniously in a peaceful paradise, untouched by evil, if they hadn't been corrupted by Europeans. Rousseau's promotion of this old, romantic, and racist idea (the ancient Greeks thought Celts were noble savages), lent Enlightenment weight to the concept. It's supported by a more modern belief that people's good or evil behaviour is only a product of their environment, and the outcome of social forces that need reconstruction; and after we reconstruct society in our own image, all will be well.

When we ascribe unwarranted virtue to a people group, our experience of the real world is likely to be disappointing, as are the lessons of history. Prior to contact with Europeans, extreme violence, including pillaging, murder, enslavement, rape, cannibalism, and population decline, were common throughout 'peaceful' Pacific Island paradises. This is not to argue that people were any worse than others, or better, but that we all have equal potential for nobility and depravity. For we are all equally made in God's image, all equally broken by the Fall, and all accountable to God for our own actions.

When cultures change, every choice provides opportunity for good or evil to flourish. While we all want to see justice and virtue, whether in the classroom or the village, it can often be difficult to discern which is which. Instead of judging whether others, or other people groups, are better or worse than us, Jesus cautions us to look at ourselves: "...*unless you repent, you will all likewise perish.*"

A few days later we travel back to Upolu. Before sunrise, Doug takes us by motorbike to Safune, where we wait for a bus. After our journey a few days ago, we're nervous, and hope travel goes more smoothly today. When a bus stops, we're delighted to see Latu's face at the window, along with Leua and Anita. The early morning bus ride is cool and uneventful, and we find the ferry at Salelologa, ready and waiting. We buy tickets without a melée, and this time sit in the shaded luxury of the passenger cabin. We arrive at Mulifanua by late morning and arrive home by lunchtime.

Feeling refreshed and re-energised after a few days break from schoolwork, we throw ourselves back into teaching with renewed vigour.

One night I finish marking test papers and find that again, Pelopia has come first in the class by a wide margin. But when I commend her in front of the class the next day, Pelopia smiles briefly, then looks at the floor as though ashamed. Of all my form class, she's easily the standout student. But I notice she doesn't smile often, and she's quieter than the others.

Is something wrong?

22
PELOPIA

*"Which of these three, do you think, proved to be a
neighbour to the man who fell among the robbers?
He said, "the one who showed him mercy." And
Jesus said to him, "You go, and do likewise."*
Luke 10:36-37

nitially, I put that down to humility and respectful behaviour. Pelopia's
a good girl - no doubt about it. She never talks out of turn and always
helps.

A model student.

When Heather initiated the classroom garden competition, Pelopia was
one of the few who turned up to work. She seems friendly with Violeta and
Valu, but often walks home alone.

She's more than an excellent student. She seems naturally curious and
keen to really understand the subject. She has real potential for a bright
future, an advanced education, and a good job.

But when I talk with her outside the class, she always looks somewhere
else - at the ground, the trees, the buildings - but not at me. While avoiding

eye contact in Samoa is a way to show respect, the way Pelopia does it seems odd to me, as though she's being too respectful.

But what would I know? I've been in the country less than three months. I barely understand Samoan culture and my language skills are poor.

Maybe it's just a Samoan cultural thing?

Perhaps a Samoan teenage girl thing?

Maybe I'm just reading something into it that isn't really there?

"Have you noticed anything different about Pelopia?" I ask Olivia one day, as we walk home. Olivia also teaches Pelopia, and lives with Valu, one of Mama Sefina's many children. Valu's bright too but doesn't come close to Pelopia.

"You mean she's the brightest girl in the class?" asks Olivia.

"No, I mean she's respectful in a way that's different to the other girls - like she's going overboard."

"Yeah, the looking to the ground when she talks? You think there's something behind it?"

"I don't know, I've just got a feeling she's hiding something."

"She lives up the hill from Matafuli'i, but I think Mama Sefina knows her family. I can make some subtle enquiries. If anyone knows anything, Mama will."

A few days later, we're eating lunch at Tammy and Shelly's house after school, when Olivia raises a finger.

"A quiet word everyone," she says, glancing through the windows to check no students are in earshot.

"I had a quiet chat to Mama Sefina about Pelopia."

"Do tell," says Helen, always keen to hear gossip.

"It's not good," says Olivia, frowning. "Pelopia's in an inappropriate relationship..."

She pauses.

"…with her father."

The air turns tense and my heart sinks. Heather puts a hand to her mouth.

"Oh dear," says Tammy, looking sad.

Helen instinctively glances out the windows too.

"I got some quiet time with Mama Sefina yesterday," says Olivia. "I asked if she knew Pelopia, and if there was anything unusual about her. She gave me a sad look and told me she'd heard a rumour."

"Could it just be nasty gossip?" asks Helen.

"It's possible," says Olivia. "But Mama told me the sort of details you don't make up. I had a chat to the Peace Corps nurse too. She says the way Pelopia avoids looking at us is a sign."

"Yeah, I've noticed that too," added Helen.

"No wonder really," says Olivia. "I mean, if Mama Sefina knows, and she lives in the next village, then the entire village knows, and probably the next village too."

"That's terrible," says Heather. "The poor girl."

"Why doesn't the mother stop it?" asks Helen.

"Apparently her mother knows but hasn't done anything; at least as far as Mama knows. She probably just wrings her hands and hopes it goes away. It's a Samoan way of coping. Deny everything and act like it's not happening."

"She needs to get away from there," I say.

"Where's she gonna go?" asks Helen.

"I don't know - grandparents, aunts and uncles?"

"It's still in the village - they all know, but it seems they haven't done anything either."

"What about the church?"

"I asked Mama, but they don't attend the Congregational Church. They go to some other small outfit."

"Is there anything we can do?" asks Heather.

"It's hard. Culturally it's up to the family to do something, or the village council."

"Maybe we could check with Tavita?" I suggest.

"Maybe, but we'd better do that quietly when no one else is around."

A few days later, when we think Tavita is home alone, we walk over and sit down to talk. As Olivia describes the problem, he shakes his head knowingly. I realise he's heard it all before - perhaps in his village, or in other villages.

"She's a bright girl?"

"Easily the brightest in the class," I say.

He shakes his head sadly.

"Sorry, I don't think there's much we can do," he says. "It's something the family and village council have to deal with. The village council at Matafuli'i will all know about it. Look, it's really hard for villages to deal with this kind of stuff. It shouldn't happen, but it does. We'll just have to hope she can get out of the situation and live with relatives somewhere else. Sorry, it's really hard for people - they don't like it, but there's no right way to get involved either."

That evening, when Tammy, Helen and John join us for a candlelit dinner (because there's no power again), I share Tavita's thoughts.

"It's something that shouldn't happen," says Helen. "Samoans can't deal with things that shouldn't happen, so they ignore them, and hope they go away."

"Until it gets unbearable, then they explode," says John. "But it's also a survival strategy. It's hard fighting things you can't control or do anything about. They'll live as though it's not happening; look the other way; turn a blind eye."

"I dunno," says Helen cynically, "I reckon they're just lazy. They'd rather gossip about it than do anything to stop it."

"You know how it is though Helen," says John. "Living in a village, you've got to live with your neighbours and family whether you like'em or not. You gotta maintain community harmony. The problem with something like incest is that it upsets everything, but no one knows what to do about it."

John's point makes sense to me. It resonates with my experience growing up in a small country community. Community harmony is vital for everyone's peaceful co-existence, and maintaining the settled order of life;

for the peace and prosperity of every Samoan village;

for the growing of food in the plantation, fishing in the sea, the building of *fales*;

for marrying and growing families;

funerals to remember departed loved ones;

the giving of gifts;

the family *lotu* each evening;

the ringing of church bells on Sunday;

the weaving of *fala*;

and the making and mending of clothes.

An inappropriate relationship upsets all these things - it's something that cracks the crust of peace and stability. If it's too hard to deal with, we ignore it as long as possible.

Like us, the others grew up in middle-class families in America or New Zealand. Like us, they've lived relatively sheltered lives so far. None of us has training or experience in dealing with issues like incest. Who does? It's something we read about in novels. We know it happens in our cultures, but we think it's rare, and certainly not spoken about in polite society. And having no firsthand experience dealing with the problem in our culture, how can we possibly help in a radically different culture? A few months after arriving in the country? I think it's facile to blame Samoan culture for not dealing with the problem; after all, what culture deals with it well?

A few weeks go by, and every time I see Pelopia sitting at her desk, I feel sad and frustrated that something can't be done. She finds it difficult to look at us when we talk, because she's afraid we'll look into the well of her soul, see the cracks in her heart, and reveal her deepest, darkest secret.

One morning as I mark the roll, and call out Pelopia's name, I hear "*le'i sau*" (not come) from Avele. I mark Pelopia absent.

The next day I hear "*le'i sau*" again, mark her absent, and hope she turns up later in the day.

The next day, when I hear "*le'i sau*" again, I scan their faces. "Does anyone know why Pelopia hasn't come?"

"*Ma'i*" (sick), calls out Peauvasa.

"Do we know why Pelopia is sick?"

"*Leai*" (no), says Peauvasa, perhaps a little too quickly.

And why is Peauvasa answering when she's not from Pelopia's village? I look at the girls at the back of the class. Peauvasa is looking at her desk. Patisepa and the others are looking out the window. They're studiously ignoring me and looking deliberately bored - like it's nothing to do with them.

Which means it probably has absolutely everything to do with them.

In front of me Avele stares intently, while Violeta and Valu look fearful - like they've just seen a ghost.

Something is wrong.

I can feel it in the air.

Something has happened to Pelopia, but it's clear these girls won't tell me anything.

Time to talk to Olivia again.

At home that evening in Fagamili-tai, Olivia sidles up to Valu, who sits quietly doing her homework in the dim light at the edge of their *fale*. The soft light of the kerosene lamp flickers across their faces in the warm, still air.

"Did something happen to Pelopia the other day?" asks Olivia.

Valu raises her eyebrows - wordlessly signalling, "Yes."

"What happened?"

"Some girls argue before the teacher come."

"What were they arguing about?"

"Ke le iloa" (I don't know), says Valu, shrugging her shoulders.

"And what happened?"

"Pelopia and Avele say, *Aua le pisa"* (be quiet), but they say, "Don't tell us what to do!"

"Is that all? Did something else happen?"

Valu raises her eyebrows again and looks worried.

"I need to know Valu, we're worried about Pelopia. What happened?"

Valu looks away respectfully. "They call out - we know you with your father. They say *kefe* (f*ck). They call her dog—like how you say in English?"

"Bitch?"

Valu raises her eyebrows.

"What happened then?"

"Pelopia cry and run out. She not come back to school."

"The class told Ian that Pelopia's been sick."

"Ioe (yes), before she run away. She tell Violeta she sick in the morning."

"Just in the morning?"

Valu raises her eyebrows again, like she knows what it means, but doesn't want to say it out loud, because that might make it real.

"Is she at home?"

"Violeta say she stay home now - not come to school."

Violeta lives up the same gravel road as Pelopia in Matafuli'i-uta, one of the many roads leading up into the mountains.

The next day, Olivia knocks on our door as we finish breakfast. With a heavy heart, she shares Valu's story. "I hope it's not what we think it is, but there's a pretty good chance it is."

A baby.

Her father's baby.

"And if you know, and I know," says Olivia, "then you can bet everyone else knows too, including those nasty girls in your class."

"I guess she's really not coming back to school," I say. "Maybe we should take her off the roll?"

I bet it was Vania, I think to myself. Her and her nasty friends.

Or Nanea. She's always good for anything dodgy.

No wonder they all looked so studiously bored the other day. They knew they'd been cruel. And they'd enjoyed it too. And they probably felt satisfied with themselves when Pelopia ran away in tears. But they were obviously feeling defiantly guilty now, trying to hide what they'd done behind faked boredom, and studious silence.

And it hurt Pelopia even more because she knew it was all true.

And now everyone knows it's true. If they doubted the story before, then Pelopia escaping in tears and not returning, is proof beyond all doubt. Before the classroom incident, while it was unspoken, they could maintain the illusion it wasn't real. These girls finally smashed that illusion, destroyed the pretence, and evaporated the vain hope that somehow, what happened wasn't real.

And now that secret, so long jealously guarded in the dark, exploded across the school classroom in broad daylight. It dashes into a thousand pieces all Pelopia's future hopes. Because all she can see now is the misery of a life trying to escape the inescapable dark shadow that would always be there reminding her of her past. Tattooed on her face and carved into her soul. No matter how many years went by, it would be there in the village, in every knowing look, every sidelong glance, every pitiful smile, or disgusting grin.

To the end of her dying days, known as the girl who slept with her father.

Even worse, she had a baby to prove it, from her father.

Always remembered.

Forever scarred.

"What about the baby?" I ask Olivia.

"Oh, don't worry, the baby'll be fine," says Olivia. "Samoan's love children. They don't have the concept of a child being illegitimate like palagis do. The child'll be loved and cared for like every other child."

"But what about in-breeding, you know, inherited diseases?"

"Oh, no, that's very unlikely. That only happens when there are generations of in-breeding."

What can we do? We feel utterly helpless.

We blame the mother for not doing anything about it.

And we blame the rest of the family - aunts, uncles, cousins for not doing anything.

And the village - because everyone is happy to gossip about Pelopia, but no one has the courage to help the poor girl.

And I blame the cruelty of the girls in my class - those sweet, smiling faces who enjoy cutting down a tall poppy, the brightest and prettiest girl in the class, and revel in the pain they inflict.

In the social climate of western culture in which I write, people rapidly rush to judgement, automatically assuming Pelopia was raped, or at least violently coerced. But the behaviour of the girls suggest reality is far more complicated. We will never know the nature of the relationship, and it's unhelpful to speculate on causal details and mechanics. What matters, is that the relationship, according to Samoan values, is inappropriate, deeply shameful, and that her father, the person who should most protect Pelopia, is the one responsible for her pain.

As I think about our own country and culture, I wonder if we do any better. I think back to the little country town near our farm and wonder how that community would have coped? Would they have managed it well?

I think not.

Does anyone deal well with such a difficult problem? What would 'good' look like in a circumstance like this?

I have no idea.

But there is one significant difference. In a large country like Australia or the United States, someone like Pelopia might have the chance of moving somewhere else, to start a new life somewhere. Perhaps even with a new name. Away from everyone else and away from her past. There's the promise and possibility of anonymity.

But not in Samoa.

And not in all the small closely knit communities where most of the world's people live. Only the rich have the luxury of choosing their friends and location in life. The same community that's there to support you, that's nurtured you since birth, and made you who you are, that same community with its vibrant gossip grapevine can also destroy you. And the supercharged Samoan grapevine is like social media today but transmitted by constant conversation. Tell one juicy story (and what could be juicier than incest?) and it travels like wildfire through the entire country, making its way to every single village, on every island in Samoa.

A few weeks pass and we hear a rumour Pelopia has a boyfriend from Fagamili-tai. The gossip vine says they have secret liaisons in the plantation at night, and that's why she's pregnant.

"I heard it from Mama Sefina," says Olivia. "But we don't buy it. Mama thinks the story's spread by the family to explain the baby."

Teenage pregnancy is common in Samoa, often ending in a shotgun wedding of some sort. We hear families sometimes play the game; girls might deliberately get themselves pregnant so they can marry the boy of their choice or their family's choice.

But in Pelopia's case, the identity of the boy is unknown and vague. It's just a rumour.

And while a baby is proof of something, and more than a rumour - gossip doesn't need proof. It feeds more ravenously on half-truth and innuendo, all the while growing tentacles and branches into every cranny and crevice, every warp and weave of the tangled fabric of village life.

Gossip fans the flaming fire of shame. The same way people have morbid curiosity for the intimate details of a celebrity's life and the sordid affairs, the fights, and the he said, she said. In the villages of Samoa, it's the neighbours lives they focus on. The people they've known since childhood, with all their slights, resentments, petty jealousies, and other harboured memories that are never forgiven or forgotten. A chance for payback, an opportunity to cut someone back to size to remind them what they are, and what they aren't, and perhaps never can be.

What can we do?

We've been in the country less than three months, we barely understand the culture, and we want to help a teenage girl. How far are we prepared to go to meddle with an indigenous culture to save a life, or effect change? What will we do to protect or save people we love and care about? We like to think we'd make positive change, but in our clumsy rescue attempt we could easily push Pelopia, or someone else, over the edge. We could make it worse. Are we being cowards, or wisely cautious?

Some say we're merely guests in Samoa, that we have no right to interfere, because she belongs to different, indigenous culture; she's Samoan and we're palagi. Recalling the good Samaritan story told by Jesus, people say she's not our neighbour, and not our story. We're guests only; spectators to an unfolding drama.

But the life of a person we love is not an academic question. Pelopia is a person in dire need, and just as the good Samaritan was a neighbour to a person from another culture in need, God has placed Pelopia on our pathway and in our care. He brought us here to be her friends and to love her unconditionally, as Jesus loved the poor, outcast and shamed people of his day. People who, in their time and place, had gone past the point of no return.

And that we try to do.

We provide a place where Pelopia will always be welcome and loved unconditionally; a place where she won't feel ashamed. Perhaps our example, small as it may be, might encourage others to do the same, to reach out to people living in similar, shameful circumstances.

We hope and pray for Pelopia that God will provide a way of escape. But compassion always comes with a price tag. When we have the courage to share deeply in the life and pain of another, we too risk pain and loss. For suicide's grim reaper lurks in the shadows of every fearful Samoan family, and Pelopia's soul is ripe for reaping.

23

THE ROAD TO SAUANO

"Come now, you who say, 'Today or tomorrow we
will go into such and such a town and spend a
year there and trade and make a profit' – yet you
do not know what tomorrow will bring."
James 4:13-14

W here's Manutagi?

She said she'd meet us here at the market around 7:30am.

"We catch the Sauano *pasi*" (bus), she said.

Manutagi is a quiet student in my form class. Eighteen years old, with thick, black, wavy hair (reminding me of my Tahitian Auntie Anna), she lives in Sauano, a small village in Fagaloa. Fagaloa is scenic area off the beaten track that few Samoans visit. Even fewer go to Sauano, but it was the one village we knew about before leaving Australia.

Twelve months earlier, our friend Murray, an officer in the Australian Navy, had installed a generator to power the little Sauano village health clinic. To avoid using the narrow, rocky road, he used a helicopter to carry the generator from his ship to the village, which apparently caused a sensation. The way Murray raved about Sauano, it would have to be the most beautiful place in Samoa, or perhaps the Pacific, and Manutagi has invited us there to spend a few days with her family.

We've been in the country a little more than three months now, but this will be our first overnight stay in a village - something Peace Corps Volunteers do in their first few weeks. We're keen to experience village culture at a much deeper level, but we're also apprehensive. Sure, we've practiced changing clothes with an *ie*, and washing in the Malua pool, but will that be enough to be discreet in a *fale* with no walls or doors?

Will we sleep on a concrete floor?

Villages are noisy, so will we sleep at all?

Then yesterday Fuli told Heather she's coming too.

"We meet half-past-seven at da market," says Fuli, who's always chatty and has a beaming smile.

We left home and caught the Nofoali'i bus around daybreak. After arriving at the Apia market, we scan the crowd setting up market stalls. With no Fuli or Manutagi in sight, we wait, sitting on a concrete ledge in the shade. The heat soon increases, along with the pungent odour from the nearby fish market.

It's 7:45 and now we're anxious.

Fuli said we need to catch the bus around now.

Has something happened?

Then we see Manutagi threading her way through stall holders towards us.

"Is Fuli here too?" I ask.

"*Leai.* Why Fuli?"

"Fuli said she's coming with us."

"*Leai - pepelo Fuli*" (Fuli's a liar).

"When does the Sauano bus leave?"

"No bus. Catch da Sauano pickup."

"Here at the market?"

"*Ioe* (yes). Leave eleven o'clock?"

"What do we do now?"

"Wait for the peoples."

"People?"

"Other peoples catch da pickup."

Resigning ourselves to wait another three hours, we sit away from the overpowering smell of fish.

It looks like Fuli isn't coming after all.

Except that Heather is pretty sure Fuli said she is coming.

An hour later Fuli appears with a bag under her arm, bubbling with excitement and chatter.

She slept in.

"Sorry."

Manutagi's face remains inscrutable as Fuli arrives, like she always expected Fuli will join us.

The hours pass slowly as we watch people come and go.

We buy something to eat. We talk, stand up, sit down, and walk around the market several times.

With the rising heat we move again to catch more sea breeze.

Eleven o'clock comes and goes without any sign of departure.

At half past eleven Manutagi hurries toward us.

"Pickup ready," she says, breathless with haste. "*Kope*" (hurry)!

Grabbing our bags, we rush off after her feeling like laggards holding everyone up.

We stop at the rear door of a rusty yellow van pulled up at the curb. Along with four other women holding bags of vegetables, we climb into the van over baskets of taro, bananas, bags of rice, a spare tire, and a roll of polythene hose. By now we're sufficiently skilled in the art of pickup travel to select a comfortable spot for the journey. Meanwhile, as the women chatter about us, we hear the word 'palagi' repeated with laughter and smiles.

There's no breeze as we sit waiting with our knees tucked up in the hot, cramped van. The temperature rises and we sweat in the stifling air.

"What's happening Fuli?" I ask.

"Wait for da people," she says.

We hope they arrive before we pass out in the heat.

When two more women climb aboard and pack themselves into the tight space, the driver starts the engine. As we move off, we eagerly drink in the cool breeze blowing through the windows. After four-and-a-half hours, we're finally on our way.

But not for long.

On the outskirts of Apia, we roll to a stop by the side of the road. The driver mutters in the front seat before the rear doors suddenly open. The carefully folded arms and legs of eight passengers begin unfolding to exit the van.

"What's happening Fuli?" asks Heather.

"We stop. We out here."

"Why?"

Ke le iloa (don't know).

As I climb out over the taro and rice, Fuli interrogates the driver.

"He say no petrol," says Fuli.

"Can we get petrol here?"

"Da shop - there," says Fuli, pointing down the road towards Apia. I vaguely recall seeing a large shop by the road some distance back.

While we join the other passengers sitting under a shady tree, the driver pulls an empty plastic container out from under the spare tire. He gives the container and some money to a teenage boy, who runs back down the road towards Apia.

Half-an-hour later the boy comes running back with a container of petrol.

Smiles break out as everyone stands up to watch the driver fill the tank. However, judging from the container's shape, it's clear he can't pour the petrol into the tank. But the driver has considered this problem, or he's done it before, because he pulls a piece of black rubber hose from under his seat. When he puts one end in the container and the other in his mouth, I see he's making a siphon.

But the hose isn't transparent, so he can't see petrol in the hose. When he sucks on the tube to start the siphon, how will he avoid getting a mouth, or lung, full of petrol?

He doesn't.

Coughing and spluttering petrol over the road, he shoves the hose end into the tank. He might risk poisoning his lungs, but the siphon works, and the petrol quickly transfers from the container to the tank. The driver tosses the hose and container in the vehicle, turns on the ignition, and the engine roars back into life. We all pile into the van, back over the taro, rice, and spare tire, to our 'seats'.

We're on our way to Sauano at last.

A few kilometres further down the road the engine stops, and we roll to a halt.

The driver turns the engine over, but it won't start. He decides to investigate by opening the hood, which is inside the van beside the driver. More to the point, it's beside me, sitting behind the driver's seat. Looking at the engine, he pulls the fuel line off the carburettor and reaches for the ignition keys.

Oh no! He's about to check the fuel pump's working by cranking the engine over. If the pump does work, raw fuel will spray all over the hot engine. If it ignites, it'll be like throwing a Molotov cocktail through the windscreen, incinerating the van and any passenger too slow to get out. Being the furthest from the rear door, I have to climb over the taro, rice, and spare tire to get out. Am I going to be burned alive?

The engine cranks over, petrol spurts all over the hot engine, but doesn't ignite. I feel a surge of relief knowing I'm not going to burn alive, and the fuel pump is working just fine.

After fruitlessly poking about the engine without finding the cause of the problem, they decide to push-start the van. But since the battery and starter motor are working, it seems futile to me. I consider using a screwdriver to check the spark is being delivered by the distributor, but I think it's best to watch and listen rather than interfere. I get out to help push.

After some futile attempts to start the van, they give up trying, and appear to just push the vehicle along the road. Not that anyone sees the need to explain anything to me. I wonder if we're going to push the vehicle filled with passengers all the way to Sauano. I hope not, but who knows?

Anything is possible.

Jogging along, we pass people by the roadside who comment about the palagi, and then burst into laughter. Every time, I feel a conspicuous object of amusement. We push the van a kilometre or two down the road. It's the heat of the day, and we're all hot, sweaty, and dusty, when we finally stop.

We appear to be at the home of a village mechanic. There's evidence of a workshop under the shade of a large mango tree, while some cars and wrecks litter the yard in various states of repair and disassembly. The shirtless mechanic emerges from his *fale* with a dirty *ie* wrapped around him. Everyone else exits the vehicle as he climbs into the van, but I stay to watch.

Using a screwdriver, he opens the distributor cap and checks the spark like I would have done. He may not look like a mechanic, but he seems to know what he's doing.

I join Heather and the other passengers, who sit in the sea breeze under the shade of a small *fale* by the road.

"What happens now?" I ask Manutagi.

"Wait," she says. Manutagi uses words like they're an expensive commodity.

"What are we waiting for?"

"Pick-up."

"But isn't that the pickup?" says Heather, pointing to the motionless van.

"Other pickup."

"There's another pickup?"

"Ioe" (yes).

"When will it come?"

"Toeitiiti" (soon).

In Samoa, "soon" means anything from a few minutes to hours, or even days. We wait again, resigned to our fate and wondering which it will be - minutes, hours, or days?

It's more than six hours since we left home, but our destination still feels tantalisingly out of reach. Three months earlier we would have been anxious and distressed by now. But we've learned to patiently accept our circumstances, because they are in God's hands rather than our own. Besides, it's a fruitless waste of energy getting upset with people or circumstances over which we, and they, have no control.

We watch the waves crash on nearby rocks, the village people passing by, and enviously eye other buses and cars going in our direction full of passengers; people who are actually going somewhere, in vehicles that actually work.

But we're lucky!

Ten minutes later the other pickup wheezes to a halt in a cloud of smoke and dust. Brightly painted in shades of pink and red, the vehicle body is a makeshift timber frame with galvanised iron panels. Two rows of passenger seats run lengthwise behind the driver, in what may have once been a Ford pickup.

Manutagi, Fuli, and others clamber into the back, over the ubiquitous bags of taro and rice, or sit on the roof. But as honoured guests, we're given the front seat. Heather sits next to the driver, while I take the passenger seat with my arm on the door.

As we take off, the door unjams and swings open. I pull it shut but find there's no latch to hold it in place. Fortunately, since the vehicle moves at a snail's pace, it's not difficult to keep the door shut with my arm, as we slowly continue our journey to Sauano.

Then the engine stops, and the vehicle rolls to a halt. Our hearts sink. Not again. What now?

But the driver seems unbothered.

He eases himself from his seat, walks to the front, and lifts the bonnet. Being curious, I get out to watch.

The engine is covered in a thick coating of black dust and oil. Hand carved wooden plugs replace long lost radiator and oil caps.

The driver pulls out a large inline filter from one of the hoses, blows on it a few times to clear it, and then puts it back. The engine promptly starts, and I climb back into the pickup. Once again, we're on our way to Sauano with hearts full of hope, even if our expectations have taken a severe beating.

Ten minutes further down the road we stop at a brightly coloured village store. Passengers unpack themselves from the vehicle and flock into the store to buy drinks and snacks. We're thirsty, so I buy a bottle of Coke. After Heather and I drink a little we pass it back to Fuli and Manutagi who consume the rest.

As the driver gets into his seat, he passes us each a small container of ice cream equipped with a little plastic spoon. We're initially unsure whether they're for us, or if we're holding them for someone else. Then, realising they're a gift from the driver, we feel touched by his kindness and generosity - something that still catches us unawares. The ice cream might be a poor substitute for lunch, but it's cold, sweet, and appreciated.

Because by now we've learned to appreciate and celebrate small things, including a vehicle that moves toward our destination. We may be on our way to Sauano again, but this time we're not surprised when the engine stops, and we roll to a halt. But the driver blows the filter clean, and we're off again.

At Falefa we turn off the main road towards a bridge crossing a river. Although the bridge looks strong, there's no railing, and parts of the road platform have fallen away, leaving just the two lines of planks to support the vehicle's wheels. We hold our breath as the driver drives onto the bridge and slowly crosses, carefully keeping the wheels on the supporting planks. We breathe again when we arrive safely on the far side.

The rough gravel road climbs up and around the hillside. The engine becomes hotter, and so do our feet. Blue smoke creeps under the dashboard into our faces and irritates our eyes. As the pickup lurches its way through potholes and over rocks, the passenger door un-jams and I work hard to hold it in place. My hands are slippery with the sweat dripping from our faces and running into our eyes. We envy those passengers behind us, and those on the roof, who have fresh air blowing in their faces.

Despite the heat and smoke, we've crossed a bridge into a new world. Below us on our left, the white wavetops of the Falefa inlet emerge from the deep blue sea, crashing on the black volcanic coastal rocks stretching into the distance. Across the inlet, a fountain of lush, green vegetation cascades down the hillside into a fringe of brightly coloured village houses. On our right, bananas, *ta'amu*, breadfruit, coconuts, vines, and other vegetation grow in wild abundance up the steep hillside. Occasionally we cross small streams winding their way down to the sea, passing under the road through concrete culverts.

After another half-hour of sauna and passive smoking in the cabin, we turn a bend and see a small bay far below us. Soon the rooftops of a village appear beside a small beach. We hope this is Sauano, but after so many dashed hopes, we dampen our expectations.

As the driver negotiates a steep descent, we pass barefoot children swinging bush knives in their hands and carrying baskets of coconuts and taro on poles. Approaching the village, we're confronted by a gate, a hotchpotch of timber, chicken wire, and fragments of iron. We hear later it prevents pigs wandering away. After a passenger leaps out and opens the gate, we enter the village down a steep gravel road, stopping in the shade of a large mango tree beside a church.

I feel a finger jab me in the ribs and see Fuli mouthing, "Sauano."

The passengers give money to the driver as they leave. I follow their lead, offering a ten tala note saying, *"Fa'afetai tele lava"* (thank you very much).

He nods, saying something in Samoan I don't understand. Ten tala is probably more than I need to pay, but in Samoa generosity is a currency too.

Fuli then pulls my arm saying, "We go here."

We follow the girls under shady trees toward a small stream crossed by two logs. We gingerly cross the logs, hoping we don't fall in the stream, and lift our eyes to see two beautiful thatched *fales* in a yard of white crushed coral.

My watch says it's well past three in the afternoon. It's taken us nine hours, a bus, two vehicles, and four breakdowns, to travel the thirty kilometres to Sauano.

Following Manutagi to a *fale*, we leave our shoes on the dark stone entrance steps decorated with white clamshells.

A middle-aged man sits cross-legged on the fale floor, and I recognise him as a fellow pickup passenger. With a wide smile and friendly face, he greets us warmly saying, "*Talofa lava.*"

Realising he's Faita, Manutagi's father, we respond and sit cross-legged on *fala* (pandanus mats) covering the floor. Shirtless, he wears a brightly coloured *ie* folded around his knees revealing a full body tattoo. It suggests he might be a *matai* with status in the village. A large woman we assume is Manutagi's mother, Sapela, steps into *fale* opposite us. Wearing a yellow tee-shirt and purple *ie*, her round, friendly face beams with obvious pleasure as she sits beside Faita, and we repeat the greeting formalities. Since they are polite Samoans, they have done their homework, and already know our names and a lot about us.

"*O a le malaga?*" (how was the journey?), asks Sapela.

"*Lelei, umi tele*" (good, but very long), I say.

"*A, sa'o*" (very true).

I reach into my pack and present our gift - a tin of *pisupo*. Sapela smiles with pleasure as she takes the gift saying "*Fa'afetai tele lava*" (thank you very much). Faita also smiles with approval, and we feel relieved that we've brought an appreciated gift.

Faita speaks only a few words of English, while Sapela speaks none. The conversation quickly exhausts our common language and grinds to a halt. I hope Manutagi or Fuli will sit with us to help translate, but they've vanished.

Sitting at the edge of the *fale* with our backs to a post, I look up into the roof. Up close, I can see the leaves are woven into individual tiles tied to the roof frame using *afa* (sinnet - coconut fibre twine). Similarly, the hand cut roof frame timbers are neatly cut to fit together and secured by *afa* tied in a symmetrical pattern. The supporting posts stand in a platform of stacked basalt rocks making a floor a metre above the ground. A layer of small, smooth stones, fills the gaps between the rocks making a flat surface. Sitting on pandanus mats laid on the stones, we notice they're a soft and comfortable surface - suitable for sitting or sleeping. Tucked up near the roof are blinds woven from coconut branches. These can be dropped down to provide shade from the sun, or shelter from the wind and rain. It's cool and peaceful, as gentle waves wash on the nearby beach, and a soft ocean breeze blows through the shady *fale*.

I feel privileged sitting in this traditional home, the style of home Samoans have lived in for thousands of years. I've heard that house building is a traditional Samoan master trade, like canoe making, or tattooing, and it's clear there are specialist skills needed to make such a home. But not only skill, but also care and pride, because while it's clearly functional, the intricate woven patterns suggest beauty is also important. Unlike our European style home, Manutagi's traditional *fale* is also free of cockroaches, spiders, centipedes, and rats, because there are no dark spaces to harbour insects or vermin.

The awkward silence is broken when Fuli and Manutagi re-appear offering freshly opened *niu* (green drinking coconuts). Being hot, dusty, tired, and thirsty, the *niu* are wonderfully refreshing, and Sapela and Faita smile with pleasure.

Having no walls, the *fale* has little space for decorations or ornaments, but there are some family photos pinned to the posts and frame. There's a wooden chest neatly placed at one end, where Sapela keeps the family linen, clothes, and other valuable possessions. As simple as it is, craftsmanship and beauty seem important to them. They might be poor by Samoan standards, but they're clearly house proud. We don't know it yet, but we're in the house of a master craftsman.

Behind Manutagi's father I see another small, thatched building - the family 'kitchen' where Manutagi's brother prepares meals. There's a fireplace sheltered from the rain, a wood pile, and a pile of saucepans. Further away is a neat looking *fale moa* (chicken house), and a *fale uila* (toilet).

Fuli reappears beside Heather and points her chin towards the sea saying, "*Ka'ele?* You want swim?"

It's getting late in an already long day, and seeing the inviting waves break gently on the quiet beach, a swim sounds wonderful.

"We go," says Fuli, promptly picking up our packs and walking off.

Thanking Manutagi's parents, we follow Fuli to the next *fale*. It's empty, except for a double mattress on the floor, already made up with sheets and pillows, and a mosquito net hanging from the roof beams. It will be our *fale* while we stay in Sauano.

"You want change clothes?" asks Fuli.

"*E leai*" (no), says Heather.

By now, we've adopted the Samoan belief that having special clothes for swimming is a ridiculous waste. If they swim at all, Samoans swim in their clothes, with men and women bathing separately to maintain discretion. Wet clothing has the added bonus of cooling us while drying.

But first, a toilet stop.

A ramshackle outhouse built of odd pieces of repurposed timber on a small concrete slab, their toilet is the simple septic tank system common throughout Samoa.

In past years the UNDP and Peace Corps ran a programme to install these systems in villages. Villagers cast the toilet bowl themselves using concrete and fiberglass moulds. The bowls were fixed to a concrete slab with the waste fed to a simple septic system using the porous, sandy soil and crushed coral, common throughout Samoa. Villagers flush the toilets by tipping a bucket of water into the bowl taken from a large drum - often filled with rainwater from the outhouse roof. It may be rudimentary, but it's sanitary, odourless, and as clean as any well-kept bathroom in the world's most developed countries.

There's a new toilet roll on a ledge, thoughtfully purchased for us. Beside it is a sheaf of papers hooked on a piece of wire. The papers are repurposed school notes from the previous year, and perhaps represent a final and fitting end to a poor teacher's struggle to impart useful knowledge.

Leaving the *fale*, the beach beckons with its soft sand, gentle waves, and children frolicking in the quiet water. As I imagine walking into the delicious cool water, Manutagi turns left, away from the soft sand and gentle waves. Instead of sitting in the cool water we clamber over slippery black rocks.

"Where are we going?" I ask.

"Swim," says Manutagi.

"What about the beach there?"

"Better place."

"Where is this place?"

"There," says Manutagi, pointing to what looks like ocean waves crashing on jagged black rocks in foaming violence. I can't see any quiet beach, but Manutagi has lived here all her life, so she should know, right?

We finally stop where the rock face drops into the sea and white foam blows in our faces. Ocean waves crash violently onto the cliff face, and we see huge lumps of loose coral being tossed about in the maelstrom.

"Good for swim," says Manutagi, pointing to the carnival of violence before us. The only outcome of swimming here will be our battered and bloated bodies later washing up on that beautiful beach we just passed.

"We can't swim here Manutagi," I tell her. "We'll be killed, but you swim if you like."

"*E leai*" (no), say Manutagi and Fuli, vigorously shaking their heads, looking genuinely shocked at the idea.

The girls confer vigorously in Samoan about what to do, before Manutagi points with her chin to some nearby trees.

"You want rest?"

"That would be nice," says Heather.

"We go here," commands Fuli, who walks under the trees and sits on a rock.

We're mystified why they thought we'd want to swim in this dangerous water, but we don't probe any further. When we first arrived in Samoa, we tried to understand everything, and anything that triggered our curiosity, of which there was plenty. However, immersion experiences, in the context of real-life activity, often better satisfies palagi curiosity than confused answers from Samoans who are mystified why we're even asking such questions. It is better to avoid asking asinine questions, and easier to watch, wonder, and wait for answers to emerge, leaving us free we enjoy the experience, come what may.

Following Fuli, we find our own shaded rocks and rest. As the sea breeze blows through our hair, we look out over the deep blue sea, and a rugged coastline of jagged black rocks and foaming water. Sauano sits nearby in a bay sheltered from the ocean waves by a large sandbar and reef.

While it's still a strange culture, we're beginning to find our place, and feel part of it. Three months earlier, we arrived in Samoa sleepless, stressed, insecure, and anxious about our uncertain future. Now, we've become more Samoan - accepting and even embracing uncertainty, because uncertainty also brings opportunity - the opportunity for God's providential grace. While it's wise to plan and think ahead about what we will do with each day, or week, it's also wise to make room in our minds for God's providential plan for our day.

This day, God's plan included a series of unexpected breakdowns, pushing a vehicle along a road, and hours of patient waiting in the company of people we don't know. When we left home this morning, we had no idea we'd be sitting on these rocks with Manutagi and Fuli, with the opportunity to talk with them as young Samoan women, to relate as friends rather than teachers.

Manutagi tells us Faita carves 'ava bowls to sell for cash income to tourists at Aggie Grey's and the Tusitala Hotel. She says Faita and Sapela built their *fales* themselves, but they sheltered in the church during Cyclone Ofa. When modern iron roofs blow off, they often take the whole roof structure with them. Without supporting roof trusses, the rest of the building then collapses. But when the thatch blows off a traditional *fale*, the frame is left intact. When the wind stopped blowing, the family quickly restored their home by re-thatching their roof with coconut leaves.

On the far side of Sauano, the land rises and slightly obscures more rooftops and another beach.

"Saletele. Other village," says Manutagi, following my eyes.

Both villages nestle at the foot of green mountains rising steeply toward fleecy white clouds flitting across the blue sky. Bright blue-green water fringes the beach where children play, darkening as it deepens near the reef. From there, the deep blue sea meets dark purple rain clouds forming on the distant horizon, sparkling with the occasional lightning flash. It's breathtaking; a place of savage, primeval splendour; beauty with a softness melting the hardest heart.

I marvel how people carved a space for two villages out of this little isolated inlet. Perhaps it represents Samoa; a nook carved out of the vast Pacific Ocean - out of the world. Thousands of years ago, a group of people arrived here and made these islands their home. They learned the skills necessary to carve boats and a living out of nature's chaos - to fish, grow taro, build *fales*, and bond in community. I wonder how long Manutagi's family have lived in this place. Perhaps a thousand years? Maybe more?

All the world could disappear and Sauano could still go on, without a care. They don't need the rest of the world to survive or live happily. But like all of us, they want things the world offers. They want a village clinic, and a generator, so they have electric lights for a few hours each evening - long enough for children to do their homework. They want Manutagi to get a high school education, so Manutagi stays with Fuli's family in Lauli'i and travels by bus to school each day. Is a high school education a want or a need?

24
REST

*"Take my yoke upon you, and learn from me, for I am gentle
and lowly in heart, and you will find rest for your souls."*
Matthew 11:29

The sun is low in the sky when Manutagi stands and says, *"Ia - we go."*

Following her back to the village, we slip off our *se'evae* on the *fale* steps and sit cross legged on a soft pandanus mat.

Then Manutagi sits beside Heather and asks, *"Ka'ele?"* While *ka'ele* means 'swim', it also means 'bath' or 'shower'.

"Fa'amolemole" (yes please), says Heather eagerly. At last, a chance to wash off all the dust and sweat, and cool down.

"We walk to pool. Not far," says Manutagi.

She walks to the other fale and soon returns with Fuli carrying towels and other bathroom accoutrements.

"For you," says Manutagi, handing me an *ie solosolo* and a towel. She gives Heather a cake of pink soap - soft and scented, not the cheap, caustic, locally made Samoan soap. Being obviously special and expensive for

Manutagi's family, we feel touched, realising the effort they're making to make us feel comfortable.

"*Kakou o*" (we go), says Fuli.

In the dim light we follow the girls gingerly across the log bridge over the stream. Crossing the road behind the church, we follow a winding track around the hillside through brush. Manutagi stops and points to a small rock-lined pool below.

"You first," she says to me.

"We wait," says Fuli, grabbing Heather's arm and pulling her back up the dark path.

As I make my way down to the pool, I hear laughter and giggling from the girls and Heather. Some joke on me?

Probably.

After the long day I'm keen to walk into the dark pool and sit down. It's shallower than our pool at Malua but fed from a bubbling mountain stream at one end. Soaping up, I dip my head under the water to emerge refreshed and clean. Wrapping the *ie* around me, I walk back up the dark path carrying my clothes. I soon see dark shadows suggesting the girls are ahead.

Manutagi grabs the precious soap from my hand as they walk down the path. I soon hear splashes and laughter coming from the pool, while I stand wet and shirtless in the dark.

Two young women and some children appear out of the darkness and brush past me on the path. The children chatter excitedly, pointing at me saying "*Palagi, palagi*" before breaking into squeals of laughter as they disappear down the path. We're probably the most interesting topic of conversation in the village tonight.

The girls soon reappear wrapped in *ie's*, wet and carrying a bundle of clothes. We make our way back down the path, now illuminated by moonlight shining on the white coral. As we near their *fale*, Faita kindly holds a kerosene lamp to light the log bridge. Gingerly crossing with our hands full, we make our way to the *fale*, where Faita hangs the lamp on a wire hook, bathing everything in a soft, yellow light.

Fuli takes our wet clothes and towels to hang on lines strung between the roof beams. Meanwhile Manutagi hangs a sheet near our bed to provide some privacy. She also releases the woven blinds on the side facing the other family *fale*, but not those on the side facing the village. We look down to other *fales* nearby where families are busy preparing or eating their evening meal.

We're glad we invested time learning to change under an *ie*. While it seems we're changing while completely exposed to a watching village, neighbours afford us the privacy they should to guests of Manutagi's family. We're covered by the courtesy code that's second nature to Samoans - you don't stare into your neighbour's house when it's obvious you shouldn't. Doing so would break the delicate harmony of relationships in a village.

Sitting cross-legged on the floor in fresh clothes, we feel wonderfully clean and refreshed. We relax as the soft, evening breeze blows gently on our faces, and feel hungry.

Fortunately, Fuli and Manutagi soon reappear carrying dishes of food they lay out on the floor before us. There are only two dinner plates, because as guests it's proper that we eat first, followed later by Faita and Sapela, then the children. Among the traditional Samoan foods, there are also some palagi items, including a dish of cream filled biscuits they must have brought in Apia. We also notice the meal is not only delicious, but beautifully presented. Such attention to small details in an isolated village is unexpected, suggesting beauty is important to Sapela.

Being the chatty one, Fuli does most of the talking while we eat. Manutagi looks on smiling, her eyes twinkling with pleasure in the amber lamplight. It's a special moment for her, having her teachers stay with her family.

And a special moment for us too. All the confusion, patient endurance, hopes, fears, and frustrations of the journey have evaporated. In the balmy evening, we sit in a village under a flickering lamp. Waves gently lap the shore behind us, and moonlight dances on the foaming wavetops crashing on the distant reef.

If this isn't paradise it must be pretty close.

"*Ma'ona?*" (finished), asks Manutagi, when we stop.

"*Ioe, ma'ona*" (yes, finished), we both nod.

She passes us a bowl of water and a small towel, and we wash and dry our hands. Meanwhile, they collect the dishes and take them back to the other *fale*. We have a moment to reflect while the family sit cross legged on the floor in the other *fale* eating their meal, talking, and laughing together.

When Manutagi wanders over to ask if we want to walk through the village, we nod "*Ioe* (yes)."

"We go now," she says, turning and calling out "Fuli, *kakou o*" (let's go).

We set off together, and while Faita holds a lamp for us to cross the log bridge, we then walk by moonlight.

The soft, warm air is thick and comforting. The large stone church building casts a moon shadow over the road, while on our left, coconut palms fringe the beach. There's enough light to see each family's *fale,* with their accompanying *fale kuka,* and *fale uila,* arranged in no discernible pattern.

It's obvious there's a transition occurring from traditional to modern building techniques. Corrugated iron is replacing coconut thatch, and concrete floors are poured over stone bases. Some rectangular *fales* have palagi style roof trusses.

As we walk along the road chatting, families finish their evening meal. Adults sit talking and smoking, while children run about carrying and cleaning. It's hard to tell if the children are working or playing. Maybe it's both.

We recognise A'a (our Form Six student) standing nearby in the moonlight throwing rice to a flock of chickens making a raucous noise. Seeing us, A'a's face breaks into a beaming smile. Like everyone else in the village, she knew we were coming, and we agree to visit her family tomorrow. The visit will fulfill an important social obligation. A'a's father is the village pastor, but we're keen to meet her parents, because A'a stands out as a diligent, thoughtful, and bright student. She might possibly pass Form Six and even get a scholarship to a university somewhere.

Near A'a there's a net strung between two posts.

"*O le a le mea lea?*" (what is that?) I ask.

"*Volipolo,*" answers Manutagi, "Volleyball."

"Who plays volleyball?"

"The kids. Peoples."

"Do you play?"

"*Ioe,* sometimes."

"Are you good at *volipolo*?" asks Heather.

"*E leai*! (no). Fuli is good."

"*E leai, ua leaga*" (no, I'm bad)! laughs Fuli.

"When do you play Fuli?" asks Heather.

"After work at home, sometimes."

"You mean school homework?"

"*Leai* (no), work for da family. Clean clothes, sweep the *fale*, make da food."

"I played volleyball at school," I add, "but I wasn't very good at it."

"Like Manutagi," says Fuli.

"Like Fuli," laughs Manutagi.

We pass a pile of timber on a concrete slab. Manutagi says it's what remains of the health clinic after Cyclone Ofa. The generator installed by our friend is there too, but broken, leaving the village with neither health clinic nor power.

"When will they fix it?" asks Heather.

"*Ke le iloa,*" (don't know) shrugs Manutagi.

We continue walking and reach the end of Sauano.

"We go Saletele," declares Manutagi.

Trudging up the small rise separating the two villages, we see a village much like Sauano. It has more flat ground, and while it appears more spacious and orderly, it's less interesting to us.

Walking down the moonlit road, we're engulfed by a flock of young children emerging from the beach herded by two teenage girls. They stare at us, laughing and chattering, and we hear, " … *palagi …palagi …* " . When Manutagi calls out to them, the teenage girls grin sheepishly as they shepherd the children, then smile at us, and continue on their way laughing and chattering.

"What was that about?" I ask.

"They are childrens," says Manutagi, as if that explains everything.

"I know, but what were they laughing about?"

"They happy because they see you. You are *palagi.*"

"Don't they see palagi?"

"*E leai* (no), not many palagi here."

On our first day in Apia we were disconcerted, and then annoyed, when it seemed like every child we passed called out, "Palagi, palagi" and burst into laughter. Now it seems as much part of the Samoan landscape as coral and coconuts. The children are laughing because they're happy to see us. And we understand we have the privilege of bringing a moment of happiness to some children by doing something as simple as going for a walk. One day palagis will be so common that children will stop laughing and calling out, "Palagi." In that silence, we'll feel a little sad for its loss.

As we wander on, other adults stare curiously at us from *fales* close to the road, and a few smile, and nod. We pass another volleyball net strung near the beach, and a large, prominent Congregational Church.

But at the far end of the village is a new, modern, LDS (Mormon) church. Like every other LDS church in Samoa, it's built to the same American design, constructed of concrete cinderblocks painted white, with a green iron roof, and a mandatory small basketball court out front. It might look fine in Utah, but in a quaint, colourful Samoan village, it seems incongruously out of place.

"Do they play basketball here?" I ask Manutagi.

"*E a?*" (what?).

"It seems strange to build a basketball court if no one plays basketball."

"*Ou ke le iloa.*" (I don't know)

"Every LDS has dat," says Fuli.

"Does anyone play basketball?"

"*Ke le iloa.*"

At the end of the village, the road rises steeply as it curves around the coastline and into the forest.

"Where does it go?" I ask Manutagi.

"Fagaloa."

"Aren't we in Fagaloa?"

"*Ioe* (yes) - more village."

"My cousin live there at Musumusu," says Fuli.

"Is it far?" asks Heather.

"*E leai* (no) not far," says Manutagi. "We go back now."

We discover the next day that "not far" is a four-hour walk. A few months ago, we would have thought a four-hour walk in the tropics daunting. But now we're beginning to agree with Manutagi that it's "not far."

Arriving back at our *fale*, we sit cross legged on the floor while Fuli and Manutagi serve us a supper of sugary, black tea, and cream biscuits.

It's clear from our walk and the number of traditional *fales* we saw that Sauano is not a wealthy village, and Manutagi's family are probably some of the least wealthy. With an annual cash income of a few hundred US dollars a year, they're classified by the UN as the world's poorest. But are they really poor?

They live in their own simple, but beautiful, and comfortable home, crafted themselves using materials growing around them, on their own land, without a mortgage or landlord.

They have all the land they need to grow taro, breadfruit, coconuts, and other healthy foods, supplemented by chickens, pigs and abundant seafood. They farm nutrient rich soil, with constant rainfall, and a warm, humid climate all year round. Working diligently, they need never fear hunger, want, or cold. Yet there's no need to engage in long hours of drudgery, seven days a week, like many poor people do elsewhere in the world in their daily struggle to survive. For wealth is best measured by choice rather than income. The Sauano villagers can work harder if they wish, but free from the bondage of drudgery, they can choose to spend their time on more meaningful pursuits.

They're also free from the bondage of gastrointestinal diseases that kill millions of the world's poor every year. They have clean water supplied from a mountain stream, free from contamination because there are no upstream settlements. And the simple, septic toilet system can't contaminate their water supply.

When the village clinic is rebuilt, they'll have primary healthcare on their doorstep, and a major hospital is only a pick-up ride away, even if the journey is a little bumpy and unpredictable.

And what monetary value can we put on their strong, stable culture? Those of us who travel overseas are easily tempted to interpret the value of any culture by the sum of its shortcomings compared to our own. But the culture of any people is the air they breathe that maintains the life of their community. For culture binds people together, not just to survive, but also to maintain peace, enable prosperity, and inspire hope. When cultures disintegrate, or change too rapidly, as has happened to many indigenous communities, people easily descend into an abyss of destructive behaviours, and are left peering into a dark and hopeless future.

So perhaps the most priceless asset of the Sauano villagers is their strong, stable culture, that binds them together by a common belief system, with its traditional self-governing community. It's one that has proven to promote the peace and prosperity of its people for thousands of years, and care for any community member in need. The threat of losing such an asset is a warning to all who chafe at the cautionary pace of Samoan economic development, and campaign for more rapid cultural change. Be careful what you wish for.

So if the people of Sauano live in poverty, it's the sort of poverty most poor people, and many wealthy people, aspire to achieve all their lives - a seductively beautiful, if simple, way of life.

It's a valuable lesson for us. We should avoid confusing simplicity with poverty.

"*Fia moe oulua?*" (want to sleep?) asks Manutagi.

"*Fa'amolemole*" (please).

"*Ia,*" says Fuli, and begins collecting plates to carry them away.

In the flickering kerosene lamplight, I realise I have no idea what time it is.

But does it matter?

I feel like we're in a timeless place, in Eliot's 'timeless moment' when the past and future are all present in the now. Perhaps we've finally touched the eternity in our hearts.

Manutagi unfolds the mosquito net and tucks the end under our mattress. There might be a gentle breeze, but it's still very warm, so we lie on top of the sheets in our clothes. Fuli makes herself comfortable, lying nearby on the floor wrapped in an *ie,* with a pillow under her head. Manutagi lifts the glass of kerosene lamp and blows out the flame.

"*Manuia le po*" (good night), calls out Fuli. "*Fai le miti lelei,*" (have nice dreams).

"*Manuia le po,*" we return.

In the other *fale,* Faita and Sapela sit together quietly talking in the soft glow of another lamp. A few feet away we hear Fuli and Manutagi whispering in the darkness. We draw some comfort knowing they're not far away, keeping watch over us while we sleep.

Lying there staring at the *fale* roof, I recall that moment on our first day in Samoa, lying in the stifling oven of Mick's flat, and wondering if we'd made a mistake coming to Samoa. The hard road we've trod since that day has been far harder than we ever thought, in ways we never imagined. But it's also been a road worth taking. While Jesus may have been speaking about life eternal when he said, "*The way is hard that leads to life, and those who find it are few,*" I think he was also speaking about life here and now. Perhaps the life He offers is not the life we have been looking for or expect. Perhaps we're looking in the wrong places. For it certainly seems the road of courage in the face of risk and hardship, of self-denial instead of personal peace and affluence, is a road worth taking. Hardship, risk, and complex relationships, place burdens on our shoulders, but those burdens seem lighter and easier when we carry them with a sure hope grounded in the knowledge of God's purpose.

In his purpose and providential grace, God chose people to share that road with us; people we did not know, and perhaps would not have chosen - like Mick, John, Tammy, and Helen. People who bear each other's burdens, who have blessed us, and we've learned to accept and love. God also gave us students like Fuli and Manutagi, who took us down the narrow, winding road to Sauano, into the very heart of traditional Samoan culture, to a home in a village where we've been welcomed and feel strangely at peace. It's like we've found our place and purpose and have finally come home. Perhaps, in this here and now, we have touched the eternity in our hearts, and tasted the rest Jesus' offers for our souls.

As I close my eyes, I drift off to sleep hearing the rhythmic sound of the sea gently breaking on the sand, and the occasional muffled voices of nearby neighbours. We feel very safe, very privileged, at peace in our hearts, and inexpressibly happy.

Nice dreams.

Miti lelei.

25

EPILOGUE

*"Consider the lilies of the field, how they grow: they
neither toil nor spin, yet I tell you, even Solomon in
all his glory was not arrayed like one of these."*
Matthew 6:28-29

Sitting in our house at Leulumoega Fou, we gaze out across the peaceful, azure-blue water of our tropical lagoon. Where it reaches the encircling coral reef, its colour changes to deep ocean blue, behind the white foaming violence of crashing surf. At night, we hear the sleepless roar of the distant reef, as it breaks great ocean rollers into little lagoon waves lapping the sand's edge.

While our surface world has abundant beauty, when we snorkel in the shallow water, we look down on another enchanted wonderland of rainbow coral, brightly coloured fish, and curious marine life. And at the reef edge, where the coral floor drops away precipitously, we see corals and fish fading into a blueing, bottomless haze, where unknown treasures beckon, and the water is pregnant with risk.

It is like our journey into chaos, culture, and compassion.

Before we left Australia, a friend from World Vision told us, "After living in another culture for a month you think you form an understanding of that country and culture. But after six months, you realise your one-month thinking was all wrong. You misunderstood everything then, but now you feel like you really do understand. But at six months you'll also feel depressed. Finally worn down by the heavy cloud of uncertainty, culture shock and chaos, you'll be tempted to abandon your work and go home. But if you persist for two years, your understanding will deepen in ways difficult to describe, and you'll realise your six-month thinking was all wrong too. And then after ten years, you realise two years wasn't enough because you still had so much to learn."

It's a perspective as valuable as it is humbling, for it suggests all knowledge is provisional, and if we're sufficiently curious to leave the door of our minds open, more learning will creep in. We need humility and patience, because cultures are deeper, and more complex, than the shape of our wildest dreams. And we need to be patient, and give ourselves time, because some life lessons take a lifetime to learn.

With that perspective, we're only three months into our Samoan culture journey. While we've wet our feet in the shallows, we're still snorkelling around on top. We've not dived deep enough to be fully immersed, and while we gaze down with curiosity, we haven't ventured far enough to grasp deep treasure in our hands.

Sure, we've learned a lot in three months, but we've probably learned as much about ourselves as we have about Samoa. More than anything, we've become aware of how much we have to learn. When we gaze into the deepening blue haze of Samoan culture, its depths seem unfathomable. We could plunge a lifetime into the place and never touch the bottom. We could do the same for our own culture, and ourselves.

But we know diving deeper has risk. Risk we might find ourselves in circumstances that threaten our comfort, safety, and peace of mind or force us to make more harsh choices, unforgiveable in other people's eyes. Risk we'll uncover more suffering and pain that will tear our hearts; more ugliness and violence; more blinded and beaten children; more sickness and suicide. Risk we'll love more people limping through life dragging a ball and chain of shame. Most of all, we risk encounters that will change us in ways we don't want to imagine. Challenge beliefs so deeply held, that we don't know we have them, ideas that threaten who we think we are, and even the memory of who we once were.

We've learned to pray for the courage to take such risks. Because to dive deeper in commitment to God's work in this, our time and place, demands the courage to risk life and limb, pain and suffering, personal peace, and affluence. We believe the work we do as teachers, being friends and family to those God places on our path, is a good and righteous struggle, and worth summoning up the courage to persevere.

Just as some of the world's harshest places are also the most beautiful, we've discovered deep beauty amid our struggle with ugly cockroaches and rats, devastating cyclones, hard teaching toil, long-suffering relationships with fragile and fallen people, and our weary patience in the chaos of life's uncertainties. Focussing on our troubles, we too easily brush past God's glorious gift of a wonderful world, of beautiful people, and the loving relationships that make life's struggles worthwhile. It's like walking through a field of lilies without seeing their presence, let alone appreciating their beauty.

I'm not talking about the surface beauty of a tropical island paradise, because when we live in that paradise, we find it equally harsh and hostile. Nor in the external cultural decoration of dance, crafts, art, song and story, observed by anthropologists or tourists, who look but don't participate.

They're like gourmet chefs who critique a dish without ever eating the meal. I speak of beauty in the threads of relationships,

> woven lovingly into life's tapestry.
> Cold water,
> heartfelt, and generously offered,
> to a thirsty soul.
> Sickly sweet tea poured lukewarm,
> from an aging kettle,
> shared with passing strangers.
> Cries from sunset *volipolo*,
> and the sound of chickens
> greeting the rising sun.
> Heavenly voices wafting from
> a classroom morning service,
> peace and harmony
> in the family *lotu* -
> the daily worship's infusion
> of purpose, meaning, and hope
> in life's trouble and toil.
> Abiding, being still,
> doing nothing except
> knowing the grandeur
> of God's work and grace,
> accepting what we cannot change,
> with each day its own trouble.
> Sleeping toddlers and babies
> watched over by children,
> and brought up by a village.

The lamplight sweet dreams of children,
soundly sleeping like sausages
on a flickering *fale* floor.
Where every child is valued,
and while there's food to eat,
no one goes hungry.
Seeing useful young children
contribute responsibly,
and commit to family wellbeing.
Patience with palagi ignorance,
"it was good you tried".
Tolerance and long-suffering
for family and neighbours,
using customary pathways
to seek forgiveness for past wrongs.
Respect for wisdom and skill
in roles, responsibility, and station.
Service and humility,
a pathway to leadership.
Bubbling meeting house speeches,
a deep investment in time
to hear all voices,
solve problems,
mend relationships,
and forgive debts.
Keeping tradition to maintain cohesion,
because culture is the foundation
of peace, prosperity, and growth,
so children know who they are,

> where they come from, and
> where they're going.

While it's true that real cultural encounter, if we engage at a depth that matters, is uncomfortable, uncertain, and often painful, it's through deep immersion we gain real treasure. Treasure unseen by passing tourists, or expat palagis who judge what they see through their own cultural lens, or misguided idealogues who only see to confirm their own mythology. For if we live as children of God's kingdom, we're committed members of his family, not guests or spectators.

To dive deeper, we will stay with families in villages, first for a weekend, and then for a week at a time. To improve our language skills, we'll take in two girls to live with us, not realising in Samoa they become our actual daughters, and we've just taken on all the responsibilities of parents. Violeta will stay and become our Samoan daughter, and we'll gain a Samoan family. We'll continue to journey with Pelopia on her rollercoaster life, wondering with every descent whether it will end in tragic loss or future hope. And so, we'll weave our own bright threads into the warp and woof, not only of our life's tapestry, but into the fabric of those we meet on our road less taken.

We learn that in the visceral grittiness of cultural encounter, we taste the fruits of living, and perhaps see life more clearly. A meaningful life may not be easy, but it can be very rich. For Jesus' words: "... *for whoever will lose his life for my sake will find it*," is as true in this life as it is for life eternal. Perhaps it's when we're most aware of life's fragility, that we feel most alive. Just as a rainbow is most glorious when seen against the darkest clouds, our life in Samoa has a raw intensity that brings us, not only into dark valleys, but to life's lofty mountain peaks.

But that, is another story.

Read more in Immersion: Salt and Light in a Troubled World

If you enjoyed ENCOUNTER you might also enjoy *Trouble on Athletics Day*, a short story from the same time in Samoa. Get it for free when you sign up with your email address at www.ianreilly.com/encounter or scan the QR code.

ACKNOWLEDGEMENTS

To my dear wife Heather, who shared this journey with me, and made the encounter and adventure possible, and whose voluminous letters were wonderful, historical source material.

To our daughter Rosemary, and son-in-law Darcy, who did a thorough and critical manuscript review, and helped make it a better book. To our daughter Elizabeth for her advice and feedback on the cover design.

I thank Marsh Moyle and the many draft story readers at L'Abri Fellowship (UK) for stimulating discussion about the relationship between culture, community and Christianity.

To my early story readers: Barry Weinstein, John Tsanaktsidis, Doug Scott, Malcolm and Judy Mellor, Lance Philp, Andrea Watts and Andrew Reilly, for their encouragement and critique.

To my beta readers who provided encouraging feedback and very thoughtful advice: Janis Brydon, Ben de Warde, Kate Scott, Janelle Arnold, and Nancy Reilly.

I thank our friend, Ape, who wrote the foreword to this book, for her encouragement, cultural insight, and contemporary views on social issues raised in the story.

To Maulolo Tavita Amosa, our former principal at Leulumoega Fou College, who supported us through our encounter, from whom I learned how to lead, and who encouraged me to tell the story with honesty and courage. To other students and teachers at Leulumoega Fou College and their families, who cared for us, and whose lives and stories we had the privilege to share.

I thank the Latai family, the Rev Latu Latai, Ms Leua Leonard, and Anita, whose kindness and guidance helped us navigate through the fog of culture, and for the pastoral care provided by their late parents, the Rev. Fekusone and Olivia Latai of Saleimoa village.

To Faita and Sapela for their kindness and generosity in sharing their family and life in Sauano village.

To the family of our dear friend, the late Tammy Lind, who gave permission to use her name as a tribute to her life of Christian service.

To our fellow Australian Volunteers, and US Peace Corp Volunteers, and teachers from New Zealand who shared their journey with us, taught us more than they can know, and whose names cannot be used for reasons of privacy.

To my mentors Myfanwy Jones and Kate Ryan, who helped teach me the craft of writing, encouraged me to push boundaries, stay on track, and select darlings for slaughter.

To Erina Reddan who taught me how to find and structure the bones of a great story. To Richard Roper for his review and advice on structure. To Kate Rizzo and Juliet Mahony for their challenging editorial advice and help finding a publisher.

To the people at Ark House Press for taking on a new author and making publication a reality.

ABOUT THE AUTHOR

Telling the story of ENCOUNTER has been on Ian Reilly's heart for more than 30 years, drawing on a lifetime of creative work as an innovative engineer, entrepreneur, teacher, visual artist, and poet (www.ianreilly.com.au). Born in Barcaldine, Queensland, and raised on a small sheep farm in rural Victoria, Ian studied engineering at the University of Melbourne before designing equipment for the Australian Army and volunteering as a science teacher in Samoa. He later completed a postgraduate degree in appropriate technology, focusing on renewable energy for developing countries. His cross-cultural experience fueled a career in international consulting and product innovation, developing world-first technologies for both startups and global corporations across Europe, North America, and Asia. In 2014, he founded the agri-tech startup Agersens, launching the world's first virtual fence for cattle, and exited the company in 2021 through its sale to Gallagher. Now retired, Ian devotes his time to writing, painting, and mentoring, creating portraits and landscapes in various media. A lifelong Christian, Ian and his wife Heather worship at Donvale Presbyterian Church in Melbourne, and have two adult daughters, Rosemary and Elizabeth.

Cover Art by the Author

A teenage girl named Fuli sits on the road eroded by the sea, looks on the wreckage of her home, surrounded by debris, while an Australian Army helicopter approaches bringing supplies. Roofing iron wrapped around a damaged power pole looks like a crucifix (page 99).

An oil painting based on a compilation of original photographs taken in the aftermath of Cyclone Ofa in 1990.